Occasional Papers on Social Administration No 70

Editorial Committee under the Chairmanship of
Professor Brian Abel-Smith
London School of Economics and Political Science

CHANGING SOCIAL POLICY
the case of the supplementary benefits review

Related titles in this Occasional Papers series available from the Bedford Square Press:

The Poor and the Poorest   *B Abel-Smith and P Townsend*
Treasury Control and Social Administration   *Roy McLeod*
The Struggle for the Ministry of Health   *Frank Honigsbaum*
Income Redistribution and the Welfare State   *A Webb and J Sieve*
Information and Advice Services   *Rosalind Brooke*
Administrative Justice and Supplementary Benefits   *Melvin Herman*
Public Assistance in France   *Cindy Stevens*
In Search of the Scrounger   *Alan Deacon*
Supplementary Benefits and the Consumer   *E Briggs and A Rees*
Making Ends Meet   *Scott Kerr*

Other recent titles in the Series:

Unmet Needs and the Delivery of Care   *Paul Chapman*
Aids and Adaptations   *Ursula Keeble*
Allocating Home Help Services   *N Howell, D Boldy and B Smith*
How Many Patients?   *John Butler*
Child Support in the European Community   *J Bradshaw, D Piachaud*
The Distribution and Redistribution of Incomes   *D Piachaud*
Dependency with Dignity   *B Wade, L Sawyer and J Bell*

CHANGING SOCIAL POLICY
The case of the supplementary benefits review

Carol Walker

Bedford Square Press | NCVO

First published 1983 by the
Bedford Square Press of the
National Council for Voluntary Organisations
26 Bedford Square
London WC1B 3HU

ISBN 0 7199 1107 9

Printed in Great Britain by Imediaprint Limited

Series Foreword

This series of Occasional Papers was started in 1960 to supply the need for a medium of publication for studies in the field of social policy and administration which fell between the two extremes of the short article and the full-length book. Since the inception of this Series of papers, it has, however, been extended to include many which might better be described as books: comparative speed of publication being one factor that has attracted authors to us. It was thought that such a series would not only meet a need among research workers and writers concerned with contemporary social issues, but would also strengthen links between students of the subject and administrators, social workers, committee members and others with responsibilities and interest in the social services.

Contributions to the series are welcome from any source and should be submitted in the first instance to the Secretary, Social Administration Research Trust at the London School of Economics.

The series is now published by the Bedford Square Press to which all queries about this and previous titles should be addressed.

For Alan

Contents

Acknowledgements

The writing of this monograph has been made possible and more enjoyable by the considerable help and advice I have been given. First, my thanks must go to those officials and others connected with the review who spared time from very busy schedules to discuss the review and the research for this monograph with me. In addition to the practical help which was provided, the officials concerned also managed to convey to me their very considerable enthusiasm for the review exercise. This has stayed with me throughout, and lightened my task.

I also wish to thank Alan Deacon, Adrian Sinfield and June Stevenson, who, at various stages, managed to provide constructive criticism of my work, whilst at the same time making me feel I was making progress, even if I sometimes doubted it. Jonathan Bradshaw and Geoffrey Beltram also made comments which helped in the final revision. Alan Palmer and Michael Partridge made comments on chapters 4 and 5, and together with David Donnison provided comments on an earlier version of chapter 7. Responsibility for the final interpretation of events and any remaining errors are of course mine. Annie Oakley typed the final manuscript with great efficiency and with an enthusiasm that far exceeded the bounds of duty. Publication has been made possible by a generous grant from the University of Leeds, for which I am grateful.

Finally, this monograph is dedicated to Alan. Without his constant support and inspiration, this monograph would not have been finished.

CW
Sheffield, 1983

Chapter 1

Introduction

In November 1980, major changes were made to the supplementary benefits
(SB) scheme, the state safety net which now supports seven million
people. The reforms, introduced in the Social Security Act 1980,
represented a major shift in the assumptions on which British social
assistance policy has traditionally been based. The Social Security
Act 1980 formally recognised that the state's social assistance scheme
was not supporting merely the residual minority ineligible for
contributory benefits, as envisaged in 1948, but was a mass scheme
coping with significant numbers of retirement pensioners, lone parents,
unemployed people and the long-term sick and disabled. The new
legislation changed the supplementary benefits scheme from a highly
discretionary scheme tuned to the infinite variety of needs of the
individual to a less flexible system based on a series of regulations
covering broad categories of need. This radical change in the
character of the supplementary benefits scheme was introduced by the
Conservative Government elected in 1979. Its origins, however, are
to be found in a policy initiative begun under the previous Labour
Administration.

In September 1976, David Ennals, then Secretary of State for Social
Services, announced that he was setting up a team of Department of
Health and Social Security (DHSS) officials to review the structure
and operation of the supplementary benefits scheme. The review
transpired to be very different from the usual civil service enquiry
and to incorporate a number of very special features which made it
a unique exercise in social security policy-making. The aims of this
study are, first, to examine the external influences and internal
pressures which led to the establishment of this enquiry; secondly,
to look at the very special way the review was structured and
conducted; and finally, to assess and evaluate the effectiveness of
the review, both as a mechanism for achieving immediate policy change
and as an influence on the future shape of supplementary benefit.

The 1976 review was the latest of numerous attempts made over almost
half a century to adapt and modify the British system of last resort
financial assistance for the poor to meet changing needs and
circumstances. Means-tested social assistance has taken several guises
over this period. It gradually developed from unemployment assistance,
the first centrally administered scheme set up in 1934, through the
1940 assistance scheme serving mainly pensioners, to national assistance
which in 1948 took over responsibility for all those out of work who
had insufficient resources to meet their needs. In 1966, the supplementary
benefits scheme was established to take over as the state's financial
safety net.

The growth of the various assistance schemes up to 1948 was the result
of deliberate government action to provide a more acceptable alternative
to the Poor Law. The rise in the number of people dependent on national
assistance and supplementary benefit since then has been due to the
failure of governments to provide an adequate national insurance scheme
or to provide adequate non means-tested support for such groups as
lone parents. The rising number of claimants has continued despite

the professed commitment of successive post-war Governments to reduce dependence on means-tested assistance.

None of the changes which were made, first to the scope and later to the structure of social assistance, were accompanied by any examination of the ability of such schemes to meet their expanding responsibilities. The review of the supplementary benefits scheme set up by the Labour Government in 1976 was the first major enquiry to put British social assistance under the microscope.

The announcement of a review was enthusiastically received by the Supplementary Benefits Commission (SBC), by the press, by the union representatives of local office staff and by many major pressure groups. Reform of the scheme was widely acknowledged to be urgent and overdue. This enthusiasm was not sustained even whilst the review was under way, and for many critics, dissipated completely when the review team's final report, Social Assistance: a review of the supplementary benefits scheme in Great Britain, was published. (DHSS, 1978) (Henceforward referred to as Social Assistance) This analysis of the review exercise examines why the review failed to live up to the expectations of many outsiders and commentators. How far was it the result of a failure on the part of the review team or, in fact, a misunderstanding of the objectives of the enquiry?

The task given to the review team was to examine the structure and operation of the supplementary benefits scheme with a view to putting forward a series of policy options which, if implemented, would enable the scheme to withstand the considerable and worsening pressures being made on it. Their brief was strictly limited. It was, according to Parker's typology, to "reform": to find "... a new way of doing something with which the State is already involved. Legislation or administrative structures are literally re-formed". (Hall et al, 1975, Ch. 2)

Two factors contributed to the mistaken belief that the review might go beyond an analysis of the internal structure to examine the role of supplementary benefit within the overall framework of income maintenance policies. First, was the terms in which this enquiry was discussed. Ministers described it as "the most comprehensive review of social assistance since 1948". (DHSS Press Release, 76/223, 15 Sept. 1976) It was set up "in the light of the problems identified by the Supplementary Benefits Commission". In the first SBC Annual Report David Donnison, who had been appointed Chairman in October 1975, had drawn together the doubts which were being expressed both internally by officials and outside by the major pressure groups, on the ability of the supplementary benefits scheme to cope, efficiently and fairly, with an increasing workload.

> "The questions we are posing raise very large
> issues for Government, with implications going
> well beyond the Commission's own direct area
> of responsibility ... We are very encouraged
> to know that the Secretary of State for
> Social Services has already accepted our view
> that special attention needs to be given to
> them, and has decided that a small team of

staff should be set up so that the
Department of Health & Social Security
can review, in consultation with us, the
issues we have begun to raise".
(p.18)

One major limitation on the scope of the review was revealed at the
press conference at which it was launched. It was made clear on that
occasion that the review team would not be examining, or making
recommendations which impinged on, other areas of Government policy.
(Lister, 1977) This ruled out, most importantly, consideration of the
relationship between national insurance and supplementary benefit.
A second limitation, which required the review team to work within
existing staff and benefit costs, became apparent to outsiders only
after Social Assistance was published.

The expectations of commentators were raised, also, by the
considerable publicity given, and the significance attached to the
exercise by Ministers and by the Supplementary Benefits Commission.
Though the review was important because, as discussed above, it was
the first detailed examination of assistance, the distinctive
feature, which the Government was so anxious to make known and which
distinguished this civil service enquiry from others, lay not in its
scope but in its structure and method. The supplementary benefits
review was to be "a model of open government". (Piachaud, 1980, p. 1)
The launch of the supplementary benefits review was given the level
of publicity usually reserved for a major independent enquiry, such
as a Royal Commission. It was a long way from the low key approach
usually reserved for internal civil service investigations. Furthermore,
the Government promised to publish the review team's findings and invite
public comment. Publication of the review team's final report was
to mark the conclusion of only the first stage. A second stage was
built in to allow public discussion on the report. This second stage
was an integral part of the review process. Labour Ministers were
committed to consider both the review team's findings and the comments
made by respondents when considering whether, and if so how, to reform
the scheme.

It was, therefore, the 'open government' strategy, and the association
with the SBC's wider analysis of the problems of the scheme, which
led many outsiders to compare the review to a full-scale external
enquiry, such as a Royal Commission, rather than the normal internal
policy review frequently carried out in the civil service. In fact,
despite impressions given to the contrary by Ministers, the limited
focus of the enquiry and the concentration on internal reform and
reorganisation were almost inevitable given the hostile environment
in which the review was set up, and the fact that it was carried out
by officials. These two factors provide the background for this
analysis. Had critics taken them into account they might still have
been disappointed but they would not have been surprised at the content
of Social Assistance.

A change of fortune for social security

Until the mid-1970s, writers on policy-making in social security
consistently maintained that progress in this field could only be
made in the direction of improved coverage and value of benefits.
Derthick, for example, postulated that

> "The anticipated reactions of the public
> prevent social security policy-makers from
> seriously considering, let alone adopting,
> alterations of the social security
> programme of a kind that would entail
> reductions of benefit for any portion
> of the constituent public".
> (1979, p. 209)

However, "income maintenance policy- relatively uncontroversial in a
period of affluence - (grew) politically troublesome in recent,
more difficult years". (Heidenheimer, et al, 1983, p. 201) In the
1970s [1] several Governments, concerned at the growing size and cost
of their social security programmes, set up reviews or introduced
programmes of reform. [2] In Britain, the preoccupation of the Labour
Government with economic policy led to slower advances or even
retrenchment in many areas of social policy. Despite several rounds
of public expenditure cuts in the two decades following the Second
World War, social security provision, with some notable exceptions,
had not only been maintained but expanded. [3] by Labour and
Conservative Administrations. Between 1970 and 1974, the Heath
Government improved the breadth of benefit provision, mainly on a
selective basis. In this period, a national rent and rates rebate
scheme, family income supplement for low paid workers and an
attendance allowance for severely disabled people, were introduced.
Similarly between 1974 and 1976, the Labour Government made a number
of improvements, with the introduction of three benefits for the
disabled, the replacement of family allowances and child tax
allowances with child benefit, and a more generous uprating policy
for long-term benefits. [4]

However, social policy developments, including social security,
assumed a lower priority under the 1976-9 Labour Administration. The
balance of payments problem, the high level of inflation, with a
declining rate of growth, led to attempts to curb public expenditure.
This was spelt out in the 1976 Public Expenditure White Paper:

> "Programmes are not immutable, ... (they)
> must be open to revision in either direction
> as circumstances require. The problem is to
> find a way of allowing this flexibility to
> respond to new events, without at the same
> time allowing ever-growing expectations for
> better services to pre-empt more and more
> resources".
> (HMSO, 1976)

Townsend described the result for spending departments thus:

> "Despite protestations from some Government
> departments, like the DHSS, that their
> planning is 'needs' conscious, the fact is
> that the exigencies of the economy, as
> decided by the Treasury, have led to the
> adoption of public expenditure control as
> a dominant form of planning approved by the
> Cabinet and imposed by Whitehall".
> (Townsend, 1980, p. 1)

This then was the beginning of a period of greater austerity and economic stringency. Although at that time existing social security provision appeared safe, there were no extra resources available to implement policy changes. In 1975, social security accounted for one-fifth of total public expenditure (it has now grown to one-quarter). Policy initiatives in this field could not be taken, therefore, in isolation from the general economic climate. Those Departments wanting to make policy changes were forced to re-examine their own internal expenditure priorities.

The reports on the future development of health and social services (DHSS, 1976a), the distribution of resources in the national health service (DHSS, 1976b) and on the future of the supplementary benefits scheme (DHSS, 1978) were all examples of this internal reassessment. This trend has been continued and intensified by the 1979 Conservative Government. Those parts of the social security scheme which have been reformed, or considered for reform, have all been on a nil-cost basis.

Government concern at the size and growing cost of social security expenditure has been accompanied by a change in political and public attitudes towards welfare programmes. By the mid 1970s, those in work found their standards of living improving more slowly as prices rose, and the Government introduced successive rounds of wage restraint. By contrast, beneficiaries of the main state benefits were fully protected from the effects of inflation. The media gave considerable attention to this inequity, and thrived on stories of those who abused the system. (Golding & Middleton, 1982) Governments have all too readily responded to such adverse criticism. Furthermore, with the increase in unemployment, Government policies on income maintenance programmes have increasingly been concerned with the disincentive effects (Heidenteimer et al, 1983) or, to use a more recent analogy, the why-work syndrome.

Social Security and Officials

Many writers have noted the importance of the official in the policy-making process in the social security field. Writing of experience in the United States, Derthick found that officials were particularly dominant when social security policies were being formulated because they were the only group technically capable of furthering developments in this highly complex area of policy. (1979) In his analysis of the

policy-making process in Britain and Sweden, Heclo found that the role
of the official was "constantly" the most important.

> "While parties and interest groups did
> occasionally play extremely important
> parts, it was the civil service that
> provided the most constant analysis and
> review underlying most courses of
> government action. Parties and interest
> groups typically required a dramatic
> stimulus, such as a spurt in unemployment,
> to arouse their interest, but administrative
> attention remained relatively strong
> throughout these fluctuations".
> (1974, p. 301)

Heclo's analysis only partly fits the supplementary benefits review.
First, the existence of the SBC, working alongside Ministers and civil
servants, itself provided an informed but independent stimulus to
policy change in this area. Secondly, whilst Governments may have
been reluctant to become involved with the development of policies
in this area, pressure groups have been less reticent. Many groups,
especially the Child Poverty Action Group (CPAG), consistently tried
to draw attention to the problems of the supplementary benefits scheme. 6
However, policy-making in social security was found to be a closed
process with little access being given to groups outside the policy-
making elite.

The predominant position occupied by "national administrators" in
this field has been attributed by Heidenheimer and his colleagues to
three special features which distinguish income maintenance policies
from other spheres of policy-making. (1976) First, in social security
matters, officials not only devise programmes, they are directly
responsible also for their administration. It is the official who
is in closest touch with the way a policy is actually working. It
is he, and not other professionals, such as doctors or teachers, who
hold the expertise. Secondly, the administration of benefits is
routinised: rules are made and administered and benefits are paid.
Finally, a system of income maintenance establishes a set of
expectations in the mind of the consumer or potential consumer; people
are given rights to benefits and such expectations have to be honoured.
There is a need for continuity in administration, therefore, which
the bureaucrat is best able to provide.

Again these three distinguishing features, only partly apply to the
supplementary benefits scheme, which was, by nature, fundamentally
different from other income maintenance policies such as national
insurance or child benefit. First, the responsibility for
administering the scheme lay, until November 1980, with an
independent body, the Supplementary Benefits Commission. However,
as the SBC did not have its own staff, it was DHSS officials who worked
in the local and regional offices and acted as advisers to the
Commission. Whilst the involvement of the official in the delivery
of the service keeps him constantly in touch with technical and

administrative problems, this will not necessarily provide any
enlightenment on the problems which might confront the customer.

Secondly, a large and significant part of the administration of
supplementary benefits in 1976 was not routinised. Unlike the national
insurance scheme, for example, many aspects of entitlement to benefit
rested not on legislation but on wide discretionary powers exercised
locally by officials, under the general direction of the SBC. Finally,
recent experience has shown that it is possible for Governments to
cut the level of benefits and renege on previous commitments on social
security (see Chapter 8). But even before, Governments allowed the
value of some benefits, in particular family allowance and child benefit,
to fall by not increasing them in line with inflation.

As will be seen, there were a number of reasons behind the decision
to ask officials to conduct the supplementary benefits review. But
an overriding consideration was the experience which they could bring
to such an investigation, and the framework within which they are used
to working. An official review was a "safe" option. Its first loyalty
would be to the conventions and demands of the central administration,
including the expenditure controls of the Treasury. It would also be
likely to produce a practical programme of operational reforms. The
main cost of this option was the inadequate representation of the opinions
and needs of claimants.

The research

The analysis of recent policy developments is facilitated by two factors.
First, it is possible to follow the progress and denouement of much
of the policy process as it unfolds. Secondly, those involved in the
policy-making process, as active participants or commentators, are
still available and are able to provide background to the information
which is made publicly available. In the preparation for this study,
I was able to discuss the creation and development of the review with
many of those involved, including all the senior members of the
review team, and officials who worked with them, with some members
of the Supplementary Benefits Commission, advisers and the
representatives of some pressure groups. It is a measure of the
commitment to the review of the officials involved, and of David
Donnison, that they were so generous with their time for this study.
They also provided useful comment on drafts of chapters 4, 5 and an
earlier version of chapter 7. I had hoped that I would be able to
obtain the views of the politicians most closely involved, but this
did not prove possible.

Without these interviews and informal discussions, which took place
mainly in 1979 and 1980, it would not have been possible to go beyond
an analysis of the outcome of the first stage of the review, namely
the publication of Social Assistance, and the events leading to the
subsequent reforms of the supplementary benefits scheme, to an
assessment of that part of the policy process which took place before
the review team started work. It was these negotiations, which took place
before the establishment of an enquiry, which determined in advance
its terms of reference and scope.

Against these considerable advantages, some difficulties have to be set. It was possible for me to consult some unpublished papers, including most importantly the 1055 written responses on Social Assistance, which were sent in to the review team. Chapter 7 draws on my analysis of those. However, policy documents were not made available for consultation. The pressure of work on the civil servants involved, when access was sought in 1979 and 1980, meant that the papers, to which access had been granted in principle, could not be extracted from the review team's files which also included some documents of a confidential nature.

The interviews have provided the main source of data on the background to, and progress of, the review process. It is inevitable that those involved in current policy decisions will explain events in the light of their own perceptions and will seek to defend their own actions. Thus, different scenarios may be advanced to explain one event and the role of the interviewee is over- or under-stated depending on his relationship to the event in question. The social policy researcher must try to distil the diverse views which may be put forward and look beyond individual explanations and justifications to build up a picture of how the policy process developed. The evaluation of the review made in this report represents the author's interpretation of the significance of events described by the various participants. As Heclo and Wildavsky have suggested, it is "the participant (who) is the expert on what he does; the observer's task is to make himself expert on why he does it". (Heclo & Wildavsky, 1974, p. xvi) The fulfilment of this task was made more difficult at times in this study as some of the initial fact-finding interviews were carried out when legislation on the reforms of the supplementary benefits scheme was being drafted. Interviewees, therefore, had to be cautious when evaluating or expressing an opinion on the outcome of the review.

A second difficulty arises in the assessment of any policy development. There is often a genuine inability on the part of the key actors involved to look back at events and establish when an idea originated or who was responsible for it. Normally, new ideas emerge slowly in the course of continuing discussions and eventually are moulded to fit the variety of views put forward by a number of people. This problem was particularly difficult to overcome when trying to disentangle the contributions made by the Commission from those of the review team because the two bodies worked closely together before and after the publication of Social Assistance.

The report

This report analyses the origins, conduct and outcome of the review of the supplementary benefits scheme, which was carried out between 1976 and 1978. Chapters 2 and 3 set out the historical development of social assistance provision in Britain and draw out some of the recurring internal problems which have beset this system of last resort financial assistance and the steps which were taken in the past to solve them. Chapter 3 also considers the continuing demographic, social and political changes which exerted pressure on the supplementary benefits scheme between 1966 and 1976 and which led many groups, including the administration, staff unions and pressure groups to conclude - for different reasons - that the scheme was in urgent need of reform.

Chapter 4 examines the factors which encouraged the Labour Government to place reform of the supplementary benefits scheme on its policy agenda, despite an unfavourable economic and social climate. The chapter explores the role of the main protagonists in the establishment of a review and the effect of the negotiations and compromises, which were made, on the shape and scope of the enquiry. Finally, it examines the special features built into this review process, in particular, the open government strategy and the public discussion which comprised the second stage, which were designed to overcome some of the limitations inevitable in an internal civil service enquiry and to build continuity into the policy-making process.

Chapter 5 examines the first stage of the review. The way the review team set about the enquiry. The relationships between the review team and the committess with which it worked and with the SBC are explored. The chapter examines the open government exercise in practice: the timing and degree of access given to the various interested parties and the extent to which they influenced the review team's definition of the problem and the kind of solutions offered.

Chapter 6 examines the culmination of the review team's work in the first stage: the publication of Social Assistance: a review of the supplementary benefits scheme in Great Britain. The chapter is not intended to provide a critical analysis of the many options for change put forward by the review team. That task has been more than adequately tackled by other writers. (Lister, 1979) The discussion sets out the main areas examined by the review team in the course of their deliberations and picks out some of the most significant options for change which were discussed, if not always pursued, in the report. In particular, the analysis looks at how the constraints placed on the review team's remit limited the range of solutions which could be put forward and how far the review team was able to reconcile or overcome the conflicting aims which emerged.

Chapter 7 looks at the second stage of the review: the period of public debate. It examines, first, how successful the review was as an exercise in public participation and open government and, secondly, the views and comments which were made on Social Assistance. The change of Government in May 1979 meant that the Labour Ministers, who set up the review and who were committed to take into account both Social Assistance and the public response when considering the future of the supplementary benefits scheme, did not see the exercise through to its conclusion. Chapter 8 examines how far the review encouraged the new Conservative Government to continue with this programme of reform and the impact which Social Assistance and its critics had on the changes to the scheme which were included in the Social Security Act 1980. The chapter also looks at the new political climate in which the 1980 changes were introduced and the part they played in the Government's overall strategy on social security.

In the final chapter, the "success" of the review is assessed from the point of view of the administration, the staff who operate the scheme and claimants and their representatives. This "success" is judged against two criteria. First, how effective and appropriate the review exercise was as a mechanism for achieving change in social policy. Secondly, the chapter evaluates the impact of the review on the new supplementary benefits scheme which came into effect in November 1980.

Will the reforms provide permanent solutions to the problems of means-tested assistance where previous attempts have failed?

NOTES

1. For the reasons behind, and the effect of the changing political and economic attitudes to social security in Great Britain, Sweden and France see Heidenheimer et al, 1983, ch. 7.

2. For a discussion of the Canadian and United States experience see C. Leman, 1980.

3. For a discussion of Government attitudes to family allowance and later child benefit see CPAG, undated.

4. The three new benefits for the disabled were the mobility allowance, invalid care allowance and non-contributory invalidity pension. From 1975 until 1980, long-term benefits were uprated in line with prices or earnings whichever was the higher.

5. For an explanation of the growth of public animosity towards the unemployed in particular see David Donnison, Address to the British Institute of Management, duplicated, 16 November 1976.

6. For a discussion of the role of pressure groups in policy-making see K. Banting, 1979, ch. 3.

Chapter 2

The History of Social Assistance

Supplementary benefit, the national scheme of social assistance in
Britain today, has evolved gradually during this century. The purpose
of this chapter is to trace this development and to relate the
difficulties faced by the scheme in 1976, when the review was set up,
to the historical development of assistance policies. It will also
evaluate the effectiveness of action taken by successive Governments
to tackle the emerging problems.

The Unemployment Assistance Board (UAB)

The starting point for the study of the development of any aspect of
social policy is inevitably subjective. Many aspects of our current
social security scheme derive from the Poor Law and the introduction
of national insurance in 1911. Later landmarks, especially the
creation of national assistance in 1948 could also be taken for this
analysis. 1934, is taken as the starting point for this, as for a
previous analysis (Lynes, 1977), because is was here, with the passing
of the Unemployment Act 1934, that three elements fundamental to social
assistance provision in Britain until 1980 were founded. These were:
the confirmation of a two tier system of income support for those
unable to support themselves; national scales of benefits; and the
administration of the scheme by a central independent authority.

The 1934 Act was a determined attempt to provide a permanent solution
to the seemingly intractable problems which for fifteen years had
beset payment of benefit to the unemployed. In an attempt to keep the
growing army of unemployed off local relief over thirty changes in
legislation were introduced between 1920 and 1934. The contribution
conditions on which national insurance benefit was paid were gradually
relaxed. As a result, by 1931 a deficit of £113 million brought into
question the credibility of the national insurance scheme itself. The
1934 Act has been described as opening "a new chapter in British
unemployment history". (Davison, 1938) It hinged on the principle
of a two tier system of income support for the unemployed. Part I of
the Act widened the scope of the insurance scheme and reaffirmed it in
Davison's words "the principle instrument of British unemployment
policy". (1938, p. 30) Unemployed persons who met the contribution
conditions would receive an insurance benefit. Part II of the Act,
(which could be cited separately as the Unemployment Assistance Act)
provided for "a separate scheme of needs payments - to be called
Unemployment Assistance". (Davison, 1938, p. 30)

Unemployment assistance was the first attempt to create a national
scheme of assistance to replace local relief. It applied "national
rules to the relief of poverty, in a scheme designed to meet the
needs of its beneficiaries in full while taking account of their
individual circumstances". (Lynes, 1977, p. 201) However, the
creation of this new national scheme was due less to any attempt to
promote equity between claimants, than to the Government's desire to
wrest responsibility for administering benefits out of the hands of
the local authorities, many of whom, it was thought, had been too
profligate in the past. [1]

Although the intention of the 1934 Act was to provide national
scales of allowance to be paid according to need, there was acceptance
at the outset that the inclusion of an element of discretion was
essential to "(modify) the standard scale rates to fit the circumstances
of the individual case". (UAB, 1936, p. 8)   The UAB's discretionary
powers were broad, covering the determination of the eligibility of
applicants for assistance, the definition of the household unit, the
extent to which resources should be taken into account and the level
of needs to be met. In addition, the final assessment of the payment
which was made could be altered in three ways. First, benefit could
be reduced so that no applicant would receive "a sum which is equal to
or greater than the amount which would obviously be available by way
of earnings". (UAB, 1935, p. 294)   The rule which was later known
as the wage stop. Secondly, weekly benefit could be increased or
decreased "in any case where special circumstances exist", a facility
which was used most commonly to increase the weekly payment to
claimants with special dietary, laundry or other continuing needs.
(UAB, 1935, p. 294)   Thirdly, claimants could be paid a lump sum
where there were "needs of an exceptional character". (UAB, 1935,
p. 294)

The third, and innovatory, feature of unemployment assistance was
that it was administered by an independent board: the Unemployment
Assistance Board. The creation of an independent board was the result,
according to some early critics, of political expediency and
bureaucratic reasoning: "A surprise move originating wholly in Whitehall.
Not social needs, but political and financial calculations inspired it".
(Davison, 1938, p. 45)   It was intended that the UAB would administer
the new scheme, including its discretionary powers, in a uniform way
"consistent with policies laid down in Whitehall". (Briggs & Deacon,
1975, p. 62)

The existence of the Board was also perceived as a buffer between
the scheme and Ministers, who were not responsible for detailed aspects
of administration.

Debate on the creation of the Unemployment Assistance Board accounted
for more parliamentary time than any other issue since the first World
War. The Government was accused of trying "... to take poverty out of
politics to make the poor dumb". (House of Commons, vol. 283,
cols. 1316-17)   It is ironic, therefore, that experience was to show
that the work of the Unemployment Assistance Board and its successors
would always be under parliamentary scrutiny and that, in practice,
successive Governments would intervene in the Board's policy. From
the outset, the 'independence' of the Board was more illusory than
real. Though the UAB was responsible for drawing up regulations, for
example, on the level of assistance, these had to be approved by the
Minister and the Treasury before being laid before Parliament. In the
debate on the first set of scale rates put before Parliament in 1934,
several Members commented on the influence of the Treasury. "I am not
suggesting", said Eleanor Rathbone, "that the Treasury has actually
interfered in the deliberations of the Board, but is not its general
attitude towards increased expenditures on social services well known,
and has not the Board been furnished with an ex-Treasury official
saturated with the spirit of the Treasury, as its deputy chairman?"
(House of Commons, vol. 296, col. 1029)   Similar scepticism was
later expressed by Millett who foresaw that "If there are fundamental
divisions of opinion as to the objective, then no matter what may be

the pretence of administrative independence, political means will be
found to affect the agency involved." (1940, p. 265)

The new unemployment assistance scheme was due to come into effect
in two stages. On the first appointed day, 7 January 1933, the Board
was to take over responsibility for those unemployed persons in receipt
of transitional payments; on the second appointed day, the able-bodied
unemployed supported by the Public Assistance Authorities were to be
drawn in. However, within three weeks of the new scheme being introduced
".... the industrial towns of England, Wales and Scotland were in an
uproar. There were protest meetings, marches, and deputations from
outraged local Public Assistance Committees ... A serious political
crisis threatened". (Davison, 1938, pp. 66-7) The level of benefits,
which was lower than that paid by some Public Assistance Authorities,
the harsh application of the household means test and the failure of
the UAB to use its discretionary powers to increase benefit as much as
had been promised at the outset, meant that large numbers of the
unemployed were either excluded from benefit or suffered a reduction
in the amount received. Instead of the new scheme costing an extra
£3 million, as anticipated by Ministers, it seemed that the UAB would
actually save money.

The outcry forced the Government to suspend the scheme and it was
only two years later, in November 1936, that revised regulations were
introduced and arrangements made for the Board to assume its full
responsibilities. This time the scheme was phased in gradually,
especially in cases where benefit was to be reduced. The scale rates
were more generous and the regulations had "a code of exceptional
circumstances". (Gilbert, 1970, p. 188) The Board sent out
guidelines to its local offices to try to establish a uniform application
of discretionary powers but stressed that such instructions were
"expressly or tacitly subject to discretionary variation in individual
cases". (UAB, 1936, p. 39)

The cautious and more generous policy adopted by the Board after the
standstill was reflected in its first Annual Reports. Considerable
attention was paid to the Board's welfare role [2] and officers were
urged "to be vigilant in discovering cases where assistance can be
offered that otherwise would be unsought". (UAB, 1936, p. 40) The
discretionary nature of unemployment assistance led to a very individual
style of administration. The UAB stressed in particular the importance
of domiciliary visits because they gave "the applicant an opportunity
of bringing to notice in the most effective way any exceptional
domestic difficulties which (called) for special consideration in the
assessment of the household's needs, and at the same time enabled the
Board's officer, after seeing the circumstances and conditions under
which the household is living, to compose a true picture of the
household and its needs". (UAB, 1936, p. 12)

The Board used its discretionary powers to increase benefit
extensively. In the first year, 20 per cent of all applicants
received a weekly addition, varying between two shillings and twelve
shillings per week, at a time when the weekly payment for a couple was
one pound and seven pence. In its second year, a special enquiry into
the needs of the 14,000 claimants who had been out of work for over two
years resulted in 10,000 of them receiving a lump sum payment. In 1937,
the Board initiated a special winter addition, which was paid to 43
per cent of all applicants. These payments were later formalised in

the Unemployment Assistance (Winter Adjustment) Regulations 1938.

The benign picture presented in the UAB's early Annual Reports contrasted with the images of hardship which appeared in novels of the 1930s and personal accounts of the impact of the UAB and its policies on those dependent upon it. (Greenwood, 1933) There was particularly strong resentment against the application of the household means-test, which caused great hardship to, and was accused of encouraging the breakup of, many families. (Hannington, 1940) Even home visits, perceived so positively by the UAB, caused resentment, when officers appeared less concerned with meeting need than ensuring that the system was not being abused. By its third Annual Report, for the year ending December 1937, the UAB was itself showing a growing concern with questions of abuse and the relationship between benefits and earnings. In 1938, the Board initiated a review of all applicants under the age of thirty to establish the reasons for their long-term unemployment. The enquiry, in fact, found that only a small number were avoiding work and, as such, were penalised. Nonetheless the Board recommended that the Government should pursue an active training and employment policy for the long-term unemployed and that in some cases payment of allowances should be made only on the condition that applicants undertook training.

Despite any discontent voiced by some of its beneficiaries, by the end of its three mature years of life at the outbreak of the Second World War, the Government and some contemporary writers believed that the UAB had succeeded in overcoming the hostility which its early policies had generated. Davison, for example, wrote in 1938: "It can be said, to the credit of the Board, that they had made a resolute attack upon their problems. They had lived down the ill effect of their unhappy start and had ... established a national assistance service which was respected and even popular; no odium whatever attaches to their allowances". (1938, p. 87) The apparent success of the Unemployment Assistance Board in paying assistance to "the most dangerous group among the poor (the unemployed)" (Gilbert, 1970, p. 191) encouraged future Governments to extend the Board's area of responsibility to new groups of claimants who, it was thought, would find this agency more acceptable than the Public Assistance Authorities.

The Assistance Board

By 1939, and the outbreak of the Second World War, the Unemployment Assistance Board had been established as the national body responsible for the payment of assistance to the able-bodied unemployed. During the war, therefore, it was to the UAB, and not the less popular Public Assistance Authorities, that the Government turned to provide assistance to those new groups in need. Such a move was not unnatural. Unemployment, which had already been declining, fell dramatically during the war, relieving the UAB of much of its work. At the same time, intensive bombing produced a new clientele, including "... many normally self-supporting and even previously - and still potentially - prosperous citizens suddenly reduced to unexpected destitution". (J Simeon Clarke, quoted in Lynes, 1977) The Government wished to avoid forcing such people to suffer the stigma of Public Assistance which in any case would have imposed an unfairly heavy burden on those parts of the country which suffered large-scale bombing. Thus, the Board became "the obvious choice ... to administer and to enquire into the need for payments to fresh groups of citizens. The Board can be relied upon to undertake new work quickly, and to act uniformly throughout the land." (Clarke, 1943, p. 126) Under the Unemployment Assistance (Emergency Powers) Act 1939, the Board was empowered to help any citizen over the age of sixteen who had been forced to move, or had lost his means of support through circumstances caused by the war.

In 1940, the Board's responsibilities were extended further as a response to growing political pressure to improve the position of old people. In 1939, the national insurance pension was considerably lower than the level of assistance, with the result that 10 per cent of all pensioners were claiming poor relief. Instead of taking the more expensive option of increasing the national insurance pension, the Government introduced legislation which, in the words of Sir John Simon, Chancellor of the Exchequer, allowed the needs of pensioners to be met by a "central organisation analagous to the Unemployment Assistance Board", (Lynes, 1977, p. 203) - in fact to the UAB itself, but renamed the Assistance Board to reflect its wider clientele. The new legislation led to "the remarkable discovery of secret needs". (The Times, quoted in Titmuss, 1950) The number of applications far exceeded the 40,000 the Government had anticipated. In the two months from the announcement of the new scheme on 10 June 1940, and the first payment of benefits on 3 August 1940, over 250,000 pensioners applied. By the end of 1940, over a million pensioners were receiving the supplementary pension, compared to the 275,000 who had received local relief from the Public Assistance Authorities.

The Old Age and Widows' Pensions Act 1940 has been said to have "transformed attitudes towards means-tested assistance and established a pattern for later legislation". (Deacon, 1982) First, it confirmed the use of the assistance scheme as a way of supplementing other benefits. Unemployment assistance had been intended as a replacement when insurance was exhausted or not payable, not as a supplement. Secondly, it led to changes in the way assistance was administered and in public and political attitudes to the scheme. The 'deserving' character of its new clientele was reflected in the Assistance Board's instructions to its staff which "... began to be coloured with significant references to the need for courteous and sympathetic behaviour towards clients. They were not there during the years of unemployment". (Titmuss, quoted in Lynes, 1977, p. 203) In 1941, the Board launched an enquiry into the circumstances of pensioners, especially the infirm, followed, in 1942, by an investigation of their clothing needs, which led to special grants being paid to over 300,000 claimants. At this time it seems that local officers did exercise more generally the spirit of their instructions, and that the personal approach to the welfare of applicants won great support. In 1946, when nearly one million old people were lifted off assistance by an increase in the national insurance pension, two-thirds asked the "Boardman" to carry on visiting. (Deacon, 1982)

The growing acceptability of assistance at this time was crucially influenced by the Determination of Needs Act 1941 which virtually abolished the household means-test and replaced it with a personal means-test, similar to that used in the current supplementary benefits scheme. Politicians and others believed that the term means-test was redundant. Addressing the House of Commons in 1943, Ernest Bevin urged members to drop the use of the term 'means-test': "The Act under which we are working now is a needs test, a regulated needs test",

(House of Commons, vol. 395, col. 1242, 1943) In 1943, the Assistance
Baord's responsibilities were extended still further to include widows
under the age of sixty with dependent children. This was the first
group of lone parent families for whom the Board assumed responsibility.

   The increase in the number of categories of claimants brought under
the protective umbrella of the Assistance Board during the war years,
led to increasing complication in its administration. The introduction
of successive sets of regulations up to 1943 made them extremely
complicated. Proposals for simplification of the regulations were drawn
up by a departmental working party and their recommendations introduced
in January 1944. The winter allowances, first introduced in 1937 under
the UAB's discretionary powers and in 1943 received by 60 per cent of all
supplementary pensioners, were replaced by higher scale rates paid
throughout the year. The rural differentiation, payment of lower rates
of benefit to those living in rural areas, was dropped. Single men and
women received the same rate of benefit, the number of children's rates
was reduced and the calculation of allowances for rent was simplified.

   Perhaps mindful of the outcry which had followed the introduction
of unemployment assistance in 1934, the Government put forward the
recommendation to simplify the scheme on the understanding that the
changes would not lead to a loss of income for any of the Board's
customers. Introducing the debate on the Draft Supplementary Pensions
and Unemployment Assistance (Determination of Needs and Assessment of
Needs) Regulations, the newly appointed Minister of Health, Mr Willink
told the House: "... in this field simplification costs money. One is
inclined to think of simplification and pruning ... as being something
which is economical, but, of course, in this field simplification is
bound to mean in a substantial number of cases a levelling up".
(House of Commons, vol. 395, col. 1189, 1943) Changes, such as the
withdrawal of the winter additions which led to a drop in benefit for
some claimants, were compensated by increases in the scale rates, which
went up more than the rise in the cost of living.

   The new attitude shown by the Board and its officers to its largest
new client group, the elderly, went a considerable way to improving
its image in the country. Politicians continued to believe that the
stigma attached to the Poor Law had not been transferred to the
Assistance Board. When, in 1948, the Poor Law was abolished and its
remaining functions were transferred to the Assistance Board, now
renamed the National Assistance Board (NAB), James Griffith, Minister
of National Insurance said "I can think of no higher tribute to the
Board than to say that it has recovered in the public esteem from the
stigma attached to it in 1934". (Quoted in Deacon, 1982)

National Assistance

If the 1934 Unemployment Assistance Act was the foundation on which
assistance was developed over the next 15 years, the introduction of
two major pieces of legislation in 1946 and 1948 offered the
opportunity for a complete reappraisal of all state income support.
Many of the problems facing the supplementary benefits scheme in 1976
stemmed from the failure of the Labour Government to seize this chance
and not fully appreciate the long-term consequences of the policies
adopted.

The first of these Acts, the National Insurance Act 1946, had its
roots in the report produced by Sir William Beveridge on Social
Insurance and Allied Services in 1942. The aim of the legislation
was, in return for a weekly flat rate contribution, to pay flat rate
insurance benefits to compensate for the loss or interruption of
earnings through retirement, unemployment or sickness, and to meet
the special expenses incurred at a birth or death. It was intended
that this scheme would provide a subsistence income for the vast
majority of those unable to support themselves through work. To
back up the scheme, the Government passed the National Assistance
Act 1948 which was to provide a safety net for those whose needs were
not met under the national insurance scheme. The national assistance
scheme provided support, not for prescribed categories of persons
but for all persons, except married women living with their husbands,
who did not work and were "without resources to meet their requirements,
or whose resources (including benefits receivable under the National
Insurance Act 1946) must be supplemented in order to meet their
requirements". (National Assistance Act 1948, Section 4)   National
assistance was extended to the remaining groups supported by the
Public Assistance Authorities, including the sick, the disabled, the
elderly who did not qualify for a state pension and lone mothers.

The National Assistance Act marked the final abolition of the Poor
Law and has been called "a major breakthrough: the end of a whole
period of social history".   (Fulbrook, 1978, p. 177)   Bessie Braddock
echoed the sentiments of many, when, in the debate on the National
Assistance Bill, she said: "I think of what we are repealing more than
of what we are proposing". (quoted in Titmuss, 1969, p. 155) Little
attention was paid to the operation of the new national assistance
scheme. First, because it was assumed to be a far superior alternative
to the Poor Law and secondly, because its role was to be "minor but
residual" as envisaged by Beveridge. Explaining the role of national
assistance, Aneurin Bevan, Minister of Health, told the House of
Commons that "the amount to be left to the (National) Assistance
Board after the whole of the needs have been met by all the other
measures - insurance allowances, old age pensions, sickness benefits -
will be very small indeed. Only the residual categories will be left".
(quoted in Lynes, 1977, p. 206)

Despite such bold statements, Government policy on national insurance
ensured that, even at the outset, national assistance did not play
merely a residual role, supporting only those unable to insure
themselves against adversity. First, unemployment benefits were paid[3]
for a fixed period, not for the duration of a person's unemployment.
Once entitlement was exhausted people had to turn to the National
Assistance Board (NAB). Secondly, and more significantly, national
assistance rates were soon raised above the national insurance rates.
By the end of 1948, three-quarters of all national assistance allowances
were topping up inadequate national insurance benefits and pensions.

The 1948 National Assistance Act and accompanying regulations drew
together the existing responsibilities of the Assistance Board with
the provisions and practices of the Public Assistance Authorities.
This change was not accompanied by any rational assessment of the
structure and operation of assistance, or any consideration of this
scheme's ability or suitability to administer means-tested benefits
to an enlarged and disparate clientele. The Government failed to
anticipate that an enlarged scheme in which the 'deserving' had to mix

with the 'disreputable', would be regarded in a different, unfavourable light to the Assistance Board which had been regarded superior to the Poor Law. Some of the problems discussed below were a result of the Government's lack of foresight.

The post war legislation reinforced the administrative division between contributory benefits and the means-tested scheme. Beveridge, the wartime coalition Government and the 1946 Labour Government were in agreement that the two schemes should be perceived differently by the public "otherwise the insured persons get nothing for their contributions". (The Beveridge Report, 1942, p. 141) National insurance was to be administered directly by officials of the Ministry of National Insurance. Assistance would be administered, once more, by an independent board. The new NAB would employ its own staff.

The application of the wide discretionary powers inherited from its predecessors, ensured that the NAB would continue with the intensive and individual administration. Home visits, for which such success had been claimed during the war years, continued to be a mainstay. By the end of 1948, for example, all the quarter of a million claimants taken over from the local authorities had been visited. In 1949, five million home visits were made. Like the Unemployment Assistance Board, the NAB stressed in its Annual Reports the importance of officers making full use of these visits to establish need, in the light of which the officer was instructed either to award a special addition or grant or, where appropriate, to refer the applicant to another more relevant organisation. The NAB officer was expected to act as a mediator between the applicant and all the local voluntary and statutory services.

While the NAB presented favourable overviews of the new assistance scheme and the work of its officers, experience at the ground level could be very different. The national assistance scheme relied on a large number of officials to operate a scheme which required them to make personal assessments of need and to provide help where appropriate. By its very nature, and its ability to adapt to individual need, the actual operation of such a scheme can differ at the local level from that promoted centrally, and may vary between regions, between offices and between officers. The success of such a scheme is wholly dependent on the attitude of its officials and their perception of the 'need' which is presented.

The popularity of the Assistance Board with many of its beneficiaries, compared to the more hostile attitude of the unemployed to the UAB, was a result of the more generous and sympathetic attitude held by officers and by the public towards the elderly, who were the majority of beneficiaries. Once the assistance scheme was responsible for both 'deserving' groups, such as pensioners, and 'undeserving' groups such as lone mothers and the unemployed, difficulties arose. Most of the NAB's staff were inherited from the Assistance Board or the Public Assistance Authorities. As these staff had operated the apparently successful assistance scheme without formal training, the training which accompanied the introduction of the national assistance scheme, concentrated mainly on the technicalities of the new Act and regulations. Although it was acknowledged that some central training was desirable to encourage a consistent approach to the use of discretion which was "as much a matter of conveying an attitude of mind as of giving precise instructions", little was done. (Stowe, 1961,

p. 336) Some 'human relations' courses were run for staff in the
1950s but those were taken up most frequently by young officers and
so did little to mollify the attitudes of the older, less
sympathetic staff. The main component of training was the
guidance given by peers 'on the job'. Speaking of his own
experience working in a local national assistance office Hill found
that the "collective values of the Executive Officers, rather than
the views of one's superiors" (Hill, 1969, p. 83) were the
greatest influence on the way the scheme was administered and their
behaviour was more repressive than management. Overall, Hill drew
a very gloomy picture of the way officers exercised their discretionary
powers. The causes of this inconsistency varied from, at one
extreme, merely differing personal interpretations of need to, at the
other, deliberate "mucking around" to make it 'more difficult for an
applicant to get assistance than to get help elsewhere". (p. 83)

Few changes were made to the national assistance scheme between
1948 and 1966. The scale rates were increased more frequently than
the national insurance rates. As these upratings took place at
different times, there was some fluctuation in the number of
claimants receiving national assistance. The 1959 uprating
represented a change in political attitude to the level of the scale
rates. Previous increases had been made merely to reflect rising
prices to maintain the real level of benefit. In 1959, John
Boyd-Carpenter, Minister of Pensions and National Insurance,
announced that the increase in national assistance would be greater
than the rise in the cost of living because "Her Majesty's
Government and the National Assistance Board have decided that the
standard of provision for the least well off members of the
community should now be in some measure improved in order to give
them a share in the country's rising prosperity ... the proposed
(increase) ... unlike any of its predecessors is not necessitated
or called for by changes in the cost of living, but as a deliberate
decision to improve the standards".   (House of Commons, vol. 607,
col, 35, 15 June 1959)

This move was the first significant step away from the Beveridge
principle that assistance rates provide only for subsistence. The
1959 increase also reflected the Conservative Government's growing
emphasis on selective benefits as a means of helping the poor. The
increase in national assistance was made instead of improving national
insurance.

The administration of benefit to the disparate groups of beneficiaries
caused difficulties at the interface of the national assistance scheme.
Such problems were compounded by pressures and criticisms facing the
scheme as a whole. As discussed above, the NAB found itself from the
outset performing a much wider role than the residual and diminishing
one predicted by its political creators. Between 1948 and 1965, the
number of weekly payments grew from just over one million, supporting
1,750,000 people in December 1948 to two million, supporting
2,800,000 claimants and their dependants by December 1965 (see Table I).
There were increases amongst lone mothers, widows under 60 and people
with disabilities, but the largest growth was amongst beneficiaries
over retirement age. Not surprisingly then, throughout this period,
no fewer than two-thirds of all assistance payments were paid in
supplementation of national insurance benefits. [4]

TABLE 1: NATIONAL ASSISTANCE – NUMBER OF PAYMENTS MADE IN ONE DAY IN DECEMBER IN SELECTED YEARS 1948 – 1965

000's

	1948	1950	1955	1960	1965
Assistance paid in supplementation of insurance benefits:					
Retirement pensions	495	677	888	1,075	1,196
Sickness or industrial injury benefits	80	114	113	139	149
Widow's benefit	81	96	75	65	98
Unemployment benefit	19	38	20	43	34
	675	925	1,096	1,322	1,477
Assistance paid in supplementation of non-contributory old age pensions	89	106	158	111	53
Assistance to persons not receiving such pensions or benefits					
Persons registered for employment	34	39	41	85	78
Persons not registered for employment	213	280	317	339	389
TOTAL	1,011	1,350	1,612	1,857	1,997

Source: Annual Report of the National Assistance Board, 1965, Appendix III

Despite the growing numbers wholly or partially dependent on national assistance, data became available in the 1950s and later which showed that many people were not taking up the payments to which they were entitled. In their research into the economic circumstances of old people Cole and Utting estimated in 1962 that up to half a million pensioners might be entitled to, but not receiving assistance. They attributed this to three factors: the complexity of the regulations which made it difficult for potential claimants to understand entitlement and eligibility; the inconsistent decision-making of the NAB's officers, particularly with regard to discretionary payments; and, finally, to the continued presence of stigma. (1962)

Partly in response to these findings a second study, carried out by the Ministry of Pensions and National Insurance and the NAB, was set up by the Conservative Government to explore the problem of take-up, particularly amongst old people. (HMSO, 1966) The survey, which was conducted in 1965, found that reluctance to claim was not confined to old people though it was amongst this group that the problem was most acute. In all, it was estimated that 700,000 pensioner households were entitled to, but not receiving, national assistance. [5]

During this period, other problems of national assistance came increasingly to the forefront, in Parliament   and in the Annual Reports of the NAB. In particular, the widespread use of discretionary payments was criticised for the burden placed on the administration and because it made the scheme difficult for claimants to understand. After 1948, the number of discretionary payments grew enormously. Between 1948 and 1965, the proportion of claimants receiving a discretionary weekly addition to benefit doubled from 26.2 per cent (265,000 claimants) to 57.9 per cent (1,157,000). Weekly additions to benefit were paid for a wide variety of expenses including nightcaps and window cleaning, but four types of expenditure predominated: laundry, domestic assistance, special diets and fuel. (see Table 2). The emergence of fuel as an item of expenditure with which claimants needed extra help did not reflect a new need.

TABLE 2: NUMBER OF WEEKLY ADDITIONS TO BENEFIT

000's

	1948	1955	1960	1965
Laundry	127 (40%)	323 (37%)	418 (28%)	520 (24%)
Domestic Assistance	73 (23%)	107 (12%)	156 (10%)	268 (12%)
Diet	110 (35%)	349 (40%)	508 (34%)	640 (29%)
Fuel	9 (3%)	n/a	350 (23%)	669 (30%)
Other	-	-	83 (5%)	113 (5%)
TOTAL	319 (100)	880 (100)	1515 (100)	2210 (100)

Source: National Assistance Board Annual Reports for the years
         1948, 1955, 1960, 1965

After the abolition of the winter additions in 1944, the number of payments for fuel dropped, but after a few years the NAB resumed the practice of paying extra allowances for fuel in the winter months. In the winter of 1964-65, a payment of four pounds was made to all those claimants in receipt of assistance who had as a member of the household a person over 65 or a young child. This was the first time that the NAB used its discretionary powers to increase benefit on a mass scale in order to compensate claimants for a delay in the uprating of the scale rates.

With the introduction of national assistance in 1948, claims for lump sum payments paid to meet exceptional need trebled. The number of such payments, which the NAB described as "more numerous and more troublesome" than weekly additions to benefit, continued to grow from over 100,000 in 1948 to 345,500 in 1965. (NAB, 1949, p. 14)

This increasing reliance on discretionary payments between 1948 and 1965 led the NAB, in what was to be its final Annual Report, to conclude that "there is now a strong case for compounding, in appropriate categories, the smaller and commoner special needs with the basic scale rates and providing a scale rate which they will all receive and which is sufficient for all normal needs, including small expenses for which special discretionary additions have up to now been made". (NAB, 1966, p. xii)

The Birth of Supplementary Benefit (SB)

The increasing evidence of poor take-up, of the increasing complexity of the scheme caused by the ad hoc growth of responsibilities and the growth of discretion, and the more frequent criticism of the national assistance scheme in Parliament, led both major parties to consider reforms. The task fell to the new Labour Administration which came to office in 1964. In Opposition, Labour's solution to the "national assistance problem (which) was first and foremost a pensioner problem" rested on the introduction of an income guarantee scheme.[6] This was intended as an interim measure which would lift pensioners and widows off means-tested national assistance until a comprehensive earnings-related pensions scheme could be introduced. However, the income guarantee scheme fell by the wayside as the Labour Government curtailed expenditure plans in response to a deteriorating economic situation. Instead limited resources were made available to reform the national assistance scheme.

The changes introduced in the Supplementary Benefits Act 1966 did not result, therefore, from any detailed consideration of the role of assistance. It was, as Webb has pointed out elsewhere, more the "negative outcome of the failure of the income guarantee". (Hall et al, 1975, p. 453) The aims of the reforms were to make it more acceptable to those it was intended to help by ridding it of its association with 'assistance' and by stressing the concept of benefit as a 'right'; and secondly, to diminish the over-reliance on discretion.

In an attempt to present the new scheme as fundamentally different from its predecessor, the name was changed to supplementary benefit - the term 'benefit' was thought to connote the notion of rights more than 'assistance'. A Supplementary Benefits Commission (SBC) with similar, but more limited, powers was set up to administer the new scheme. Unlike the NAB, the Supplementary Benefits Commission had no power to make or amend the scale rates. This duty was placed with Parliament.

The second objective of the reforms was to obviate the need for the widespread use of discretion to increase the level of benefit paid to large numbers of claimants. A long-term addition of nine shillings was introduced to be paid to all supplementary pensioners and to all those under pensionable age who had been on benefit or assistance for more than two years - except where claimants had to register for work. This automatic addition was intended to replace the majority of weekly additions previously paid for special needs. When introducing the legislation, it was stressed that the long-term addition was not "... a preferential rate of benefit for long-term cases ... (but to) ... avoid the need for detailed enquiries into special expenses of the kind which have to be made by the Board in cases under National Assistance". (Lynes, 1977, p. 211) Where there were exceptional circumstances, the SBC retained discretionary powers to make an exceptional circumstances addition to meet that need, if it exceeded the level of the long-term addition.

Apart from these changes, the detail of the new supplementary benefits scheme differed little from national assistance legislation or the policy of the NAB. The Act put into law the distinction between supplementary pensions and supplementary allowances, which had existed in practice under the NAB. For example, under the 1966 Act, the Commission was empowered to decrease or withhold part of the benefit paid to supplementary allowance claimants, a sanction which could not be applied to supplementary pensioners. In addition to the administrative responsibilities which the Commission inherited from the NAB, it was given a policy role: "to offer advice to Ministers on matters which may arise out of the experience in dealing with the many human problems in its field which raise issues outside the administration of the scheme itself". (SBC, 1967, p. 22) The way in which the Supplementary Benefits Commission applied this policy role, together with an evaluation of the effectiveness of the 1966 reforms, are examined in the next chapter.

Conclusion

This chapter has traced the development of assistance from the strictly limited groups covered in the 1934 Unemployment Assistance Act, through the years of the Assistance Board and the National Assistance Board to the national and almost comprehensive supplementary benefits scheme. As can be seen this development has occurred with little rational planning. Successive Governments have been more concerned with the structure of national insurance and with lifting claimants off an existing stigmatised service, first the Poor Law and then 'assistance', than any detailed consideration of what was being erected in its place.

Many of the problems which have faced our social assistance schemes over the past 45 years can be traced back to the introduction of unemployment assistance in 1934. The shortcomings of the 1934 solution were pointed out by Millett who in 1940 warned of "The possibility of future strain arising from these illogical arrangements". (p. 296)   The problem, as Gilbert has pointed out, was that the introduction of unemployment assistance provided a solution to the political problem of paying benefits to the unemployed, rather than the social problem of unemployment or poverty and in so doing "closed most of the alternative doors to the creation of a real needs service". (1970, p. 191)   Nevertheless, successive Governments accepted the 1934 solution as the most expedient way of supporting large groups of people. Successive social assistance schemes have been regarded as the natural home for any contingency need and have been required to make up for the inadequacies of the national insurance scheme. There was, however, at no time any consideration of the suitability of such schemes for the task or of possible alternatives.

Developments since 1934 have confirmed a two tier income support system: national insurance, with a safety net of means-tested assistance. From 1940 onwards, the major task of assistance has been to supplement inadequate insurance benefits. In 1938, 8,400 beneficiaries (1.5 per cent) received unemployment assistance in addition to an insurance beenfit. By the end of 1945, 1.5 million elderly people, many of whom were in receipt of a state pension, were receiving an allowance from the Assistance Board, and the Board was supplementing one-third of all pensions. Between 1948 and 1965, over two-thirds of all assistance payments made were in supplementation of national insurance benefits. In 1965, one-quarter of all pensioners and over 13 per cent of the unemployed received assistance, a situation which was to deteriorate in subsequent years.

The failure of successive Governments to pay adequate insurance benefits increased dependence on means-tested assistance. The failure to pay adequate levels of assistance created a second problem which has recurred. [7]   In all assistance schemes, discretion has been used in a large number of cases to meet 'normal' not 'exceptional' needs as intended. Although upratings protected claimants against rises in prices, they did not afford beneficiaries any improvement in the general standard of living. Even the 1959 uprating which was to allow the poor "a share in increasing national prosperity" was insufficient to bring any lasting improvement in the relationship between benefits and average earnings. [8]

If the standards of living afforded by the two schemes of financial assistance were roughly comparable, the national insurance and national assistance schemes differed significantly in their administration. Unlike national insurance which could be administered impersonally and remotely, the administration of assistance has always been much more individually based, with a heavy reliance on home visiting and detailed enquiry into personal circumstances. Inevitably then the quality of the service provided depended to a great extent on the personal application and qualities of the staff. Despite efforts especially under the NAB to standardise the use of discretion to ensure equitable treatment of claimants, there were limits to the effectiveness of any guidelines. In such a service, it is easy for a disparity to occur between the intention of the legislation, the central administrative authority on the way a policy should be implemented, and the way it is exercised at the local level. Thus it was possible for politicians to believe that the problems of means-tested assistance had been overcome, when claimants still regarded the scheme and the means-test with animosity.

Although the essential difference in administration between the two income maintenance schemes had been deliberately fostered by successive Governments with a Board, and later a Commission, established to administer assistance, the independence of these bodies was, in some important respects, illusory. Not only have Governments become involved in the timing and amount of upratings, but they have constantly expressed concerns on particular aspects of policy, such as the special problems of old people or the problem of abuse. The Unemployment Assistance Board, and its successors, have not operated in a vacuum, but have had to respond to concerns of the day, especially where these have been expressed by their political masters. As the Unemployment Assistance Board stated in its first Annual Report, in carrying out its duty to meet need the Board's officers had to do "what responsible public opinion at the time would wish them to do. The Board is, in this respect, a trustee for the public conscience ... It is also a trustee for the taxpayer". (1935, p. 19)

In the past forty-five years, various attempts have been made to improve social assistance provision. However, these attempts have tackled only the presenting problems, such as complexity (in 1944 and 1966), the extensive use of discretionary powers (in 1944 and 1966) or the unacceptable image of the scheme (in 1966) or previous last resort schemes (in 1934 and 1948). They were not accompanied by any rational assessment of the efficacy of the various assistance schemes. The 1966 reforms attempted once more to encourage take-up and increase confidence by presenting assistance with a new image and emphasising benefit as of right. As 1948 had seen the death of the Poor Law, so 1966 presided over the death of assistance. But future developments were to show once again that a change of name and superficial changes in administrative practice and structure were not sufficient to solve the long-term problems of the adequacy of and acceptability of the State's safety net.

NOTES

1.   For a fuller discussion of this point see Briggs & Deacon, (1973).

2.   Under the Unemployment Assistance Act, the Board was charged with the duty of "creating a new social service for the assistance of unemployed persons ... not only for the relief of their material needs, but also for the promotion of their welfare", UAB Annual Report 1935, p. 6.

3.   For a fuller discussion for the reasons for this restriction see Deacon, 1981.

4. In the parliamentary debate on the 1959 increase, it was suggested that the name of national assistance be changed to reflect its essentially 'supplementary' role, a suggestion rejected by the Minister because "the institution itself (the NAB) by the devotion to duty of its officers, is earning an increasingly good name". House of Commons, Hansard, vol. 607, col. 39, 15 June 1959.

5. In 1965, further findings were published on take-up in B. Abel-Smith and P. Townsend, (1965).

6. For a full account of the demise of the income guarantee and events leading to the creation of supplementary benefit see P. Hall, (1975), ch. 4.

7. For a discussion of the origins of the supplementary benefits scale rates see DHSS/SBC (1977) pp. 6-11 and appendix 3.

8. Tony Lynes disputed that the 1959 increase had been as beneficial as Ministers maintained. (Lynes, 1967).

Chapter 3

Supplementary benefit: pressures for change

The aim of the Supplementary Benefits Act 1966* was to construct a new
system of assistance which was qualitatively different from its
predecessors. It was hoped that the emphasis on legal entitlement and
the decreased role for discretion in the new scheme would encourage
take-up of benefit and make the scheme more comprehensible and more
equitable. Unfortunately, the improvements which were made
immediately after the introduction of the new Act proved to be less
significant than first assumed, and certainly more shortlived than
the architects of the new scheme had hoped. The aims of this chapter
are to look at developments between 1966 and 1976, first to examine
why the 1966 reforms failed to provide a permanent solution and
secondly to trace the emergence of internal and external criticism of
the scheme.[1] As will become clear many of the problems were not new,
and comparison to previous years could often be made.

Take-up of supplementary benefit

The discovery of significant numbers of pensioners who were not
taking up the benefit to which they were entitled was the main reason
why both major political parties took the reform of the national
assistance scheme on board in the mid 1960s.

It was believed initially that the establishment of supplementary
benefit had been successful in improving take-up. Douglas Houghton,
Chancellor of the Duchy of Lancaster in the Labour Government claimed
that "the abolition of the National Assistance Board, and the deletion
of the word 'assistance' from the dictionary of Social Security, has
had remarkable success. Some half a million more people applied within
a few weeks". (1967) The claim that the introduction of the new
scheme had been, in itself, enough to improve take-up was soon
challenged. Atkinson estimated that, although the total receiving
benefit had increased by 20 per cent between September and December 1966,
in fact between one-half and two-thirds of the increase in the number
of retirement pensioners in receipt of a supplementary pension between
December 1965 and November 1968, was due to the more generous scale
rates and not to the greater acceptability or knowledge of the new
scheme. (Atkinson, 1970, p. 61)

Whilst there are obvious difficulties in calculating precise levels
of take-up, statistical studies based on Family Expenditure Survey
data, carried out for the Supplementary Benefits Commission (SBC),
have revealed that take-up of benefit did not exceed 76 per cent for
the whole of the ten years under study (see table 1). Since 1976, the
take-up level has fallen. In 1979, it was estimated that overall only
70 per cent of those eligible had taken up their entitlement, and that
900,000 pensioners (35 per cent of those eligible) and 320,000 of those
below retirement age were failing to claim over £355 m. (Social Services
Committee, 1982, p. 51)[2]

* Re-enacted with minor amendments as the Supplementary Benefits Act 1976

TABLE 1: TAKE-UP OF SUPPLEMENTARY BENEFIT

	1973	1974	1975	1976	1977
1. Entitled to but not receiving SB	1030	910	930	920	1040
2. Receiving SB	2760	2670	2700	2900	3000
3. Total	3790	3580	3630	3820	4040
4. Estimated level of take-up: 2 as percentage of 3	73%	75%	74%	76%	74%
5. Estimate benefit unclaimed	£165m	£180m	£240m	£250m	£345m

(Source: SBC Annual Report 1978, Tables 12.8 and 12.9)

In a study of eligible pensioners not in receipt of supplementary benefit, it was found that the main reasons for not claiming were that many were unaware of the scheme, or of their own entitlement. Others had negative attitudes towards supplementary benefit and its public image, or to the assessment procedure. Others did not consider themselves to be in need. Such attitudes did not extend towards rent and rate rebates, which three-quarters of the respondents were receiving and professed to be quite content with. (Broad, 1977; see also Kerr, 1983) The SBC suggested that eligible claimants were less likely to claim when the amount of benefit due was small or where the claimant's entitlement lasted for less than four weeks (DHSS/SBC, 1978). Against this must be weighed the very substantial losses suffered by some claimants, especially amongst families with children. (see table 2).

The scheme's customers

Despite the existence of one million families who were not taking up their entitlement, the number of claimants in receipt of a regular weekly payment continued to grow between 1966 and 1975 and has greatly accelerated since then. (see table 3) The problems which beset the scheme in 1976, however, were due less to the overall increase in claimants, and more to a number of demographic and economic factors which changed the balance between the number of supplementary allowance cases and supplementary pensioners. Between 1966 and 1975, the number of claimants increased by 12 per cent. Within this, the proportion of supplementary pensioners fell from 73 per cent to 60 per cent, while the proportion of supplementary allowance recipients increased from 27 per cent to 40 per cent of all claimants (see table 4). In 1981,

TABLE 2: ESTIMATES OF TAKE-UP OF SUPPLEMENTARY BENEFIT BY FAMILY CONSTITUTION 1977

Group	Total likely to be entitled ('000)	Proportion receiving benefit	Number eligible but not receiving benefit ('000)	Estimated benefit unclaimed (£per annum)	Average weekly amount of unclaimed benefit
Pensioners: total	2,280	73%	610	£100m	£ 3.10
married	440	66%	150	£ 25m	£ 3.10
single	1,850	75%	460	£75m	£ 3.10
Non-pensioners: total	1,760	76%	420	£245m	£11.00
MC* no children	140	74%	40	£ 25m	£12.20
MC with children	310	76%	70	£ 65m	£17.10
SP** no children	930	71%	270	£135m	£ 9.40
SP with children	380	89%	40	£ 20m	£10.00
All MC	450	76%	110	£ 90m	£15.50
All SP	1,310	76%	320	£155m	£ 9.50
All with children	690	83%	120	£ 85m	£14.50
All without children	1,060	71%	310	£155m	£ 9.70

* Married couples   ** Single person

Source: SBC Annual Report 1978, Table 12.11

TABLE 3: RECIPIENTS OF REGULAR WEEKLY PAYMENTS ON A DAY IN THE MONTH SHOWN, WITH AND WITHOUT NATIONAL INSURANCE BENEFITS

000's

	Nov 1966	Nov 1968	Nov 1970	Nov[1] 1972	Nov 1974	Dec 1975	Dec 1979	Dec 1981
All supplementary benefits	2,495	2,637	2,739	2,911	2,680	2,793	2,850	3,720
All supplementary pensions	1,819	1,860	1,902	1,909	1,807	1,679	1,720	1,740
Retirement pensioners and NI widows aged 60 and over	1,631	1,682	1,745	1,807	1,712	1,586	1,630	1,640
Others	187	178	156	102	96	94	97	95
All supplementary allowances	676	777	836	1,002	872	1,113	1,130	1,980
Unemployed: with NI benefit	77	73	73	87	73	135	80	234
without NI benefit	102	147	166	305	228	406	486	1,084
Sick and disabled: with NI benefit	156	172	164	137	95	77	52	66
without NI benefit	142	150	159	161	165	165	155	155
NI widows under age 60	59	61	63	62	42	30	19	16
Women with dependent children	125	157	191	227	245	276	306	369
Others	16	17	20	22	24	24	32	61

Notes: 1. From November 1972, the figures exclude unemployed claimants who received no payment of SB during the week preceding the count.

Source: Social Security Statistics, 1966-1981, Table 34.30

TABLE 4: RECIPIENTS OF REGULAR WEEKLY PAYMENTS ON A DAY IN THE MONTH* SHOWN, BY CLAIMANT GROUP

		1964	1966	1968	1970	1972	1974	1975	1979	1981
All supplementary benefits	000's	1,961	2,495	2,637	2,739	2,911	2,680	2,793	2,850	3,720
All supplementary pensions	%	70.5	72.9	70.5	69.4	65.5	67.4	60.1	60.4	46.8
All supplementary allowances	%	29.5	27.1	29.5	30.5	34.4	32.5	39.8	39.6	53.2
- unemployed	%	6.7	7.2	8.3	8.7	13.5	11.2	19.4	19.8	35.4
- sick and disabled	%	14.3	11.9	12.2	11.8	10.2	9.7	8.7	7.3	5.9
- widows	%	2.9	2.4	2.3	2.3	2.1	1.6	1.1	0.7	0.4
- women with dependent children	%	4.8	5.0	6.0	6.8	7.8	9.1	9.9	9.7	9.9
- others	%	0.8	0.6	0.6	0.7	0.7	0.9	0.8	1.1	1.6

Source: Table 3 above

* November except 1975 December

the number of claimants below pension age exceeded those above the
retirement age for the first time ever, and by 1982 the number of
unemployed claimants exceeded the number of supplementary pensioners.
The reasons for this shift and the implications for the scheme are
considered below.

Four main groups go to make up the supplementary benefit scheme's
customers: those over retirement age, the unemployed, lone parents
and the sick or disabled.

Retirement pensioners formed the largest single group from the
introduction of national assistance in 1948 until 1982. There has
been a steady increase in the number of supplementary pensioners
dependent on supplementary benefit in each year except 1973 when
the introduction of a national rent and rates rebates scheme
produced a once and for all reduction. This growth was in fact slower
than the increase in the total number of retirement pensioners as the
effects of the graduated pensions scheme and the growth of occupational
pensions kept many above the supplementary benefit level. It has also
been due to a declining take-up by pensioners discussed above. In 1975,
only 22 per cent of all retirement pensioners received a supplementary
pension, compared to an average of 28 per cent between 1969 and 1972,
(SBC 1976, p. 42)

It was amongst unemployed claimants, and particularly those with
children, that the sharpest increase occurred. Between 1966 and 1975,
they trebled overall, and the number of unemployed families with
children on supplementary benefit increased fourfold. Since then, and
particularly since 1979, this increase has accelerated. Growing
reliance on supplementary benefit by the unemployed was caused by a
250 per cent rise in the level of unemployment, and the continued
failure of the national insurance scheme to provide benefits which
were adequate in duration and in cash terms. In 1966, 38 per cent
(179,000) of those registered unemployed were wholly or partially
dependent on supplementary benefit. From 1974 onwards the scheme
supported almost one half of those registered unemployed, and in some
subsequent years up to 1976 and since has supported a greater number
than the national insurance scheme.

Amongst the unemployed, two groups which were wholly dependent on
supplementary benefit grew significantly during the first ten years of
the scheme. First were those who had exhausted their entitlement to
unemployment benefit either through repeated spells of unemployment or
sickness or by a continuous period out of work of twelve months or
more. Between 1966 and 1975, the number of long-term unemployed persons
rose from 48,000 to 161,200. School-leavers made up the second growing
group amongst the unemployed whose needs were not met by the national
insurance scheme. (See Table 5)

Although numerically a smaller group, the number of lone parents
receiving supplementary benefit grew almost as quickly as the number of
unemployed in the first ten years of the new scheme.   By 1977,
almost half of all lone parents were dependent on supplementary benefit
for all or part of their income. In 1966, 125,000 lone parents
(excluding widows) received a supplementary allowance, comprising 5 per
cent of all supplementary benefit recipients; by 1975, this number had
more than doubled to 276,000 and lone parents (excluding widows)
represented almost 10 per cent of all recipients.

TABLE 5: NUMBER OF SCHOOL-LEAVERS REGISTERED UNEMPLOYED

	Annual Average	August
1968	8,600	36,200
1970	9,000	36,300
1972	19,100	60,900
1974	13,700	56,000
1975	45,300	158,200
1976	81,600	194,500
1978	93,700	210,900
1980	120,100	252,000

Source: Department of Employment Gazette, 1968-80

Conversely, the number of widows dependent on supplementary benefit fell. This was mainly because national insurance widow's benefit was higher than short-term supplementary benefit. However, like some claimants in the sick and disabled group, some widows found themselves in the trap between the short-term and the long-term rate of benefit. Because periods of time in receipt of other benefits could not be used to qualify the recipient for the higher rate of supplementary benefit, widows never became eligible even if their resources were below the long-term rates of benefit. Many widows are less likely to have to turn to the supplementary benefit scheme because, as they tend to be older than other lone parents, with fewer or older dependants, and as widows' benefit, unlike supplementary benefit, is not affected by earnings, they have greater opportunity and incentive to work.

The fourth main group receiving supplementary benefit are the sick and disabled, composed mainly of people of working age who are incapable of work because of illness or physical or mental incapacity. The number dependent on supplementary benefit alone during this period increased by about one per cent a year. The number receiving supplementary benefit in addition to a national insurance benefit, however, more than halved to 77,000 in December 1975 with the introduction of an invalidity benefit which is higher than the short-term supplementary benefit rate. However, it has since been estimated that 70,000 people fell into the 'invalidity trap', discussed above. This ended in 1983 when the Government announced that time on invalidity benefit would be used to qualify for the long-term rate of supplementary benefit.

The changing population of claimants dependent on supplementary benefit had implications for the image of the scheme, which is discussed below in relation to the welfare backlash of the 1960s and 1970s, and for its administration. Supplementary benefit was very expensive to operate. In 1975, it cost £1 to administer every £7.50 paid out in benefit. (SBC, 1976) These costs varied widely according to the category of claimant: from £36 a year per supplementary pensioner to £134 a year per lone parent. (See table 6) Over two-thirds of the work done by supplementary benefit staff was estimated in 1976 to be on supplementary allowance cases, which comprised at that time around 40 per cent of the case-load. This disparity in costs was due to three factors: the number of discretionary additions requested by supplementary allowance recipients and the number of discretionary deductions made; the administrative controls operated with regard to certain groups; and the frequency and complexity of supplementary allowance claims.

Supplementary allowance recipients made more claims for lump sum exceptional needs payments (ENPs) than did supplementary pensioners. (See p. 40) The situation was reversed with exceptional circumstances additions. The reasons for this are discussed below in the section on discretion. Its relevance to this discussion of the disparity in cost of administering benefits to different groups of claimants arises from the SBC's finding that "ENPs take more than twice as much time and effort to administer as weekly additions to benefit". (SBC, 1977, p. 110)

Under the Supplementary Benefits Act 1976, the SBC was empowered to increase benefit for all claimants. Deductions could be made in supplementary allowance cases only. Besides the penalties imposed on some unemployed claimants (see p. 40), deductions were made also to allow the Commission to make payments direct to a third party; 'payments direct' could be made on behalf of all claimants. In practice 83 per cent of such payments made to fuel boards in 1977 were on behalf of supplementary allowance cases. In a survey carried out by the SBC Inspectorate in 1977 on the incidence of deductions, it was found that they occurred most frequently in the 21-39 years' age group, especially where there were children in the family: "One parent families featured prominently". (SBC, 1978, p. 111)

The second factor contributing to the higher administrative costs for supplementary allowance claimants was the tighter control and closer supervision given to guard against abuse of the scheme. The unemployed were not given order books. Entitlement to benefit was dependent on signing on at the local unemployment benefit office at designated intervals, after which a giro would be sent out by post. The costs of paying by giro cheque have been estimated more recently at 51 pence each when produced by a central office computer and 58 pence each when produced manually in the local office. The costs of paying by order book were estimated to be 19 pence and 34 pence respectively. (Social Services Committee, 1980) Unemployment review officers were employed to ensure that unemployed claimants were looking for work. Liable relative officers were employed to trace the husbands of separated or deserted wives to secure maintenance payments.

Finally the increase in the number of supplementary allowance claimants led to a disproportionate increase in administrative costs because such claims are more complex. Claimants in this category tend to go on and off benefit more frequently: the unemployed and sick fall in and out of work and lone parents may form a new relationship or take up employment. In an internal study, the SBC Inspectorate found that

TABLE 6: <u>NUMBERS AND COSTS OF DIFFERENT GROUPS OF CLAIMANTS ON SUPPLEMENTARY BENEFIT IN DECEMBER 1976</u>

Claimants	Total numbers	Percentage of all claimants	Total annual gross cost * £m	Total annual administrative cost £m	Average annual administrative cost per claimant £	Percentage of total administrative cost
Pensioners	1,687,000	57%	639	61	36	29%
Unemployed [1]	654,000	22%	750	82	120	39%
Lone parent families not included in other groups [2]	303,000	10%	430	41	134	20%
Sick claimants	243,000	8%	167	19	80	9%

Note: *Total gross cost = Benefit and administrative costs before any money has been recovered from local authorities in respect of rent and rate rebates, the National Insurance Fund or relatives with a liability to maintain their spouses and children

1 Estimated figures
2 Excludes one parent families included in other groups

Source: <u>SBC Annual Report 1976</u>, table 2.1

unemployed and lone parent claimants were far more likely to have
more than one successful claim in the course of one year. (See Table 7)

TABLE 7: NUMBER OF SPELLS ON SUPPLEMENTARY BENEFIT WITHIN A TWELVE
MONTH PERIOD, BY REASONS WHY CLAIMS COMMENCED

Number of spells	Retirement	Incapacity for work	Lone care of children	Unemployment	Other
1	98%	90%	80%	58%	81%
2	1%	3%	11%	24%	19%
3	–	6%	6%	12%	–
4+	*	1%	3%	6%	–
TOTAL	100%	100%	100%	100%	100%
Number of claimants	208	161	151	315	18

* less than ½ per cent

Source: Review of the Supplementary Benefits Scheme: Background Paper No. 8
table 6

Thus, in the twelve months to December 1976, 5.7 million claims for
benefit were received, only a small minority of which came from people
over retirement age, while over half came from the unemployed. (SBC,
1977, p. 179)   The unemployed featured particularly prominently in the
number of claims for benefit for two reasons. First, unemployed
supplementary benefit claimants are "drawn mainly from the bottom end
of the labour market where pay is low, jobs are insecure, skills are
limited and trade unions are weakest: 60 per cent of them are
registered for unskilled work". (SBC, 1978, p. 43) Such workers are
three times as likely to have repeated spells of unemployment within
a twelve month period. Secondly, claims from the unemployed for
supplementary benefit fluctuate seasonally, whereas for other groups
it is relatively constant. Part of this fluctuation can be explained
by seasonal fluctuations in the rate of unemployment. More

important for the administrative pressure it placed on the scheme
was the additional impact of large numbers of students and school-
leavers claiming at one time, particularly in the summer when local
offices were least able to cope.

The rapid increase in the number of students registering as
unemployed and claiming supplementary benefit in the vacations
followed a publicity campaign by the National Union of Students
(NUS) in the early 1970s. In August 1975, students accounted for one
in twelve supplementary benefit beneficiaries registered as unemployed.
The SBC made it clear in its second Annual Report that it did not
regard "student support as a proper function of the supplementary
benefits scheme". (1977, p. 29) The influx of students in the summer
months when large numbers of staff were on holiday was identified as
particularly problematic. In the summer of 1976, nearly 150,000
students were paid benefit despite the SBC's reservation that
"difficulties of testing availability for work means that supplementary
benefit can be paid in these cases whether or not the student is really
looking for a job". (1976, p. 119) In the 1976/77 academic year, the
SBC was successful in securing changes in student grant arrangements
which reduced the number of students who could claim during the
Christmas and Easter vacations. (SBC, 1976, ch. 8) As a consequence
23,000 students received benefit over the Christmas period in 1976
compared to 155,000 in the previous year.

Following the raising of the school-leaving age to 16 in the 1973/74
academic year, school-leavers were able to claim benefit immediately
and therefore also added to the sudden influx of claimants in the
summer months. This influx, reported the SBC, led to "our local
offices - as well as Careers Offices, experiencing severe operational
difficulties". (1976, p. 54) The SBC also doubted the wisdom of
paying benefit to school leavers because "some 30 per cent of those
registering for work ... cannot be regarded as immediately seeking
work" and secondly, because "the availability of supplementary benefit
may even be an inducement for them to say that they intend leaving
school, as benefit is not payable to those intending to remain at
school". (1976, p. 54)

The initial claim and assessment is the most complex element in the
administration of supplementary benefit: the number of dependents,
earnings, savings, rent, contributions records, work records must,
amongst other facts, be verified. For the supplementary allowance
applicant this is likely to be more complicated than for the average
supplementary pensioner. Most revisions to benefit assessment occur
in the early stages of a claim. For example in 1976, 65 per cent of
all revisions occurred during the first 13 weeks. (SBC, 1978, p. 13)
It is not surprising then that mistakes are most frequently made in
the initial assessment. The complexity and frequency of claims by the
unemployed particularly would also account for the finding by the SBC
Inspectorate that revisions to benefit following the discovery of an
error were twice as high for the unemployed as for any other group.
(BG No. 19)*

---

*BG refers to the published background papers to the SB review: see Appendix 1

The growing use of discretion

As the discussion in the previous chapter shows, the conflict inherent in trying to administer a highly discretionary system to large numbers of claimants with a wide variety of needs was causing concern even before the introduction of supplementary benefit in 1966. (see for example, p.22), and provided part of the rationale behind the changes made.

By 1975, the discretion versus rights debate was being waged still more vigorously when it became clear that the 1966 reforms had provided only temporary respite to the increasing use of discretionary powers. Before looking at the arguments of the debate, the reasons for the failure of the Supplementary Benefits Act 1966 in this respect are examined.

The Act did produce an initial sharp drop in the number of exceptional circumstances additions from 1,157,000 in November 1965 to 594,000 in November 1967, despite an increase in the number of claimants. The downward trend continued up to 1971. Subsequently, however, the number of ECAs steadily increased until, in 1975, over 1.5 million ECAs were made and 39 per cent of all claimants were in receipt of a weekly addition to benefit. (See table 8)

TABLE 8: NO. OF CLAIMANTS IN RECEIPT OF AN EXCEPTIONAL CIRCUMSTANCES ADDITION (ECAs)[*] IN A WEEK IN NOV/DEC

	Total with ECA	% of all SB claimants	On long term rate (a)	On short term rate
1968	527	(20.0)	452	75
1970	445	(16.2)	381	63
1972	482	(16.6)	407	75
1974	912	(34.1)	841	71
1976 [(b)]	1,431	(48.7)	1,226	205
1978	1,666	(56.8)	1,431	235
1980 [*]	2,109	(67.6)	1,757	351

Source: Social Security Statistics, 1982 table 34.40

[*]   From 24 November 1980, ECAs were replaced by additional requirements under new rules introduced in the Social Security Act 1980

(a)   Prior to 1 October 1973, the long-term scale rate was the basic scale rate supplemented by a long-term addition

(b)   Estimates for UE cases. Figures shown are approximations

The main reason for the increase in ECAs was the rise in the number of extra heating additions. (See table 9)

TABLE 9: NO. OF RECKONABLE EXPENSES [a] TAKEN INTO
ACCOUNT IN CASES IN WHICH ECAs WERE IN
PAYMENT ON A DAY IN NOV/DEC 1968-1979

	Extra heating 1	Special diet 2	Laundry 3	Domestic help 4	Other 5	Total Cols 1-5	Anomaly/ Trans- itional payments
1968	143	239	92	33	33	540	363
1970	196	308	106	31	33	674	188
1972	232	326	104	31	36	729	143
1974	708	350	162	16	36	1,272	120
1976[b]	1,233	373	154	11	74	1,845	116
1978	1,546	386	143	23	66	2,165	5
1979	1,637[c]	377	142	29	67	2,252	3

Source: SBC Annual Report 1979, Table 16.1

(a)   Reckonable expenses are the amounts in respect of particular
           special expenses taken into account in the calculation of
           ECAs, before deduction of the LTA (then scale rate margin)
           where this is applicable

(b)   Estimates for UE cases. Figures are approximations

(c)   In addition an estimated 192,000 householders aged 75 or
           over, or who have a dependent aged 75 or over, or a child
           under 5 years of age, received a heating addition
           retrospectively from 12 November 1979

Following the increase in fuel prices which resulted from the Conservative Government's decision to phase out subsidies to the gas and electricity industries from 1973, and growing concern about the dangers of hypothermia amongst the elderly, amendments were made in the National Insurance and Supplementary Benefits Act 1973. The margin in the long-term scale rate (which under the provisions of the same Act replaced the long-term addition) was no longer offset against reckonable expenses for extra heating. As the majority of extra heating expenses at the time were for amounts less than the value of the long-term addition, there was an immediate doubling of payments for extra heating. In 1974 the SBC simplified the qualifying criteria for standard heating additions, which had accounted for a large number of errors in the calculation of entitlement and this, together with the publication of new explanatory leaflets and improved liaison with social services departments, led to a further increase. By December 1975, the number of extra heating additions alone was over three-quarters of a million.

Under the supplementary benefits scheme, claimants could also receive a lump sum payment to meet exceptional need. Between 1966 and 1976, the number of such payments trebled. This increase was due to two factors. First, the changing population of claimants. (See Table 10) In the twelve months to December 1975, 11 per cent of pensioners received one or more ENPs. Twenty-five per cent of supplementary allowance beneficiaries received such a payment during the same period: 48 per cent of lone parents, 20 per cent of the sick and disabled group and 16 per cent of unemployed claimants. Secondly, ENPs were a prime target for the growing welfare rights movement (see p. 48) and orchestrated campaigns were launched by some groups to encourage take-up.

In the discussion on the growth of discretion generated by the Commission, less attention was paid to the powers to reduce benefit. (SBC, 1976, ch. 7) Deductions were made either as a sanction against some claimants, most frequently the unemployed, or to help claimants manage their income. Reduction or withdrawal of benefit as a sanction was covered by paragraph 4 (1) (b) of the Supplementary Benefits Act: "Where there are exceptional circumstances ... a supplementary allowance may be reduced below the amount so calculated or may be withheld". This power was used most frequently in cases of voluntary unemployment, that is where the claimant was dismissed because of his own misconduct or left work without due cause. In these cases, benefit was reduced by 40 per cent for up to six weeks. When the Commission judged that a claimant had refused suitable employment, benefit could be withheld completely. In 1967, 13,600 unemployed claimants were subject to the voluntary unemployment deduction; in 1975 the number had risen to 26,200. This increase was due entirely to the increase in the number registered as unemployed. Between these two years the proportion affected actually dropped from 6 per cent to 5 per cent. Over the whole period the percentage varied between 4 per cent and 7 per cent. (SBC, 1975, p. 69)

The Supplementary Benefits Commission was also empowered to reduce benefit in order to make payments direct to a third party. This power could be used with or without the claimant's agreement and was applied mainly to payments of rent direct to the landlord or for fuel to the relevant authority. On the recommendation of the Finer Committee on One Parent Families, the SBC used this power more freely and the number of 'rent direct' cases doubled from 26,000 to 51,000 in 1975 (see table 11). This number had almost doubled again by 1978 when rent was paid direct to the landlord in 92,000 cases.

The massive rise in fuel prices between 1974 and 1977 increased the problems poor consumers faced in meeting their bills. Special arrangements were negotiated with the fuel boards to prevent disconnections of the most vulnerable groups of supplementary benefit claimants. The SBC was allowed to make direct payments to cover the cost of current consumption plus, where appropriate, an amount to cover arrears. In 1975, 37,000 claimants had deductions made to cover fuel costs. No figures are available for 1976, but by 1977

TABLE 10:   TOTAL EXCEPTIONAL NEEDS PAYMENTS ISSUED & NUMBERS ISSUED PER 1000 CASES 1968-80

	ALL CASES		PENSIONERS		ALLOWANCES	
	No. of ENPs 000s	ENPs per 1000 cases	No. of ENPs 000s	ENPs per 1000 cases	No. of ENPs 000s	ENPs per 1000 cases
1968	470	178	140	75	330	423
1970	560	204	181	95	380	452
1972	740	254	212	110	532	532
1974	830	310	260	144	570	655
1976	1110	377	288	170	827	661
1978	1200	409	294	169	905	760
1980	1130	362	243	144	885	623

Source: Social Security Statistics 1982, Tables 34.30 and 34.97

TABLE 11:   DIRECT DEDUCTIONS MADE FOR RENT, FUEL AND CLOTHING

| Year [1] | Rent Direct | | | | Fuel Direct | | | | Savings for Clothing | | | |
| | SP* | | SA** | | SP | | SA | | SP | | SA | |
	Number	Average £	Number	Average £	Number	Average £	Number	Average £	Number	Average £	Number	Average £
1971	2,000	2.09	13,000	3.31	......not available......				-	-	2,000	0.65
1972	5,000	2.34	16,000	3.54	......not available......				↙	0.41	3,000	0.75
1973	4,000	2.36	16,000	3.25	......not available......				-	-	3,000	0.73
1974	5,000	4.15	21,000	5.23	......not available......				1,000	0.50	5,000	0.93
1975	6,000	5.76	45,000	6.56	7,000	1.91	30,000	2.28	-	-	9,000	1.16
1976	......		......		...... not available industrial action				......		......	
1977	9,000	6.84	78,000	8.46	17,000	2.58	85,000	3.44	↙	1.50	25,000	1.25
1978	10,000	7.12	82,000	9.17	12,000	3.68	85,000	4.09	1,000	1.21	27,000	1.36
1979	9,000	8.36	82,000	10.32	10,000	3.73	70,000	4.67	1,000	0.96	31,000	1.66

Source: Correspondence with the SBC

Notes: 1. Figures relate to deductions made in November, except for 1975 December

     *   Supplementary pensioners   **   supplementary allowances

    ↙   Less than 500

Numbers relate to numbers of deductions not numbers of cases

102,000 such deductions were made. Claimants often had no say in how much would be deducted, especially where there were arrears. The sum held back was the result of negotiations between the local office and the fuel board. The average deductions made for fuel, which of course do not reflect "the number of cases in which amounts considerably in excess of the average figures are made", (SBC, 1977, pp. 146-7) were £3.53 per week for electricity and £2.83 for gas in November 1977.

In the mid-1970s the Commission used its powers to make savings deductions for other expenses, especially clothing. The powers given to the SBC in this regard were to enable it to intervene "in cases of mismanagement or misuse of benefit to make on the claimant's behalf savings to meet a particular need. Such arrangements (could) ... be made where a beneficiary agrees to it, or they may be applied compulsorily where a claimant persistently failed to provide out of the weekly supplementary benefit for normal requirements". (SBC, 1976, p. 67) Whilst the number of such deductions remained small compared to the total number of claimants, the rate of increase was very fast: from 2,000 in 1971, to 9,000 in 1975 to 25,000 in 1977 (see Table 11).

As the number of discretionary payments increased from 1966 onwards, so increasing numbers of claimants exercised their right of appeal to an independent appeal tribunal. (See Table 12) Between 1971 and 1975, the number of appeals lodged and the number heard almost trebled. Each time an appeal is lodged the decision must be re-examined by the local office. In 1975, 35 per cent of appeals were revised before the Tribunal hearings; of the 65 per cent which were heard almost one-fifth were successful. The most common reasons for an appeal were to challenge the amount of benefit awarded or the refusal of benefit (52 per cent in 1976) or to challenge the refusal of or level of an ENP (45 per cent in 1976). As table 12 shows, whilst Tribunals used their power to overturn the Commission's decisions slightly less frequently between 1973 and 1976, they were most likely to do so on appeals against the refusal of or the level of a discretionary payment. The success rate for ECA and ENP appeals in 1976 was 34.7 and 27.6 per cent respectively, compared to 18.9 per cent for all appeals. The findings of a special study carried out for the review team on a small sample of appeals reached a similar conclusion but found also that the success rate of 28 per cent for all ENP appeals rose to 50 per cent when only appeals against the amount of the Commission's award were examined. (BG no. 12)

The frequent revision of local office decisions on discretionary payments was objected to by the SBC and its officials on two grounds. First, that it undermined the morale of staff, who reached decisions in line with national SBC or local office policy, to see them later overturned by a Tribunal which was not so constrained. Appeals against discretionary decisions were regarded "as a second look at the facts, in effect a second claim rather than an appeal as normally understood". (DHSS, 1978, p. 86) Secondly, it was felt that Tribunals were undermining attempts by the SBC to regulate the use of discretion at the local level. Officers were expected to exercise their discretionary power in line with guidance laid down by the SBC. Tribunals were not so constrained and could reach more favourable decisions than those open to officers following instructions.

Dissatisfaction with the Tribunal system itself by staff and by pressure groups (see Fulbrook, 1972) culminated in the very critical

TABLE 12: ANALYSIS OF RESULTS OF APPEALS

Year	Appeals lodged	Cases heard	Decisions revised by Tribunal	Decisions confirmed by Tribunal
1971	39,150	22,420	4,186	18,234
1972	59,136	33,735	5,212	18,523
1973	50,752	24,486	3,854	19,632
1974	55,743	25,611	4,493	21,118
1975	68,975	32,759	6,568	26,191
1976	101,112	55,125	10,450	44,675
1977	114,734	62,896	12,071	50,825
1978	115,467	62,308	12,526	49,782
1979	94,178	50,639	10,840	39,789

Source: SBC Annual Report 1975, p. 93, Table 42. SBC Annual Report 1979, p. 122, Table 13.1.

Note: Appeals lodged but not heard may be withdrawn by the claimant, ruled outside the Tribunal's jurisdiction or the decision may be revised by the local office.

findings of Government sponsored research published in 1975 (Bell, 1975). In 1976, a group of officials drawn from the DHSS and the Lord Chancellor's Office was set up to review the supplementary benefit appeals system. Plans for changes and improvements in the appeal system were announced by Stanley Orme, Minister of Social Security in January 1977. The changes were the first attempt to meet the recommendations of the Bell Report to judicialise the system. Legal chairmen were to be introduced gradually and other members were to receive more training. The changes allowed "a direct right of appeal from the Tribunals to the High Court on a point of law". (See SBC, 1977, Appendix k), and the Minister did not rule out "further consideration of a second-tier appeal to a higher tribunal". (ibid)

The trend towards judicialisation of the appeals system had important ramifications for the policy function of the Supplementary Benefits Commission. If a body of case-law was built up, as in the national insurance appeals system, the Commission would be in the position of having to adapt its policy and much of its autonomy would be removed to the appeals system. Improved training of chairmen and members, and increased representation for claimants (also recommended by Bell), would mean that Tribunals might decide against the Commission more often, because appeals where the claimant was represented were almost twice as likely to be successful as appeals where the appellant attended alone.

The pressure caused by the increased number of discretionary payments and appeals led to David Donnison re-opening the discretion versus rights debate soon after taking office. Donnison took the argument to the public in the Annual Reports (see, in particular, SBC, 1977, pp. 11-14 and ch. 7), in his speeches and, in the pages of the specialist weeklies he debated with pressure groups and academics.[6] The protagonists agreed on the problems. They differed, however, on the immediate solution. Three main criticisms were made of the prevailing reliance on discretion; it undermined the concept of benefit as of right; it was an inadequate response to inadequate benefits.

One of the underlying principles on which supplementary benefit was founded was that claimants were entitled to benefit as of right. The use of discretion to meet predictable and basic needs undermined that principle. As the SBC acknowledged, the administration of discretion was "on the basis that the initiative generally lies with the claimant" (DHSS/SBC, 1973, para 60), with the result that it was those with the greatest knowledge, or who demanded most, not necessarily those in greatest need who benefitted most. For example, unemployed claimants tended to receive fewer lump-sum payments than other groups of supplementary allowance recipients, despite the fact many had unmet needs. For example, a study of unemployed families found that three-quarters of those with children lacked even the minimum standard of clothing laid down by the SBC. (See DHSS/SBC, 1977).

The differential application for discretionary payments was exacerbated by the considerable disparity in the number awarded by the twelve DHSS regions. For example, in 1976 the number of ENPs as a proportion of the workload ranged between 14.7 per cent and 22.6 per cent. The variations between local offices within regions was even greater. "The highest local office ratio ... (could) ... be as much

as ten or eleven times that of the office with the lowest ratio".
(SBC, 1976, p. 111) The pressure groups argued that claimants should
have a legal right to an adequate benefit and not depend on the
vagaries of administrative action to get help with essential
expenditure. (See Lister, 1975)

The Commission made attempts to standardise the exercise of
discretion at the local level. It issued voluminous and detailed
guidelines to its staff. These complex codes of instruction provided
no direct guidance to claimants because they were unpublished (except
in a much abridged and simplified form in the Supplementary Benefits
Handbook) and were thus criticised by pressure groups and certain
sections of the press because of the secrecy surrounding them. With
staff, who did have access, they were equally unpopular. First, for
their sheer volume. In 1975, about 10,000 pages of new or revised
instructions were issued to local offices. (Expenditure Committee 1977,
vol. II, p. 399) The result of such an "uneasy amalgam of policy and
procedures ... difficult to use ... difficult to understand ...
written in a style that manages to be at the same time lengthy and
vague ... (was that it was) little used and still less liked". (BG no. 23)

The most important criticism of discretion levied by the pressure
groups was that it was a cheap, inequitable and inefficient way of
compensating for inadequate scale rates. The large number of
discretionary payments to meet such basic needs as clothing and heating,
together with more frequent intervention by the SBC to help claimants to
budget their weekly benefit, were seen as symptoms of the more serious
underlying problem, namely that many claimants found it very difficult
to manage on the basic scale rates. This conclusion was drawn by the
SBC itself: "the supplementary benefits scheme provides, particularly
for families with children, incomes that are barely adequate to meet
their needs at a level that is consistent with normal participation
in the life of the relatively wealthy society in which they live. This
impression is borne out by the extent to which we find it necessary
to make use of our discretionary powers to provide more than the
minimum levels of benefit determined by the scale rates". (DHSS/SBC
1977, p. 28)

The pressure groups saw the solution to the problems caused by over
reliance on discretionary payments in an increase in the basic benefit
levels. At that time, the problem of already inadequate scale rates
was exacerbated by the high rates of inflation which were a feature
of the 1970s, especially in the early years of the 1974-79 Labour
Administration. Though the 1974 uprating was brought forward to
July and there were two upratings in 1975, with inflation running at
26 per cent in the summer of 1975, standards of living soon fell
between upratings. It was only in 1975 that the Labour Government
took steps to ensure that some claimants, at least, would share in
the rising standards of living enjoyed by the rest of the community.
From 1975, the long-term benefits were increased in line with prices
or earnings, whichever rose faster. However, the uprating of short-
term benefits remained unchanged. Claimants on benefit for under
two years and the unemployed who never qualified for the higher rate,
received no extra help. No changes were made either in the value of
benefits paid to children. [7] Whilst the rates of supplementary benefit
have increased slightly faster than prices, and had improved in
relation to earnings since they were set in 1948, in November 1976 the
level of benefit paid to a married couple on the short-term and
long-term rates as a proportion of net earnings was only 49.8 per cent
and 60.0 per cent respectively.

By 1975, Donnison and the SBC saw a reduction in discretionary payments as the key to solving the complexity of administration. This was regarded as one of the most urgent issues to be tackled. As discussed above, the administration of this part of the scheme accounted for a large part of the complex codes issued to local office staff and a disproportionate amount of office time. In fact in 1976, ENPs and ECAs represented only 5 per cent of net benefit cost, and 6 per cent of administrative costs. What was clear to the SBC was that previously increased demand had been met by increased numbers of staff, this was not the solution they thought would be feasible in the less favourable economic climate of the mid-70s. It was equally clear that staff would not tolerate any further deterioration in their work conditions, and the only way to alleviate prevailing and growing pressures would be to find ways of simplifying administration. This leads, then, to discussion of the influence of staff in creating a demand for reform.

Internal pressure from staff

When the Ministry of Pensions and National Insurance and the National Assistance Board were merged in 1966, 25,000 staff were employed to administer contributory benefits (including non-means-tested benefits, such as family allowances) and 12,500 to administer supplementary benefit. By December 1975, the regional directorate of the DHSS employed 500 staff, the regional and central offices employed 3,800 working on all benefits, and the 927 local social security offices employed over 60,000 staff, roughly half of whom worked on supplementary benefit. The growth in the number of staff working on contributory benefits was in line with the new benefits which were introduced and the number of claimants. The increase in the number of staff working on supplementary benefit was much greater than the increase in the number of claimants, over 100 per cent versus 12 per cent. (Expenditure Committee, p. 400) This disproportionate increase was due to the increase in the number of discretionary payments and deductions, the more complex caseload, the number of bulk reassessments which were made following the more frequent upratings and the introduction of new or improved benefits which affected supplementary benefit claimants. The scheme also assumed some ad hoc responsibilities, such as the administration of butter and beef tokens.

The increased pressure and complexity of work, together with simultaneous demands to curtail the growth in the number of civil servants led to discontent amongst staff. The Staffside Unions imposed various forms of industrial action, most commonly by instituting overtime bans or banning the use of casual staff, on which many local supplementary benefit offices depended. Following such action in 1972, the Departmental Whitley Council, representing staff and management set up a joint working party to "examine the possibilities of simplifying methods of work and procedures with a view to reducing the burden of work in regional and local offices". (ibid, p. 952) Following further industrial unrest in 1974 and 1975 a joint official and staffside examination was set up to look at how the pay, grading and structure within the department's social security operations matched the demands of the work. As a result, clerical and executive officers working on supplementary benefit were awarded an extra £100 per annum, in recognition of the difficult burden they had to bear.

In 1975, the Government introduced cash limits as part of their strategy to cut public expenditure. Social security benefits themselves could not be subject to such limits because expenditure is determined by the level of benefits and the number of claimants. A cash limit could, however, be imposed on the administrative costs. The DHSS was required to make savings of £5 million by 1977-78 and £14.4 million by 1978-79 (at 1975 prices). Because the supplementary benefits scheme was such a voracious consumer of staff resources and extremely expensive to administer, it was inevitable that substantial savings would have to be made, and that, because of staff attitudes, could only be made if, at the same time, the workload was reduced.

The growth of the welfare rights movement

Two developments outside the supplementary benefits scheme contributed to the internal pressures for reform: the growth of the welfare rights movement and the 'welfare backlash' discussed below. The growth of the welfare rights movement from the late 1960s onwards was significant both in drawing the attention of Governments to the needs of the poor and in drawing the attention of claimants to their rights to welfare benefits.[8] Many voluntary groups such as the Child Poverty Action Group (CPAG),[8] Gingerbread and the Disablement Income Group (DIG) were formed to tackle the issue of incomes of the poor; existing groups, such as the National Union of Students and the National Council for One Parent Families, became concerned with issues of income maintenance and the way the administration of the supplementary benefits scheme affected the groups they represented.

In 1970, CPAG published its first National Welfare Benefits Handbook, which provided a guide to supplementary benefit and other welfare benefits. It has been revised annually ever since. The Penguin Guide to Supplementary Benefit written by Tony Lynes, a past director of CPAG, was first published in 1972. Other national groups such as the National Federation of Claimants Unions, Age Concern, the Disability Alliance and numerous local groups produced their own rights guides.[9] The SBC itself published the first Supplementary Benefits Handbook in May 1970. Local authorities gradually began to appoint welfare rights officers to improve the availability of information on benefits. The growth in size and influence of the welfare rights lobby was regarded by the SBC as one of the key factors in the increase in the number of claims for discretionary payments and in the number of appeals. In the 1976 report, it was frankly admitted that the current highly discretionary system was "viable for so long as additional payments were exceptional, for needs which were 'felt and expressed' by claimants themselves and while claimants broadly accepted decisions by local officers. It must be highly doubtful, however, whether it could continue to be so if pressures for welfare rights ... were to develop ... on a continuing basis". (SBC, 1977, p. 115)

One of the most influential and consistent critics of the supplementary benefits scheme throughout the 1970s was CPAG. campaign for higher family allowances, by the early 1970s the main problems dealt with by its Citizen's Rights Office, a welfare rights advisory and advocacy service, related to supplementary benefit. The group published a series of pamphlets highlighting the problems of the scheme. (eg. Coleman, 1971, Field & Grieve, 1972, Elks, 1974)

The main criticisms directed at the scheme were concerned at the level of benefits, the size of the scheme and the manner of its administration. CPAG argued, citing individual cases tackled by the Citizen's Rights Office, that there was "accumulating evidence of the inability of the supplementary benefits system to provide a fair, efficient and humane service to claimants". (Lister, 1975, p. 28) CPAG carried out research and collated evidence on the way the SBC administered the scheme and used its discretionary powers and concluded that in several respects "claimants (were) unjustly being denied their rights" under such rules as the wage stop, the four-week rule and the cohabitation rule. (p. 30) Criticism of the administration of the scheme stemmed not just from the unreasonable pressure put on offices because of the large numbers of claimants, but from the two conflicting roles assistance schemes have always been asked to perform: on the one hand to meet need, and on the other to prevent abuse. In trying to ensure that claimants were genuine, for example in not being able to find work, there was a danger that such vigilant administration would screen out also those in need, or at least present such a barrage of administrative checks that the problem of stigma as a deterrent to claiming would be further exacerbated.

The welfare backlash

Pressure on the supplementary benefits scheme and on social security as a whole came from outside in the form of a welfare backlash, or as the events of 1976 have been called "scroungerphobia". (Deacon, 1978) The supplementary benefits review itself was announced in the summer of 1976 when "public concern at the possible abuse of ... benefits became more intense and was expressed more widely than at any time since the 1920s". (p. 120) The press campaign that fuelled such feelings continued to the end of that year. (See Golding and Middleton, 1982)

Such hostility was not new. The history of the social security system has been chequered with outbursts of hostility towards welfare benefit recipients and administrative campaigns to limit fraud and abuse. In the 1920s over three million claimants were refused benefit on the grounds that they were not genuinely seeking work, though there was little evidence to show that such work existed. (Deacon, 1976) The late 1960s and early 1970s saw the issue of fraud and abuse within the social security system coming onto the agenda more frequently and gain greater public support. Each time such a campaign gained momentum, so the Government took steps to show its concern and introduced measures to crack down on possible abuse or misuse of the system, regardless of the actual evidence which existed on the extent of the problem. The introduction of the four-week rule and the cohabitation rule in 1968 followed a 'welfare backlash' similar to that of 1976. Newspapers and politicians painted emotive pictures of "... genuine old-age pensioners reduced to tears by pushful young men elbowing them to one side, some with bulging wallets". (Gresham Cooke MP, Hansard, vol. 586, col. 914, 20.10.69)

The next wave of concern which arrived in the early 1970s led Sir Keith Joseph, the Secretary of State for Social Services, to set up a Committee to examine "Abuse of Social Security Benefits". Under its Chairman, Sir Henry Fisher, the Committee was asked to "review the measures taken by the DHSS and the Department of Employment to prevent and detect abuse through wrongful claims to social security

benefits" and "to recommend any necessary changes" (Fisher, 1973)
This Committee, whose approach was not on the whole sympathetic to
claimants [10] concluded that the amount of abuse was very small as a
percentage of total expenditure on benefits but still serious because
"substantial sums of money are misappropriated each year". (p. 5)

The virulent outbreak of "scroungerphobia" of 1976 reached a peak
when newspaper headline writers were attracted by the claims of Ian
Sproat, Conservative MP, who claimed that 20 per cent of supplementary
benefits claims were fraudulent and that 50 per cent of the unemployed
could find jobs if they wanted. Though these claims were later to be
discredited [11], they undoubtedly contributed to the general hostile
environment in which the Labour Government set up a departmental
Co-ordinating Committee on Abuse in 1976.

Much of the criticism made of the social security scheme in the
press in 1976 was concerned not only with fraud and abuse but also with
the level of benefits and their administration. Golding and Middleton
found that the most explicit theme in the media during this period
was the generosity and inefficiency of the welfare apparatus. (1982)
In the month that the review of the supplementary benefits scheme was
announced, the Daily Express carried the headline "Social Security ...
the giant that's gone out of control" (30 September 1976) and the
Daily Mirror declared that welfare is "so complicated that the system
can no longer be policed". (17 September 1976)

In 1976 the Labour Government was imposing a third year of pay
restraint; tax thresholds were falling and, in return for help from
the International Monetary Fund, significant cuts were made in public
expenditure. However, while those in work were limited to wage increases
of £6, social security payments were increased in line with inflation,
which for some claimants amounted to more than the £6 pay limit. The
fall in the standard of living felt by many workers undoubtedly contributed to the resentment towards those unable to support themselves.
It is difficult to quantify how widespread such feelings were. They
were important, however, insofar as they contributed to a climate in
which the Government felt obliged to take action. The link between
the welfare backlash and the necessity for reform of the supplementary
benefits scheme was made explicit later when the findings of the
supplementary benefits review were published. In the foreword to the
report, the Labour Government Ministers wrote: "We have already
published our proposals to counter fraud and abuse. But the
complexities ... of the supplementary benefits scheme ... are not
helping our efforts". (DHSS, 1978)

Conclusion

In its first ten years of life, the supplementary benefits scheme was
subjected to pressures from within and from outside interests. The
numbers of claimants dependent on supplementary benefit continued to
grow, and grow significantly for those under pension age. The
increase in the numbers of unemployed claimants, in particular, showed
no signs of abating. Government sponsored research showed that many
claimants, especially those in receipt of the short-term rate of
benefit were finding it extremely difficult to manage on the basic
scale rates. This, together with the more generous application of

discretionary additions for fuel and increased activity by the welfare
rights lobby to encourage take-up of discretionary payments, led to a
situation where once again nearly a half of all claiments were receiving
exceptional circumstances additions on top of their basic benefit and
the number of exceptional needs payments had more than doubled. The
growing number of parliamentary questions on the scheme, themselves
promoted by adverse press publicity or by a vigilant welfare rights
lobby monitoring the scheme, and staff dissatisfaction left senior
departmental officials, the SBC and finally Ministers in no doubt that
the 1966 reforms had not been the panacea they were intended to be.

Attempts were made through the various official channels during these
ten years to monitor the scheme and make adjustments in the light of
emerging difficulties. The DHSS operational research unit, the SBC
Inspectorate and the Management Information Service of the DHSS
examined various aspects of the scheme ranging from in depth studies
of specific administrative practices to evaluations on the deployment
of staff. Ad hoc study groups were also set up. The scheme was
subject to a number of simplification exercises, the last of which
led to the creation of a staff suggestions scheme to glean from staff
ideas for simplification at the local and regional level. By 1976, out
of 2,000 suggestions sent in, 600 were seriously considered, over a
third of which were accepted. Whilst most of these related to
contributory benefits, special efforts were made to process those
relating to supplementary benefit. Progress on simplification of the
supplementary benefits scheme was slow, however, because "it is easier
to put forward an idea for simplification than it is to overcome the
financial and legal restraints necessary to implement it. ("New Window",
DHSS Newsletter, September 1976) A Steering Group was set up to take
up those suggestions which the Joint Working Party could not pursue
because they required a policy or legislative change. Sir Patrick
Nairne, Permanent Secretary to the DHSS, said in evidence to the
Public Expenditure Committee that "in regard to the supplementary
benefits scheme we felt that we had to look at the structure of the
scheme itself. We could not see sufficient prospect of achieving
simplification simply through looking at organisation and methods
and simplifying procedures". (Expenditure Committee, p. 450)

The SBC, itself, tried to adapt its own policy, or initiate legislative change on specific issues. These included the abolition of
the wage stop (1975), improvements in heating additions (1970, 1971
and 1973), improved diet additions (1976), changes in the cohabitation
rule (1975), changes with relation to students' entitlement (1976).
It was clear that such ad hoc changes were not, in themselves,
sufficient to relieve the scheme of its very heavy burden, or meet
outside criticism. A much more fundamental approach was needed if the
supplementary benefits scheme was not to collapse.

Notes

1. Not all Government statistics were collected on the SB scheme for 1976 because of industrial action. In the discussion and tables which follow the 1975 figures are used; all apply to Great Britain.

2. On coming to office the Conservative Government decided that figures on take-up should be collected every two years, instead of every year as before. The 1979 figures are the latest available (in May 1983).

3. See SBC, 1977, pp. 114-5 for a discussion of two such campaigns, in Batley and Coventry, and of the SBC's concern lest such action should spread.

4. A small local study in Coventry revealed that half of the supplementary allowance recipients had not heard of ENPs and only a quarter had heard of ECAs. Similar findings were obtained in a local office case-study carried out by OPCS (Ritchie & Wilson, 1979).

5. A decision could be revised by the local office if "it was made in ignorance of or was based on a mistake as to some material fact", SBC, 1976, p. 93.

6. New Society ran a series of imaginary   letters which picked up this issue, written by B. Jordan "Dear Claimant", 24.8.79, 31.8.78, 7.9.78, to which Donnison responded "Dear Bill Jordan", 21.9.78.
    See also D. Donnison, "Against Discretion", New Society, 15.9.77 and Bill Jordan, "Against Donnison", New Society, 13.10.77.

7. For a more recent discussion on the adequacy of the SB scale rates see Burghes, 1980, and for the children's rates, Piachaud, 1979.

8. For a discussion of the role of CPAG in getting poverty onto the political agenda, see Banting, 1979.

9. For example, National Federation of Claimants' Unions, Unsupported Mothers Handbook and Claimants Unions Guidebook; Age Concern, Your Rights (annual); Disability Alliance, Disability Rights Handbook (annual).

10. The Committee concluded, for example, that the number of claims for ENPs was "only further evidence of the same lack of capacity which led to the claimants going on to social security in the first place". Fisher, 1973, para 370.

11. Investigation by the DHSS of 485 cases of alleged fraud submitted by Mr Sproat found 44 cases of fraud, 22 of which were already under investigation. DHSS Press Release, 77/186, 22 June 1977.

Chapter 4

The creation of a review of the supplementary benefits scheme

By 1975, it was clear that the creation of the supplementary benefits
scheme had not solved either the problems that had beset national
assistance up to 1966 nor the pressures which had emerged over the
next decade. It was also clear that the solution lay in more radical
action than the kind of administrative changes or more ad hoc legislative
changes which had taken place. What was needed was for the Government
Ministers responsible for social assistance policy to be persuaded to
take the reform of the scheme on board and to set up an enquiry.

The move from issue recognition to issue adoption is the first
crucial step in the policy-making cycle. (Nelson and Lindenfeld, 1979)
Governments are confronted by a plethora of issues for consideration
only some of which can be adopted. Social security, and especially
social assistance policy, is an extremely contentious and sensitive
area of Government policy. Contentious because it arouses
diametrically opposed positions, as discussed in the previous chapter,
which vary from calls for more generous benefits to demands for more
stringent control. Sensitive because it covers the most vulnerable but
often disparaged members of society. Unlike some other social security
benefits, most notably pensions, improvements in social assistance
offer no electoral rewards to political parties. Although in 1975 the
supplementary benefits scheme supported some 4½ million people, and by
1982 was supporting nearly 7 million, and millions more come into
contact with the scheme during the course of any one year, there is
no electoral advantage to be gained in trying to woo this group. By
contrast, politicians are extremely concerned with the views of the
general public, and "Although what 'public' feeling actually is about
an issue can rarely be determined empirically, what it is thought
to be by authorities is more important in the short-term". (Hall
et al, 1975, p. 484) With regard to welfare benefits, the little
empirical evidence which does exist suggests that, in Britain, at
best, the general public is ignorant of the facts and, at worst,
believes that the system of benefits is too generous and encourages
the undeserving. (Schlackman, BG no. 6) An EEC survey found that more
people in Britain than in any other country accept pathological
explanations of poverty. (EEC, 1977)

The fact that reform of the supplementary benefits scheme found its
way onto the policy agenda despite its unpopularity was due to the
entry on to the scene of a new set of protagonists and the strategy
which they adopted to overcome the antipathy of Ministers and the
opposition of other Government departments.

The Protagonists: the architects of a review

In 1975, after being the subject of much external and internal
criticism over several years, the problems of the supplementary
benefits scheme and the need for change were at last taken up by those
in a position to influence the policy-making process: by a new
Chairman of the Supplementary Benefits Commission (SBC) and the senior
DHSS officials working with the Commission.

The impetus for getting supplementary benefit reform onto the Government's agenda came with the appointment of David Donnison as Chairman of the SBC in October 1975. With his experience as Deputy Chairman behind him, and both academic and practical experience of various aspects of social policy, [1] Donnison was soon "beginning to understand supplementary benefit well enough to formulate strategies for the future". He was also convinced that "reform of some sort was on the way for sure, and urgently. We had a couple of years in which to achieve some nationwide agreement which would lead to contructive and orderly changes. After that it would be too late". (Donnison, 1982, pp. 40, 46)

Donnison was not the only person in a key position to be persuaded of the need for reform. One of the civil servant's routine duties is to monitor policy and suggest changes before problems become insurmountable. Sir Patrick Nairne, the Permanent Secretary in the DHSS, "already knew that the whole supplementary benefit scheme would have to be overhauled". (Donnison, 1982, p. 51) The importance of securing his support has been spelt out by Donnison: "one of a permanent secretary's most important tasks is to sense which sectors of the enormous front he commands are going to 'go live' ..., and get the best people into key positions there. Policy is usually formulated much lower down among principals and assistant secretaries". (p. 51) The opportunity for key staff changes arose with the retirement of three of the senior officials working with the SBC in 1975 and early 1976. Donnison was instrumental in ensuring the appointment of personnel who would be sympathetic to his style of administration and to implementing changes. With the personal intervention of Barbara Castle, then Secretary of State for Social Services, Donnison secured his choice of candidate, Geoffrey Otton, to the key post of Chief Adviser to the Commission. Otten had much relevant experience including his work with the CDP Programme in the Home Office and later as establishments officer responsible for general deployment of staff in the DHSS. He was regarded by Donnison as an "open government man", and, unlike his SBC predecessors who had been defensive about change, was an 'enabler'. He began work in January 1976. In the summer of that year, two new undersecretaries were appointed, both had long experience in the DHSS. Geoffrey Beltram had worked on supplementary benefit policy and Michael Partridge in the Regional Directorate.

Even such a united and influential group of protagonists was not in itself sufficient to ensure that, having been exposed to the problem, Ministers would be willing to act. Here Donnison had a powerful weapon. As a condition of accepting the post of Chairman, and against internal Departmental and Treasury opposition, he was given freedom to publish an independent Annual Report in which he could "comment on developments and express views about priorities". (Hansard, vol. 891, col. 262, 2.5.75) From the outset he took full advantage of this widened remit to examine critically the role and administration of the supplementary benefits scheme in the context of wider provision for the poor. Despite some criticism at the concentration of the report on the problems of the administration rather than their impact on claimants, the Annual Reports were widely welcomed. The five Annual Reports published under his Chairmanship provided a wealth of factual information and critical assessment of the scope and administration of the scheme. In the first, Donnison personally

drafted the most crucial chapter in which he set out his analysis of
the problems facing the scheme and the issues which required urgent
action. (SBC, 1976, ch. 2) This critical appraisal by the SBC was
applauded "for its boldness in ringing out an alarm over the
conditions of our social security system which will reverberate
throughout the rest of the welfare system". (Community Care, 6.10.76)

Donnison took the argument outside the Commission. The ideas in
the 1975 Annual Report were first floated in the James Seth Memorial
Lecture given at the University of Edinburgh in February 1976. (Later
published as Donnison, 1976) In his own account of his time as
Chairman, Donnison remarked that he soon reached the conclusion that
"the Commission had so few powers to do anything: our influence
would therefore depend heavily on gaining a hearing through the media".
(Donnison, 1982, p. 30) Early in 1976, he engaged in a public
correspondence with members of the Child Poverty Action Group and
academics in the columns of Social Work Today. Articles were also
published in New Society and other specialist press and journals.
With the help of a sympathetic press adviser and office lunches "with
editors of all the main newspapers and some of the radio and television
people", he was successful in his goal of convincing them "to focus
their attention upon issues more significant than the stories about 'sex
snoopers' investigating claimants' love lives which seemed to be the
standard social security news item at this time". (Donnison, 1982,
p. 30) The aim, and the result, was not 'a good press', but to get
publicity and that was undoubtedly achieved. Virtually all the
national newspapers covered the publication of the first Annual Report.
The Daily Express carried a story about "the giant that's gone out
of control" (30.9.76) and the Daily Mirror reported that "welfare
is so complicated that the system can no longer be policed". (17.9.76)
Could any Government afford to ignore such headlines? Could the
Government responsible for appointing Donnison, ignore the profound
concern which its "official watchdog" [2] was now showing publicly under
his leadership.

The united call for reform from the Commission and its officials,
together with the opening of the debate publicly, were crucial
prerequisites for getting Ministers to take this issue on board.
The problem which the protagonists then had to resolve stemmed from
the air of economic stringency which dominated all Government thinking
at the time, as since. Until the 1970s students of social policy as
well as policy-makers had discussed developments only in positive terms
of improved coverage or higher benefits. But in that decade the
deteriorating economic circumstances in many developed countries led
them to reconsider their social security provision. (See, for example
Leman, 1980; Heidenheimer et al, 1983) Britain, faced with the 1976
IMF crisis, was no exception. At such a time of economic stringency,
it became clear that those departments wanting to make policy changes
would have to re-examine their own internal expenditure priorities.
(See Chapter 1) This trend was of course continued and intensified
by the 1979 Conservative Government, under whom plans for reform of
various parts of the social security scheme were all formulated on a
nil-cost basis. [3]

Government scope to cut social security expenditure was limited.
At that time, especially with a Labour Government commanding only a
narrow parliamentary majority, cuts in the real value of benefits,
such as those made in 1980 by the Conservative Administration, were
not proposed. The value of some benefits was allowed to fall in
some years during Labour's term of office and a change in uprating
policy netted a £500m saving in 1975. An enquiry into the
supplementary benefits scheme offered Ministers the opportunity to
show that this growing sector of social security was under scrutiny
and to control future expenditure on marginal benefit costs and
administrative costs. The main benefit costs of the social security
system could not be controlled by cash limits, the main tool used by
the Labour Government to curb departmental expenditure, because the
level of expenditure is protected by law and governed by the number
of claimants and the level of benefits. The area of benefit costs
which could be brought under firmer control was the 5 per cent given
out in discretionary payments. More significant was that cash limits
could be, and were, applied to the administrative costs of the scheme.
As discussed in the previous chapter, the DHSS was required to make
substantial savings in this area. As supplementary benefit is the
most expensive benefit to administer, that had to bear a considerable
part of the cuts. An exercise to simplify the scheme through policy
changes offered the Government an effective way of controlling this
voracious consumer of civil service manpower.

Hitherto the establishment of enquiries into any aspect of Government
spending inevitably led to demands for extra resources, as evidenced
in Heclo and Wildavsky's study of Government spending:

> "Both sides (the Treasury and the spending
> departments) know ... that efforts to secure
> stable increases can often be begun by
> commissions of inquiry ... All such
> committees ... recommend increased spending
> ... Commissions make good forums for launching
> publicity campaigns ... Even an inter-
> departmental committee of officials can be
> expected to highlight any real need for
> improvement ... the result is the same, more
> money recommended for the favoured cause".
> (1977, p. 90)

The structure of the review, and the scope of the enquiry, were the
result of compromises reached between the protagonists anxious to get
changes underway and the two main opponents, the Treasury and the Civil
Service Department, anxious to protect the public purse. They were
not alone in fearing the expenditure implications of an enquiry. For
example, when the review was announced the Times said that

> "(it) is bound to provoke controversy.
> People who believe that the social security
> system is already too broad are expected to
> interpret the review as a means of seeking
> to increase public expenditure, since any
> simplification would involve higher
> expenditure rates".
> (16.9.76)

A review is set up

Enquiries into aspects of Government policy and areas of Government concern take a variety of forms: from wholly internal official reviews to fully independent Royal Commissions. In between lie various hybrid forms which, in some way, combine both internal and external expertise eg Plowden Committee, (1961) and Beveridge, (1942) Under the 1979 Conservative Government a new more managerial type of investigation was instituted. Sir Derek Rayner, Managing Director of Marks & Spencer, was brought in to look for ways of streamlining civil service procedures in all areas of Government. He reported direct to the Prime Minister. Similarly a team of top businessmen was brought together to examine ways of making NHS practices more efficient. Although Labour Ministers agreed to an enquiry, there was no Government commitment to the reform of supplementary benefit, and several of those interviewed reported there was no ministerial interest in the aims of the review. Thus, the battles which were fought on structure and scope were between the officials and the SBC fighting for action and the Treasury and Civil Service Department fearful of the consequences.

A review of the supplementary benefits scheme was announced in September 1976. The enquiry was to be internal, conducted by a small team of DHSS officials. An external source of influence was provided by the SBC. Originally, Donnison had envisaged that the SBC would carry out the enquiry. Instead an internal official review was agreed with which it would work closely, but from which it would remain independent. The SBC would be free to make its own public response.

The structure and style of the SB review represented a novel approach for official reviews. It retained the advantages of a civil service review but introduced some new features to mitigate some of the disadvantages. The review was conducted in two stages. The first comprised the investigations carried out by the review team and publication of their own report Social Assistance: a review of the supplementary benefits scheme in Great Britain (DHSS, 1978). In the second stage, which grew considerably once it was underway, the review team sought the views of the public and the many interested groups on their proposals. The precise form and extent of this consultation were not laid down beforehand but evolved gradually. These two stages were distinct but integral parts of the enquiry. Labour Ministers were committed to take account of both the review team's report and the public response. (DHSS, 1978, foreword).

The decision to conduct an internal enquiry rather than an independent external investigation was made for both practical and political reasons. In practical terms, an internal review was favoured because the size of the team could be restricted and the conclusion of the study hastened. Although some external enquiries have been concluded in a similar time to that eventually achieved by the review team, for example the Fisher Committee on Abuse of Social Security benefits was concluded within two years, (1973) this is very much the exception. External enquiries generally take longer because many diverse interests have to be represented who then have to agree a final report distilled from the wide range of evidence which is collected. The Warnock Committee which looked at the education of handicapped children and young people had 27 members, assessors from six Government departments and 15 co-opted members. (HMSO, 1978) By contrast there were only two permanent members of the review team. Together with the undersecretary with whom they worked, they were responsible for the final report. They did not have to receive the endorsement of Ministers, the SBC or other Government departments. This was extremely unusual as civil service enquiries normally culminate in an official 'departmental' report. Because final responsibility was left with individuals, and because of the second 'open government' stage, some contentious questions could be deferred for further consultation and deliberation. They were also able to put forward a wider range of alternative options for discussion than would have been possible in either a Green Paper or the more usual departmental consensus reports, which require the total agreement of all those involved before publication. The time pressure imposed on the review team still showed in the investigation and the report which followed. In particular, some issues deferred for later consideration because agreement could not be reached quickly were in fact never followed up. (See Chapter 8)

The second practical reason for an internal review was, as one official said: 'it was the natural way of going about it'. Various other aspects of social security, including pensions, earnings related supplements, child benefit and tax credits, had already been looked at internally by the normal pattern of ministerial and official committees. At the time of the review, other policy divisions in the DHSS were looking at short-term benefits, the industrial injuries scheme and benefits for people with disabilities. The SB review was a similar sort of technical exercise. In the light of the growing administrative pressures already stretching the limits of the scheme and to prevent further deterioration with the anticipated growth in unemployment and reductions in civil service manpower, the review was, in one official's words, 'no more than an exercise in good housekeeping, which the bureaucracy is so good at'. That was "not the usual kind of 'Royal Commission' subject in which the purpose is to ascertain and weigh the views of many different interests and sections of the community". (Clarke, 1978, p. 38)

More important than the practical considerations which were taken into account when the structure of the enquiry was determined were the political compromises which had to be made. Accommodations were made, first, to enable an enquiry to be set up at all and, secondly to try to ensure that the findings of that enquiry would be acted upon. Though the social security Ministers had been persuaded to set up a review, the impetus had not come from Government and there was no commitment to find extra resources. The most important hurdle the advocates of a review had to overcome was the initial one of winning the agreement of the Treasury and the Civil Service Department (CSD) to the establishment of an enquiry to examine this area of policy. Policy developments are theoretically the responsibility of the spending departments but, in practice, the Treasury determines what is possible through its control of resources. The main concern of the Treasury in the initial discussions was to ensure that a review should not, overtly or covertly, lead to demands for increased expenditure. Similarly the CSD, which at that time was responsible for manpower, was concerned that there should be no call for additional staff. Although increasingly Royal Commissions and external Committees of Enquiry were asked to pay due attention to the "effective use of resources" (Warnock, HMSO, 1978, p. 1) or have "regard to the cost and other implications" (Pearson, HMSO, 1978, p. 3), a small internal review team structure allowed the Treasury the greatest degree of control and influence over the scope and recommendations of the enquiry. One official remarked that 'the Treasury would not permit an enquiry which would come up with proposals like Finer's'. (HMSO, 1974) It is not obvious when Treasury and CSD officials acceded to demands for a review that they were aware that its findings would be made available for public discussion - at that time no-one realised quite how extensive the debate would be. By the time they realized the extent of the open government exercise, it could not be stopped.

Besides being the only type of enquiry to which the Treasury would give approval, an internal enquiry had certain advantages which fitted the aims of both the SBC and its officials. An internal review was more likely to put forward proposals which were realistic and feasible in terms of Government priorities and the demands of other Government departments. It is part of a civil servant's routine approach to his work to take into account what will be acceptable to Ministers and fit in with overall Government and internal departmental policy objectives. "Knowing the Minister's mind", Heclo & Wildavsky have written, "(and) intense, incessant, incurable Minister-watching (are) ... almost a normal body function for top civil servants". (1974, p. 131) The weakness of Royal Commissions in this respect was pointed out by Clarke. "The civil service assessors (on Plowden) wanted to get positive answers; and so the enquiries could formulate recommendations (sic) which .. could lead at once to Government action ...; without civil servants participating, (other enquiries) have often found difficulty at this last, but most important stage". (1978, p. 38) If there was to be reasonable chance of the review leading to changes, the review team had to win the support of the many other departments whose responsibilities overlapped with those of the SBC. Such areas were numerous as, over the years, supplementary benefit became the catchall for the failure of other departments and services to meet the needs of the poor or to take the effect on poor families into account when framing their own policies. For example, the level and coverage of education benefits, student grants, national insurance provision, fuel costs, all have implications for the supplementary benefits scheme. It was essential to retain the tacit support of these departments for the aims of the review, if not with all the detail. It has been argued that civil servants work to the convention that "nobody should do anything unless he is certain that everyone else who is likely to be concerned, even remotely, has been first 'put in the picture' ". (Wilson, 1969, p. 367) As civil servants, then, members of the review team were able to keep their Whitehall colleagues in touch with progress. By taking into account comments and criticisms and by not trespassing on other department's areas of responsibility, the review team could minimise the possibility of opposition to proposals at the policy implementation stage.

An internal enquiry also had the advantage of offering some continuity between the review itself and the policy implementation stage. Officials stay on to fight any existing battles and are at the centre of the policy-making process to foster progress. Once an external enquiry has reported to Ministers, the Committee or Commission is disbanded and though its members may continue to debate and defend proposals in public, as for example happened following publication of the Warnock Report (HMSO, 1975) and the Seebohm Report (HMSO, 1968), they have no further formal role. [4] Traditionally, civil servants do not serve on external enquiries - the Fulton Enquiry on the Civil Service (HMSO, 1968a) was an exception - and as a matter of policy the

officials who service such Committees are not involved with the
implementation of measures covered by the enquiry. By contrast, the
key personnel working on the supplementary benefits review stayed on to
take part in the public and interdepartmental and ministerial discussions
which took place, advised first the Labour and then the incoming
Conservative Ministers and helped to draft the reforms to the scheme
introduced in 1980.

The continuity provided by personnel is only meaningful as long as the
policy process survives. Donnison and his officials were aware that
"Reforming a major part of the social security system takes longer than
the lifetime of any government". (Donnison, 1982, p. 53) and that many
pitfalls could present themselves. Thus, a major consideration in
determining the structure and scope of the review was the need to enable
the policy process to survive changes of officials, of Ministers or even
of Government. The protagonists, only too familiar with the demise of
the Crossman pension plan of the 1960s, were concerned that this initiative
should not suffer a similar fate. [5] Continuity in the policy process
was sought in two main ways: first, by depoliticising the issue so that it
could be broadly acceptable to any political party, and secondly, by
building up an impetus for change which it would be hard for any
Government to ignore. This second point is examined later in the
discussion on the open government strategy.

Although the idea of a review of the supplementary benefits scheme
was being mooted early in the life of the 1975 Labour Government the
protagonists, as one official said, still had 'one eye on the next
election'. In policy terms, the three years remaining to the existing
Administration was not a long time, especially with its slim majority.
The problem was identified by Michael Partridge: "Legislative changes
are difficult to secure in this area and need lengthy debate even with
a sound Government majority; and are impossible without this ... social
security reforms can be long delayed if they become a political
football". (1979) The review was kept free of political affiliations
in two ways. First, as discussed earlier, the review was conducted by
'impartial' officials who were, themselves, responsible for the contents
of the final report and its findings. This point was stressed by Labour
Ministers before and after its publication. Unlike Green Papers and other
consultative documents associated with party policy, the review team's
findings were seen as a neutral assessment which could therefore be
adopted by any administration.

Royal Commissions are often regarded as having a "party political role
which ... is concealed as far as possible behind a neutral facade".
(Chapman, 1973, p. 9) Their findings may be shelved if there is a
change of emphasis in Government policy - as happened with proposals
put forward by the Finer Committee on One Parent Families (1974) - or
if there is a change of Government. The Royal Commission on the
Distribution of Income and Wealth, set up by the Labour Government, was
disbanded by the incoming Conservative Administration and the report of
the Royal Commission on the National Health Service also set up by the
Labour Government received little sympathy from a Conservative Government
committed to cutting public expenditure and sympathetic to the enlargement
of the private sector in health. (Merrison, 1979) Placing the
responsibility for the review's findings with officials enabled the Labour
Government to show concern in an extremely sensative area of policy whilst
still remaining neutral and uncommitted to any particular line of action.
Such a strategy allowed the Commission to be closely involved, in a way

it could not have been with an external enquiry, whilst also maintaining
its independence from the findings. (See chapter 5) If the review was
not to become a 'political football' it was crucial also that the range
of reforms presented should be within a framework which would fit into
the wider policies of both the Labour Government and the Conservative
Opposition. The review team was able to ensure their findings were
acceptable to Government through the normal official channels but it
would have been improper for them to confer with members of the Opposition.
Here the SBC could assist by meeting with Conservative MPs and members of
the Conservative Research Department to keep them informed of developments
and feed back their reactions to the review team.

An exercise in open government

Although the SB review was carried out by officials, it was not like a
normal internal enquiry. First, it did not lead to a 'Departmental' or
'Government' report, but merely a set of options for change drawn up by
a team of people who happened to be civil servants. The significance of
this distinction was discussed above. An even greater departure from
normal practice, however, was the decision to conduct the review as an
exercise in open government. Far from being kept secret or confidential
like most other internal enquiries, the review was very publicly launched
by David Ennals, then Labour Secretary of State for Social Services and
Stanley Orme, Minister for Social Security. In addition, a second stage
was built into the review process, during which the review team's final
report was published, its findings widely disseminated and the views of
the public and interested parties sought. The Ministers pledged to take
into account both the review team's findings and the public response when
framing proposals.

In other areas of planning, public participation has been a common
feature, but, as Donnison has pointed out, it has not figured in the
development of services provided for the 'more vulnerable claimant group'.
(1975, p. 315) Developments in social security policy have normally
resulted from incremental changes evolved within the administrative
apparatus rather than from any wider public debate. (See, for example
Heidenheimer et al, 1976) The introduction of supplementary benefits in
1966, for example, was made without any consultation. (See Hall et al,
1976, p. 460) Opening up the policy-making process, and inviting public
participation inevitably takes up a considerable amount of time. Why
then was it adopted for this very contentious area of policy, when both
the Commission and its officials were anxious for reforms to be
implemented urgently?

Precisely how the open government strategy originated is not clear.
During the course of the interviews conducted for this study, Ministers,
officials and David Donnison were all credited with the idea. What is
clear is that there were a number of different reasons behind its
adoption, which variously found favour with the partisans involved. The
overriding argument in favour of making the review public arose from the
position and influence of the SBC. It would simply not have been
practical to keep the review and its work secret whilst the Commission
had the freedom to comment publicly on policy developments which affected
claimants. Neither could the low profile normally adopted by internal
enquiries be maintained whilst at the same time they worked closely with
the Commission, which could raise any issues in the Annual Reports. In
addition, Donnison and the officials who worked with him were genuinely

sympathetic to a more open approach to policy-making, as exemplified in the style of the Annual Reports.

For Ministers, and the Labour Government, the review could be pointed to as an example of their commitment to more open government: a pledge which was being treated with increasing scepticism at that time by the press. At the same time, because the findings were to be published without any endorsement or commitment from Government, a wide ranging debate could be initiated on an extremely sensitive area of policy without Ministers having to debate where their own priorities lay and without any obligation to take action.

It was argued earlier than an internal review was set up as it was the only type of enquiry that the Treasury and the CSD would sanction. The open government strategy, and in particular the second stage for public consultation and discussion provided a possible way of overcoming some of the disadvantages of a civil service enquiry. Most obviously, the issue was put on the public agenda, and not carried on confidentially within the bureaucracy. More important was that the protagonists hoped that it would mitigate some of the shortcomings inevitable in the kind of solutions which a team of officials could offer. It was assumed that exposing to extensive public scrutiny a set of proposals, based on the stringent cost and staffing criteria laid down by the Treasury and the CSD, discussed below, would lead to such opposition that those departments would recognise the impracticability of reforming supplementary benefit without a significant injection of resources. It was hoped that concerted external pressure could be used by Ministers as a lever to secure extra resources. From the outset, it was accepted that reform would involve losses for some claimants. A period of public discussion would indicate the extent and type of changes which would be acceptable and where reductions would and would not be tolerated. As is shown in Chapter 8, whilst many of the review team's proposals were implemented despite public opposition, others, which politicians and officials thought would not be publicly acceptable, proved to be less contentious than had been envisaged and were also implemented.

The main reason for the Commission and its officials supporting the open government strategy in general, and a second stage of public consultation in particular, was because it provided another way of building continuity into the policy-making process. It was hoped that the period of public discussion would transform general unco-ordinated feelings of dissatisfaction into effective pressure for change and that it would thus educate politicians of both major parties, staff, claimants and pressure groups into the need for, and the urgency of, change and, as one official said 'build up a head of steam to support action...', which could not be ignored by any Government.

The aims of the review and its terms of reference

From the previous discussions, it is clear that all those involved in the setting up of a review - Ministers, the SBC and its officials, represent-atives of the Treasury and the CSD - were all aware that the structure of the enquiry would have a critical influence on the scope of the investigation and the kind of reforms which would be considered. In the end, an internal enquiry, with the crucial inclusion of a stage for public consultation was the compromise solution, which had advantages and disadvantages for all parties. The remaining question to be settled related to the terms of reference. Here again it was a case of finding the most advantageous compromise to get the exercise underway. Any difficulties could be tackled later.

When a Royal Commission or Committee of Enquiry is set up the terms of reference are clearly laid down. In some cases, there may be disagreement among members on their interpretation (see, for example, Pearson Report, 1978) and Committees vary in how imaginatively they interpret their remits. The Pearson Commission took a narrow view compared, for example, to Beveridge. (1942) The Fisher Committee, whilst working strictly within its area of study, adopted a very broad interpretation of the request to have regard to the "economic use of available resources": "We do not see ourselves as limited to a consideration of what can be done with the resources at present available; we understand 'available resources' to mean those resources which are from time to time made available in the light of all relevant circumstances, including the recommendations of this committee". (Para. 29)

Written terms of reference are not always laid down for internal enquiries; where they are they may change over time. Normally, this causes little problem as the findings of such investigations are intended for internal dissemination only and are not generally exposed to public scrutiny. No precise remit was laid down for the review team. On this occasion, however, the lack of clearly defined and published terms of reference was to lead to considerable dissatisfaction and confusion when the proposals in the final report, Social Assistance, were put forward for public discussion.

From the outset, both the SBC and Ministers suggested that the SB review would be wide-ranging. In its 1976 Annual Report, for example, the Commission welcomed the decision of the Secretary of State for Social Services to "set up a review of the whole supplementary benefits scheme and its interaction with other Government policies and programmes". (SBC 1977, p. 1) In an article published in the same year as the review was set up, Donnison himself had stressed the importance of examining the supplementary benefits scheme in context and not in isolation from other policies for the poor. "We can only formulate consistent policies for the relatively small part of the social security system which falls to the SBC within the context of a more comprehensive planning process to which many departments should make a contribution". (1976, p. 354) The significance of the exercise was stressed by Ministers when Social Assistance was published: David Ennals, Secretary of State for Social Services, and Stanley Orme, Minister for Social Security, described it as the culmination of "the most searching analysis of the role of social assistance in this country since the National Assistance Act came into operation in 1948" (DHSS Press Release 76/223, 15.9.76) It was also, of course, the first such analysis since 1948.

Members of the review team have said that the nearest approximation to written terms of reference was the statement made by Ministers in the press release which announced the formation of a team "to review the issues identified in the Commission's (1975 Annual) Report". These were then listed: "the proliferation of discretionary decisions, the growing complexity of the scheme, the overlapping of the responsibilities of the Commission and of other agencies of central and local government quite apart from the growth in the numbers helped by the Commission". (DHSS, 76/223, 15.9.76)

In the opening sentences of <u>Social Assistance</u>, the review team made clear that their study was more limited than that suggested by earlier statements. Out of the "general remit to conduct a comprehensive review of the supplementary benefit scheme" set by the Secretary of State for Social Services, the review team set themselves six objectives: 1) to examine the scope and purpose of the scheme and its method of operation, including its relationships with other central and local services; 2) to produce a simpler scheme which would be more readily comprehensible by claimants and staff, with rules capable of being published, whether in the form of regulations or otherwise; 3) to deploy more effectively the financial resources likely to be available over the next few years; 4) to reduce the rising demands on staff, having regard to available financial resources; 5) to devise arrangements which, in the light of the Bell Report (1975) would lead to a more effective appeals system; 6) to examine the role of the SBC, including its agency and other duties not directly connected with supplementary benefit". (DHSS,1978, p. 1) The inference drawn from this narrow definition of objectives, following the very considerable publicity given and great significance attached to the review by the Government and the SBC, was that the review team **were** responsible for limiting the terms of reference, and especially imposed on themselves a no-cost constraint. The many commentators who made this assumption were in fact incorrect. As mentioned above, to obtain Government and even more importantly Treasury approval to any review of supplementary benefit meant that the enquiry was structured specifically to limit its scope and avoid demands for increases in resources.

This analysis was only publicly confirmed by David Donnison some time after the review had been completed. "If we were to get anything done about supplementary benefit we would have to pick limited targets. There was no point in calling for massive expenditure, or a new Beveridge report reviewing the social security system". (1982, p. 54) In the terms of one of the protagonists, a compromise was reached with the Treasury and the Civil Service Department. The publicly announced 'general remit' remained but alongside two, unannounced, 'implicit understandings'. It was agreed first, that the enquiry would look <u>only</u> at the supplementary benefits scheme and not present proposals which would have implications for those policies with which the scheme overlapped, such as national insurance. The review was to examine supplementary benefit <u>not</u> social security policy as a whole. Second, it was agreed that the review team's recommendations should be based on existing cash and manpower limits. Michael Partridge tried publicly to deflect criticism for the no cost basis of <u>Social Assistance</u> which, he said, was the result of "consultation with other departments ... (and) which was widely misunderstood as having been chosen by the review team themselves". (Partridge, 1979) It can be seen, therefore, that the Ministers' publicly announced 'general remit' had been narrowed even <u>before</u> the review team actually started work. But it was only later that it was fully recognised, even by the officials themselves, that "a no cost" report was the inevitable result.

The review team decided not to make these limitations public, in the hope that they would be able to circumvent them. This happened to some extent with, for example, the inclusion of references to comprehensive housing and fuel benefits, but eventually was less than hoped. At this preliminary stage, it was thought that the no cost remit need not be made explicit because it was intended that the final report would merely produce a series of costed options, some of which would involve extra expenditure and others of which would lead to savings. However, when the review was underway it was decided that, as an aid to public discussion, the report should also "pick out the underlying themes and ... group some of the main options together in model schemes". (DHSS, 1978, p. 2) In drawing together the package of recommendations included in the final chapter of Social Assistance, the straightjacket imposed by the nil cost constraint became obvious. In order not to be vetoed by the Treasury, the package had to be self-balancing. Additional options for change involving an overall increase in expenditure were put forward but as a second and less likely possibility. Members of the review team later suggested that packages for change requiring additional resources could have been recommended only if the report had not been published but presented confidentially direct to Ministers or if there had been a ministerial commitment to that end (which there was not). As Michael Partridge pointed out to critics "Policy decisions about committing extra public resources of money and staff are for Ministers: civil servants can have no mandate on that". (1979a)

The limitations of an internal review

The SB review was widely welcomed when it was set up, but much of the enthusiasm waned once it got underway and for many it disappeared completely when the final report was published. (See Ch. 7) One of the main complaints was that the investigation was too narrow and many groups called for a much broader and comprehensive investigation, such as a Royal Commission, to look at supplementary benefit in the context of other policies, in particular national insurance and the taxation system. There were, as discussed above, numerous reasons why some sort of external, independent Committee of Enquiry was not set up. The review did not have the ministerial commitment essential for the establishment of a Royal Commission, and for overcoming Treasury opposition. Moreover, such a structure would not have been appropriate given the aims of the review. A Royal Commission could have carried out the kind of investigation which many critics felt was necessary, and might have devised, in the SBC's words, "some grander strategy" for reform. (SBC, 1979a, p. 14) However, the aims of the review which was set up were much more restricted and immediate: to "search for internal reforms to (the SB) scheme" and to devise "a fairer more rational system". (p.14) A hybrid structure, like that adopted for Plowden or Beveridge, might also have been considered as both these enquiries did have some objectives in common: they dealt with practical questions and were looking for positive solutions. But the reform of supplementary benefit had a far lower priority for Government than either of the other committees. While the review did mix external and internal expertise, in this case the officials were in charge, with the SBC trying to wield influence but having no power. In the case of Plowden and Beveridge, the enquiries were conducted by men "of great standing and authority and experience of the subject matter" (Clarke, 1978, p. 38) and who were responsible for the final decisions. The structure of the review was the 'best deal' which could be reached with Ministers, the Treasury and the CSD. The most realistic alternative would have been no review at all.

The introduction of the innovative open government element into this policy process was intended, and, as will be seen later, did mitigate some of the disadvantages of an internal review. There, remained, however, serious limitations. There now exists a wide body of literature on the role of the civil service in the policy-making process. The Whitehall bureaucracy has been criticised as an inherently conservative and parochial institution. Specific criticisms have included the narrow social background of new recruits, the lack of specialism and the inability or unwillingness of the bureaucracy to change. Willson has pointed to the lack of room for initiative and individuality. "The top civil service are an extremely close homogeneous group, whose membership is subject to constant fluctuations but whose pattern of behaviour remains more or less constant". (1969, p. 367) This, it is argued, is the inevitable result of the official fitting into, and being accepted by the civil service 'community'. (Heclo & Wildavsky, 1974, ch. 1) The top civil service policy-makers form a very small group. Though individuals frequently move from job to job they continue to work within this framework and need the support of their colleagues. They cannot therefore afford to alienate their peers. Their behaviour on one issue will affect future successes and failures. Through negotiations and dicussions, officials have to obey the civil service 'rules of the game'. (Heclo & Wildavsky, 1974, p. 94) Failing to do so will hinder their chances of winning future policy battles and indeed their promotion and advancement prospects. "Whatever his origins, by the time a civil servant has risen to the policy-making levels he has been conditioned into professional conformity". (Willson, 1969, p. 359) This is the context of official decision-making. Even the officials who comprised the review team, who were widely regarded as extremely capable and were committed to their task, and who devoted so much energy to their newly created public functions, were first and foremost part of that community.

The structure of ministerial and departmental decision-making is, also inward-looking. Ministers and officials seek to protect and further the interests of their own department. Civil servants are not expected to intervene in policies outside their own specific area of responsibility. This applies equally well to other sections of their own department as to separate departments. Thus, although in practice the policies of the national insurance scheme and supplementary benefit are inseparable, changes in one having ramifications for the other, they are, within the DHSS structure, totally separate. This convention gave the review team a further rationalisation for adhering to their narrow remit. Thus less attention could be paid to the shortcomings of other policies which were undermining the effective operation of the supplementary benefits scheme, or to solutions which had external implications that might be considered appropriate. In the two specific instances of fuel and housing costs the review team did cross departmental boundaries. Why these, and no other exceptions were made, is considered in the following chapter.

Steps were taken in the 1970s to foster cross-departmental policy-making. In 1970, the Conservative Government introduced Programme Analysis and Review (PAR) and set up the Central Policy Review Staff (CPRS). The aims of PAR, later abolished by the 1979 Conservative Administration, were two-fold: "to aid collective ministerial decision-making ... to focus issues for joint ministerial decision and test departmental activities against ministers' collective strategy" and

"to undercut the inertia of existing government programmes by
undertaking a 'regular spring-cleaning of objectives' ". (Heclo &
Wildavsky, 1974, p. 289) PARs were normally carried out on issues
which involved large public expenditure and crossed departmental
boundaries and as such would have been a possible mechanism for reviewing
the supplementary benefits scheme. As a tool for policy analysis
PARs had two disadvantages. First, they were under the close control
of the Treasury which would have restricted the SB review even more
and secondly, they were conducted in secret which as discussed above
was considered disadvantageous in this case. The aim of the CPRS is to
present reviews of policy, untrammelled by departmental boundaries.[6]
CPRS would, therefore, have been in a position to look at supplementary
benefit in relation to other departments. CPRS is, however, only
a small unit and much of its limited time would have been spent on
learning and understanding the many technicalities of the scheme,
not the kind of intellectual role it was set up to perform. The key
members of the review team had previous experience of the supplementary
benefits scheme. Although CPRS has the advantage of being able to
present reports direct to Cabinet, its recommendations then have to
be considered departmentally and could only be successful if agreed
by all the relevant departments (which in this case would have been
unlikely) or if the Cabinet was prepared to make them high priority,
again unlikely if it had implications outside the supplementary benefits
scheme itself.

Paradoxically, departmental parochialism within the civil service
'community' gives rise to extensive consultation. Such consultation
takes place both horizontally, across all interested departments,
and vertically up the departmental hierarchy. In the case of the
supplementary benefits review, members had formal consultations through
an interdepartmental steering committee (see p. 71) and the usual
informal consultations and soundings. The need to consult continuously
and widely means that the range of possible options gets simplified
and more structured as it becomes further removed from the point of
access. Those consulted tend to concentrate on those aspects which
affect their own interests and seek to protect their own department,
rather than try to solve what they might regard as the internal
problems of another department, in this case the supplementary benefits
scheme.

In theory civil servants are impartial. Their job is to present the
facts to their Ministers on the basis of which policy decisions can
be made. In reality, in the very collection and presentation of material,
the official, like social scientists and researchers, must make value
judgements as to the significance of the facts to his responsibilities
and aims. (Rose, 1969, pp. 183-196) The definition of the problem,
the identification of those groups whose opinions should be sought,
the options for change available, are not value-free judgements. The
official is aware of the views of other departments and this limits
his freedom of action. He is also constrained by prevailing
departmental policy. An official cannot make recommendations in one
area of policy which go against the flow of policy elsewhere in a
department. To do so would lead to a rejection of the idea and loss
of credibility of the individual. Even so, this need not prevent him
raising questions or pointing to the implications of the general
direction of policy on one specific area.

of the new rules proposed by the review team would have left many claimants worse off, in some cases substantially so. Apart from recommending the appointment of special welfare officers, who would have no greater access to additional resources than other staff, the review team did not follow through the impact of reductions in benefit to those already living on the poverty line. Putting certain needs and groups of people outside the scope of the supplementary benefits scheme may ease administration, it does not mean that the problems no longer exist.

The lack of consideration given to the impact of some options on claimants was revealed in several changes which were advocated solely on administrative grounds. The proposal to defer payment of benefit to school-leavers, involving a loss of benefit of over £10 per week for up to fourteen weeks, was recommended mainly because of the administrative burden placed on the scheme by the sudden influx of claimants in the summer. It was required also to release jobs which could then be assigned to special welfare officers. The proposals to abolish special diet additions and laundry additions were also based solely on administrative criteria. The staff savings involved, though not quantified, were discussed but there was no consideration of the impact which the loss of a dietary addition (which in 1978 could be worth over £7 per week in exceptional cases) would have on the chronically sick claimant.

In the earlier discussion of official reviews (see Chapter 1), it was argued that policy change initiated within the bureaucracy is incremental. Social Assistance shows that the supplementary benefits review was no exception. The review team did not challenge any of the underlying assumptions on which the scheme was based. Throughout the report one eye was kept on those aspects of the scheme which attracted media and public criticism. Many options were not pursued because it was feared that they might add to the incentive problem - even though the review team agreed that this was a marginal problem which should be solved by higher wages and not lower benefits. Rejecting an increase in the earnings disregard for unemployed men, the review team concluded: "Part-time working by men ... is rare. There is no evidence that an increase in the disregard would induce any change in their behaviour, but there is some danger that any increase in the total income from benefit and part-time work might discourage claimants from moving back into full-time work ... We do not therefore think a significant increase in the disregard for the unemployed can be justified on merits, even though it might be justifiable on grounds of simplicity". (p. 64) Although the review team did make the important recommendation that the long-term rate of benefit should be paid to the unemployed, in many other proposals it was accepted that they should receive different, and inferior, treatment. For example, the unemployed were not included in the proposal to allow payment of benefit when on holiday abroad nor in the proposal to taper the earnings disregard.

The review team was concerned also that the proposed changes should not encourage abuse. Thus, the options put forward to promote more equality in the treatment of married women demanded that the controls, such as the full-time work exclusion clause and the voluntary employment rules which then applied only to the male partner, be extended to both partners to ensure that the new provision was not used by the

Conclusion

By 1976, it was widely accepted within Government that the supplementary benefits scheme was in a state of crisis. However, the SBC and its officials still had to persuade Ministers to take the issue on board and then overcome Treasury and CSD fears about the expenditure implications of setting up an enquiry. Agreement was eventually secured because the protagonists accepted crucial restrictions on the structure and scope of the review.

A civil service enquiry confined to an internal examination of the supplementary benefits scheme only, and which worked within existing staff numbers and benefit costs was not the ideal solution sought by the Commission and senior officials, or called for by outside commentators. It was, however, the best that could be negotiated without direct Government underpinning, which in this case anyway, was considered inappropriate. The 'most important factor' said one associate 'was to get it underway and then see what happens'. The establishment of any kind of review was regarded as the first step on the road to reform and in the context of 1976 (described by one of the protagonists as the 'nadir of the British economy') was, in itself, a considerable achievement.

An internal review had certain practical advantages over external, 'independent' enquiries. In particular, because the final report, Social Assistance, was attributable to 'impartial' civil servants, the findings were kept free of party affiliations. This, together with the politically-neutral terms in which the proposals were framed, facilitated continuity in the policy-making process. It also made it less likely that this issue would fall by the wayside in the event of a General Election even if it led to a change of Government.

Whilst the political neutrality of the review, contributed to the survival of the review process, it was not sufficient to guarantee that changes would indeed follow. The main reason, therefore, for the open government strategy, including a second stage of public participation in the review, was to provide an impetus for Government action and to ensure that,having been placed on the agenda, the reform of supplementary benefits would not fall victim to Government inertia.

There is no doubt that, despite the advantages, the scope of the enquiry was limited because it was conducted by officials. The conventions governing the official's relationships with other departments, the need not to transgress the 'rules' of Whitehall, inhibited the review team from overcoming to any degree the restrictions placed on the remit. As will be seen, even the adoption of an open government strategy and the active involvement of the SBC had little effect in broadening the framework of the review team's recommendations. There was no shift in the power base of the policy-making process, the officials retained control. Had the review been structured on the lines of the Plowden Committee, where officials and independent members worked together as equal partners, then it might have presented a fairer balance between the needs of the administration and the needs of the claimant. As it was the review team's concern with the benefits of the review to claimants was limited to the advantage they would derive from more efficient and rational administration. The more pressing financial needs of claimants could examined possibilities for change against only two benchmarks: the cost to public expenditure and the need for simplification which would bring administrative costs under control. It is clear that the cost restriction inhibited both the range of options for change even raised for discussion and then the selection of those which were recommended for implementation. The consequence for the report was the options were assessed not primarily for the effect that they would have on claimants but for the effect on the administration of the scheme in terms of cost, staff numbers and workload.

The review team found that the limitations of their remit often conflicted with their own priorities, in particular with their 'underlying theme': the need for simplification. The exclusion of recommendations impinging on policy areas outside the scheme precluded consideration of the two major simplifications: an increase in national insurance benefits to lift beneficiaries above supplementary benefits level, and an increase in the supplementary benefit scale rates which would have obviated the need for widespread reliance on discretionary additions. Earlier examinations of the supplementary benefits scheme had revealed limits to the degree of simplification which could be achieved without an increase in resources or a reduction in the level of benefit to at least some groups. In its evidence to the Expenditure Committee, the DHSS stressed this point:

> "There is ... a basic dilemma in the quest for
> simplification in the social security field.
> Major simplification can normally be achieved
> only by reducing the complexity of qualifying
> conditions for benefits. But this usually
> means 'generalising' the benefit so that
> selectivity is reduced and benefit costs
> increased or people are cut out of benefit".
> (Expenditure Committee, 1977, p. 401)

Unlike their predecessors in 1944 (see p. 50) the review team, and indeed the Commission, accepted 'rough justice' was inevitable and some claimants would have to be left worse off in order to improve the position of others. In order to make improvements in certain parts of the scheme, savings had to be made elsewhere. The problem which the review team then had to solve was where the right balance between simplicity and equity lay. Where they eventually struck the balance depended on the degree of simplification to be achieved, the minimum cost at which it could be introduced without being "too abrasive" (p. 5) and also on which group of claimants was affected. [6] As discussed earlier, the review team identified families with children as the group in greatest need and they tried to protect their level of benefit as well as directing any extra resources towards them. The option of reducing the number of children's rates was, therefore, dropped. (See p. 88) On the other hand, a short-term scheme was put forward as a high priority despite the fact that, on 1978 estimates, over 30,000 claimants would lose £7 per week or more. Even larger losses would be suffered by school-leavers and those with capital over the recommended level of £2,000. Long-term claimants, particularly pensioners, were the largest group who would lose, mainly from the alignment of the national insurance and supplementary benefit scale rates. Though the individual losses were small, they made up an estimated saving of £30m for distribution elsewhere.

Chapter 5

The Review - the first stage

In the previous chapter it was argued that the scope and objectives of
the review had been restricted <u>before</u> the review team actually began
work. However, within the parameters laid down, the review team
could influence both the emphasis and the detail of the final report.
It was they who decided on how the problems to be studied were defined,
on how information and views were to be collected and which options for
change should be included in the final report. In consultation with
senior officials, the review team also determined the timing and the
kind of access which would be given to the various concerned groups as
part of the open government strategy.

A new policy unit composed of a "small but exceedingly able team of
officials" drawn from the DHSS was set up to conduct the review.
(Donnison, 1977) The creation of such a policy unit, which requires a
'decision made at the highest level', indicated that this matter was
being treated with a degree of urgency. Key members of the review
team were able to work full-time on this project and not be distracted
by other more immediate day to day demands. Though no specific time
limit was set, the review team was aware of the importance of presenting
a final report as quickly as possible to ensure publication and
discussion well before a General Election.

The 'small' review team comprised two permanent full-time members:
Alan Palmer, an assistant secretary and leader of the team and John
Westbey, a principal. Additional support was given by other officials
ranging from the grade of principal to executive officer, who worked
on the project for part of its life. There were normally four people
working on the review at any one time. The review team was given
normal clerical support. It had no research personnel assigned to it
full-time but had the support of the department's statistics and
research branches. The team reported to an under-secretary, Michael
Partridge, who played an active, as well as supervisory, role and who
provided a link between the team and the two committees with which they
worked: a steering group and a research sub-group.

Steering groups are a usual feature of civil service enquiries but
the steering group working with the review team was unusual in both
its membership and its function. The Chairman of the steering group
was Geoffrey Otton, then Chief Adviser to the Supplementary Benefits
Commission and later second Permanent Secretary of the DHSS. Its
members were under-secretaries (a higher grade than is usual) from
all those Government departments with which the supplementary benefits
scheme overlaps, including the Department of the Environment, the
Department of Education, the contributory benefits side of the DHSS,
and most importantly the Department of Employment, which has 'the
major and continuing links' with supplementary benefit. Other
departments with a lesser interest were either invited to specific
meetings to discuss certain issues, for example a representative of
the Home Office attended the discussions on the eligibility of immigrants
to benefit, or were circulated with relevant papers. The most
influential participants were the representatives of the Treasury and

the Civil Service Department (the department responsible for civil
service manpower). Also represented was the Central Policy Review
Staff which is usually involved with the "more important Departmental
policy review". (CPRS, 1977)

The composition of the steering group was unusual, also, because
two of its members were not civil servants: David Donnison, Chairman
of the SBC, and Tony Lynes, a political adviser. The presence of
outsiders, and of David Donnison in particular, was resisted by some
departments because it would, and did, alter the role played by the
committee. The inclusion of David Donnison was described by one
official as 'an unsecret political weapon' which the review team and
Donnison himself could use to keep the discussion open and push the
boundaries of the enquiry to their limits. It provided a disincentive
to members of the steering group vetoing or suppressing discussion on
any issue (though this occasionally happened) because David Donnison,
with his freedom to make independent public comment on policy issues
concerning the supplementary benefits scheme, could take the debate
out of the committee into the public arena. By keeping topics on
the agenda, members of the steering group retained some control over
their development.

As well as the differences in the composition, the steering group
differed from others also in the function which it was asked to
perform, and that stemmed from the fact that the review team's own
task was unusual. Generally the purpose of an internal review is
to present appropriate solutions to specific policy objectives. The
review team's job was wider: to analyse the main structure of the
scheme and to identify and suggest a range of options for change.
The role of the steering group at its six-weekly meetings was, as one
official described it, to use 'the accumulated wisdom of Whitehall
... to literally steer (the review team) through the maze' of material
and possible scenarios for change. The steering group did not <u>direct</u>
the review team. It did not set the review team's agenda of work.
Its role was largely responsive: to act as a forum where the review
team could test out other departments' reactions to their work and
proposals. Where there was united opposition to a proposal, it was
dropped by the review team. To have pursued such issues would have
been counter-productive. The aim was to find proposals which could
be put into operation, and which would, therefore, require the
co-operation of other Government departments at a later stage.
Pursuing contentious issues would also have taken up much valuable
time which a very small review team could not spare. Thus,
consideration of a scheme which combined supplementary benefit and
family income supplement was dropped. The discussion on other issues,
such as that on housing costs, was reduced to the lowest common
denominator in order to ensure inclusion in the final published
report.

The other committee with which the review team worked was a sub-
group set up by the Social Security Research Policy Committee, "to
consider the need for research in connection with the review of
the supplementary benefits scheme". (SBC, 1978, p. 112) Only two
such sub-groups have been set up - the purpose of the other was to
examine take-up of benefits. The research group was very large.
Chaired by Michael Partridge, its members included representatives
from the SBC Inspectorate, the DHSS regional directorate, policy

branches and statistical branch, as well as representatives from the
Central Office of Information, and the DHSS Chief Scientist's Office.
David Donnison who, as a member of the Social Security Research Policy
Committee, recommended the creation of this sub-group, was also a
member, as was Kathleen Bell, who had chaired enquiries into National
Insurance and Supplementary Benefit Appeals Tribunals, and Adrian
Sinfield, now Professor of Social Policy at the University of Edinburgh.
The group met just four times before publication of Social Assistance:
first in November 1976, just after the review team had been appointed
and finally in January 1978 when the review team were completing their
analysis of the first stage. In January 1980, the sub-group was
reconvened, this time to explore ways of monitoring the changes to
the supplementary benefits scheme to be introduced in the Social Security
Act 1980.

Like the steering group, the research sub-group was largely reactive.
It provided a forum where the review team could set out its demands for
information and consult expert opinion on what research evidence was
already available, and what it was possible to generate. The restricted
timescale within which the review team itself was working meant that it
was not feasible for the research sub-group to launch large-scale research. [1]
Instead, the sub-group concentrated on collating all the relevant research
which was already under way or recently completed within various Government
departments, universities and other research establishments - not an
insignificant task. The team drew on internal reports prepared by the
SBC Inspectorate, the Economic Adviser's Office and by other supplementary benefit policy units, many of which were made available as background
papers to the review. Three-quarters of the forty background papers
subsequently made available to the public were produced internally.
In addition, the National Children's Bureau submitted a special report
to the review team on the position of sixteen year olds in households
in receipt of supplementary benefit or family income supplement drawn
from its National Child Development Study. (SBC, 1977, Appendix B)
The sub-group was instrumental in getting published the results of a
survey of social security claimants which had been conducted by the
Office of Population Censuses and Statistics (OPCS) in April 1974.
(Ritchie & Wilson, 1979)

The sub-group commissioned two small scale 'market research' type
surveys from commercial research organisations. The first, carried
out in 1977, explored the attitude of the general public to the social
security scheme. (Schlackman, BG no. 6,1978) The review team were
anxious to obtain a range of views from the 'public' as opposed to
those of pressure groups or the stereotype images presented in the
press. The second survey, which is discussed at greater length in
Chapter 7, explored the views of claimants to some of the proposed
changes to the supplementary benefits scheme raised in Social
Assistance. (DHSS, 1979a)

The review team's relationship with the SBC

Whilst the SBC, and in particular its Chairman, played a catalyst
role in the creation of a review, it was made clear from the outset by
Ministers that the review was not being undertaken by, or on behalf
of, the Commission. However, many commentators wrongly attributed

responsibility for Social Assistance to the Commission. (Jordan, 1978)
The confusion arose out of the very close relationship which existed
between the Commission and the review team. When announcing the review,
Ministers said that they were acting in response to the problems set
out in the SBC's first Annual Report, that the review team would be
working closely with the Commission and that the second Annual Report
would comment on progress. (DHSS, PR 76/223, 15.9.76) Besides this
'constitutional' relationship, the review team and the Commission had
a close working relationship. In practice, David Donnison was most
actively involved. First, because he was a member of the two
committees with whom the review team worked, and secondly because,
as the only member to be employed full-time (in fact four days per
week) on Commission duties, he worked in the same building as the
review team and, together with his Private Office staff, had frequent
informal discussions with its members. His personal commitment to
the review exercise was displayed in a number of speeches made whilst
the review was under way and the very active part he played during
the public debate.

The review team and the Commission shared some personnel. The SBC
did not directly employ the officials who advised it (or the staff
in the local offices). The Commission's Chief Adviser, two under-
secretaries and staff in the Chairman's Private Office were "made
available to the Commission by the Secretary of State whom they also
advise" (my emphasis). (SBC, 1976, p. 4) One official described the
position of civil servants working with the SBC as 'schizophrenic'
because of their dual loyalties. On one day an official might draft
a letter from the Commission to the DHSS on an aspect of policy; on
the next he might be drafting the reply. Even the two senior officials
working with the Commission were in this position. The Chief Adviser,
Geoffrey Otton, was also Chairman of the steering group. Michael
Partridge, the under-secretary who supervised the review team, chaired
the research sub-group and represented the review team in discussions
on the steering group. The members of the review team 'wore two hats:
one part Commission, two parts department'. Staff in the Chairman's
Private Office drafted papers for the review team; members of the review
team drafted parts of the SBC's Annual Reports and even the SBC's independent
response to Social Assistance. (DHSS/SBC, 1979) David Donnison sat on both
the research sub-group and at each monthly meeting of the Commission, the first
item on the agenda for discussion was a report from the review team.

Given these interconnections, the 'independence' of the review from
the Commission arose not from the working relationship between the
two, but from where final responsibility for the enquiry, the contents
of the report and its recommendations lay. Ultimate responsibility
for all these key stages lay with the review team who could over-ride
the views of the Commission. For the SBC, its own 'independence'
was important from the outset and gained greater significance over
time as it became apparent that the review team would not be able to
tackle or make recommendations on many of the wider issues raised in
the 1975 Annual Report. The Commission increasingly distanced itself
from the content of Social Assistance and concentrated attention, not
on the review team's report, but on its own published response.

The presence of the Commission and the independence it maintained
provided an effective counter-balance to some of the restrictions
implicit in an internal enquiry discussed in the previous chapter.
The SBC and Donnison were able to broaden or keep open the debate on
many issues both with the review team and the steering group. It was

only pressure from the Commission, mindful of a recent EEC draft directive, that persuaded the review team to tackle the question of equal treatment between men and women in the scheme despite great reluctance to take on board such a complex issue. It was also the public support of the Commission and pressure from Donnison which helped persuade the steering group that the final report should include a discussion, albeit brief, of new ways of providing help with housing costs (an issue close to Donnison's policy interest before joining the SBC) and with fuel costs. Ideas, which the review team was considering, were often floated by the Commission in its Annual Reports, in its regular discussions with pressure groups and staff in local offices as well as with members of the main political parties. This served the purpose, first, of discouraging either the review team or the steering group from dropping any issue for which Donnison or the SBC was prepared to fight. It also generated early feedback.

When Social Assistance was published, many of its proposals were already familiar because they had been floated by the SBC. The Commission raised publicly all the major new proposals which would appear in the final report, some of which it had originated, including the deferment of payment of benefit to school-leavers (SBC, 1977, pp. 53-54), the replacement of many exceptional needs payments (ENPs) by six monthly lump sum payments (p. 118), the need for more equal treatment (Ch. 6), and a unified housing benefit (pp. 140-141).

Evidence

One of the main tasks of any enquiry is to collect together evidence and gather information. Royal Commissions and other external enquiries generally make a very broad sweep to obtain views from as wide a range of commentators and experts as possible. Advertisements may be placed in the press or circulars and invitations sent out to stimulate written submissions, on the basis of which some groups or individuals will be invited to give oral evidence. Such invitations can lead to the collection of many volumes of evidence which then have to be sifted and considered. The Warnock Committee, for example, received 400 written submissions. The Pearson Commission received 863 written submissions from 766 organisations and individuals and heard 113 oral submissions. Many parliamentary committees, in particular the new select committees set up in 1979, take evidence from a wide range of people and groups, within and outside the Government and bureaucracy. The Industrial Injuries Advisory Council places advertisements in the press when conducting an investigation inviting evidence. Unusually, in 1981, an internal enquiry on the administration of benefits for the unemployed, invited comments from academics and pressure groups. (DE/DHSS, 1981)

In contrast, most internal civil service reviews do not make a general call for evidence. Instead, consultations are held with selected key interest groups and experts. The review team did not call evidence for two reasons. First, for the practical reason that the number of personnel involved, without the research support which is often provided to external enquiries, working to a tight schedule, could not handle the amount of material that might be generated. A decision which, in administrative terms, was proved right by the 1055 written responses which were sent in after publication of Social Assistance. (See Ch. 7)

Secondly, they did not do so because, as one member said 'it was not that kind of review'. The first task of the review team was "to analyse the main structure of the scheme and to identify options for change". (DHSS, 1978, p. 1) They regarded it as an internal fact-finding operation and as such only the views of those who could contribute to such a functional assessment were sought. Other writers have asserted that general calls for evidence yield more 'opinion' than fact (see Slack, 1969). Sir Henry Fisher was extremely sceptical about the evidence submitted to his Committee on Abuse of Social Security Benefits:

> "It has become increasingly apparent, that
> while there are a number of organisations
> which are deeply concerned with what they
> conceive to be defects in the Social Security
> system and in the way in which claimants are
> treated by the departments, and which are
> ready to produce well argued evidence in
> support of their point of view, there is no
> such body of organised opinion ready to
> marshal arguments in favour of a stricter
> control over abuse. Whilst not disputing
> the correctness of much of what our
> witnesses have said, we believe that they
> have presented us with a partial point of
> view".
> (1973, p. 2)

Such a wide consultation during the first stage would only have confused the initial marshalling of the 'facts' and as such could be deferred.

Thus, during the initial fact-finding exercise, the review team concentrated their efforts on the most influential internal groups. During the investigation they worked closely with the SBC. They had discussions with representatives of other Government departments both informally and formally through the inter-departmental steering group. With the help of the research sub-group, all the most relevant research findings and statistical information were collated. Here too the most lucrative source of data were the Government research and statistical services. In addition, the review team took extensive steps to obtain the views of local and regional DHSS staff. This latter step was felt necessary because, despite efforts by the SBC to standardise the administration of the scheme nationally, the way the scheme actually worked in practice, especially in the application of discretion, could only be assessed by examining its operation at the local level. The operation of the scheme often varied according to local tradition, (for example, in some cities regular ENPs were given to claimants for clothing), the size of the caseload and the type of claimants. (See Adler, 1975) Thus, the perception of both staff and claimants would be different in the relatively relaxed atmosphere of the local office in a seaside retirement town from the frenzied atmosphere of a city centre office with large numbers of unemployed and ethnic minority groups. The review team visited local offices in all the DHSS administrative regions to obtain the views of those 'in the firing line' of what the problems were and what improvements they would like to see. Members of the review team also initiated residential staff training courses where they could get staff views on the scheme and test staff reactions to the issues under consideration. The review team obtained the official view of the DHSS Staffside Unions (Staffside) through special meetings and the formal consultation machinery which at that time was widely used in the DHSS: a system of participative management which had been instituted following the industrial unrest of the early 1970s. (See Ch. 3) According to this formula, informal consultation was extended even to the discussion of policy developments: "Policy priorities and objectives, together with their practical implications, are discussed ... The aim is to secure the fullest possible understanding between staff representatives and management of the implications of policy for the staff and agreement to the operational consequences". (DHSS memo to the Expenditure Committee, 1977, p. 390)

The review team was extremely concerned with finding out what the 'public' really felt about supplementary benefit and its recipients and explored with the research sub-group the most appropriate way of obtaining such views. It was decided that a private research organisation should be appointed to carry out a small survey to investigate "the views of the general public, which will include claimants, former claimants and non-claimants, some or all of whom will be or will have been taxpayers". (Schlackman, BG no. 6, 1978) The research objectives were:

> "a) to investigate public knowledge about the supplementary benefits scheme in terms of who receives it, how it is claimed and how the scheme is financed and administered.
>
> b) To examine public attitudes to different aspects of the system, including means testing and the principles of discretionary payments.
>
> c) To investigate attitudes towards claiming among those who have not so far had reason to do so.
>
> d) To investigate the experiences of those who have claimed SB and the way in which this has influenced their views of the adequacy of the system.
>
> e) To assess the information obtained in order to provide guidance on the likely public response to the types of changes envisaged by the Supplementary Benefits Review".
> (p. ii)

It was hoped that this survey, based on twelve group interviews, and 32 individual in-depth interviews, approximately one-quarter of which were with claimants, would give, albeit limited, empirical evidence of public perceptions of the scheme and of what changes would be acceptable, to counter the one-sided and negative view which was being represented in the press in 1976.

Less strenuous efforts were made to secure 'the views either of outside pressure groups or claimants at this stage. The review team believed that these would be more effectively canvassed after their own ideas and proposals had been formulated. Five groups submitted evidence nonetheless: Child Poverty Action Group (CPAG) (Lister, 1977), Trades Union Congress (TUC) (BG 36), DHSS Staffside Unions (BG 37), the Campaign for the Homeless and Rootless (CHAR) (1978) and the Granada Television programme 'This is your right' (BG 40). CPAG, one of the main groups which met regularly with Donnison, also had a lengthy and detailed meeting with the review team. Meetings were also held with the British Association of Social Workers (BASW) and the Association of Directors of Social Services (ADSS). In addition to this limited number of meetings, the review team set up a seminar at the School of Advanced Urban Studies at the University of Bristol again to discuss progress and test out its thinking. This seminar was limited to an invited audience which included civil servants, local government representatives, social workers, academics and representatives of pressure groups. The review team presented six papers for discussion,(BG 31-35) covering broad aspects of the scheme (its scope, assessment, legal structure and discretionary payments). In October 1977, David Donnison spoke at a seminar organised by the Fabian Society on the theme of the supplementary benefits review.

Outsiders were given the opportunity to participate in the review process only after publication of Social Assistance, when their views were sought at a series of meetings, in an invitation for written submissions and in a small survey of claimants. The success and effectiveness of this period is discussed at length in Chapters 7 and 8. Here it is important to consider how disparity in the timing and kind of access given to the different interested parties influenced the early development of the decision-making process. The Commission, top officials in interested Government departments and staff were involved in defining the problem, and in considering feasible solutions. By the time the consultation process was thrown open to all interested parties - after publication of Social Assistance, the agenda had been effectively set. Whilst members of the review team (Partridge, 1979) and David Donnison publicly argued that commentators need not be tied to the proposals or to the parameters within which they had been drawn up, as will be seen, (Walker, 1982) in practice, respondents found it difficult to widen the debate.

The Agenda

"The most careful policy analysis cannot make all the options, plus their merits and defects, explicit. The policy options which are chosen for consideration are not a complete or a random set of all possibilities. Policy analysis is neither perfectly efficient nor value free". (Hall et al, 1975, p. 77) The definition of the problem, the choice of options selected for consideration and the type of solutions offered are determined by those involved in the policy process. In the case of the supplementary benefits review, such decisions were made by the review team, in consultation with senior officials and the Commission. Although neither the steering group nor other departments were directly involved in these decisions, for reasons discussed earlier (Ch. 4) the review team had to work within predetermined parameters and in accordance with the expectations of, and what would be acceptable to, Ministers and other interested departments, particularly the Treasury.

And, as Bachrach and Baratz have pointed out, the proposals which are
not put forward because of anticipated opposition are just as significant
as those which are included: "To measure relative influence solely
in terms of the ability to initiate and veto proposals is to ignore
the possible exercise of influence or power in limiting the scope of
initiation". (1970, p. 15)

The restricted parameters within which the review team were required
to operate ensured that they would be limited to suggesting only
incremental reforms. Hall has described how such an approach limited
even a much more independent enquiry like that conducted by Seebohm
on the Personal Social Services. (1976, p. 40) The alternative
'rationalist' approach would have involved asking such fundamental
questions as: what are the aims of the supplementary benefits scheme?
What changes are needed to facilitate the achievement of such aims?
Such questions inevitably would have had ramifications for supplementary
benefit expenditure, for the national insurance scheme and other
Government departments and policies. Thus, as the review team
increasingly came to interpret the problems within the limited parameters
set, so they concentrated only on curing symptoms not tackling the
causes of the difficulties. The problem they tackled was not the
increasing number of people dependent on supplementary benefit,
but given this increasing dependency, how could the scheme be adapted
to cope with the increased demands being made upon it. Similarly,
they did not tackle the problem of why so many people were dependent
on discretionary payments to meet everyday needs, but only, given this
increasing reliance, how to solve the administrative headaches which
resulted.

The review team's analysis was defined from an internal perspective.
This was the inevitable result of conferring, at this stage, only with
those concerned with the administration and operation of the scheme
or with the interdepartmental ramifications of their proposals for
reform. The review team, thus, made the needs and concerns of the
administration their first priority and solutions were sought which
would alleviate operational difficulties. Had the review team consulted
with the outside groups earlier, they might have defined the problem
differently: for example, in relation to the needs of claimants.
As it was help for claimants was increasingly confined only to the
benefits which it was assumed would follow from a more efficient
administrative apparatus. This emphasis first with the needs of the
administration rather than the needs of claimants was regarded as
inevitable by one member of the team: ' Civil servants are governed
by political constraints that don't apply to pressure groups or others,
or the SBC, who would say that claimants must come first. The review
had to be more balanced'. It follows that it should not have been
surprising that the review team did little to challenge the underlying
assumptions on which the administration of supplementary benefit had
been traditionally based, such is its control functions. Neither
did they consider the conflict which arises between its duty to meet
need and public and political demands to prevent abuse. Finally, the
problems of take-up and stigma, which had been the driving force behind
the 1966 reforms, were considered only peripherally.

As Banting points out: "The prevailing definition of the problem
circumscribes the options considered and the stakes involved; getting
policy-makers to accept a particular definition of the problem is the

first step in getting them to accept a particular type of solution".
(1979, p. 10) The review team's definition of the problems confronting
the supplementary benefits scheme was strongly influenced by the SBC.
Government Ministers had linked the setting up of the review with
publication of the first SBC Annual Report and in setting the agenda
for their enquiry, the team's self-confessed starting point was the
chapter on Policies and Priorities written by David Donnison which
identified the "strategic issues ... which will have to be tackled
during the coming years". (1976, Ch. 2) The fact that the review
team were to stray so little from the SBC analysis confirmed for at
least one key member of the Commission that 'we'd got it broadly right'
However, as discussed above the analysis itself had been criticised
for presenting only a partial viewpoint. In particular, the Commission
was accused of failing to present the scheme from the point of view
of the consumer and for failing to examine "whether the Commission
can provide the sort of service we would want for ourselves or our families".
(Field, 1976). For reasons discussed above, the SBC's omission was not
rectified by the review team and they too concentrated on administrative
and operational problems. The key issues which were identified in
the 1975 Annual Report were the growing reliance on the Commission's
discretionary powers; the increasing complexity of the scheme; the
Commission's frontier problems, specifically with local authority social
services departments, employment services, local authority housing
benefits, and education departments; and the effect of the trend to
judicialise the appeals system on the SBC's policy function. During
the course of the enquiry, and especially in the discussions with staff,
the review team concluded that any attempt to simplify the scheme and
reduce the use of discretion would require a revised legal structure.
The need to examine the effects of changes in the supplementary benefits
appeals system was also subsumed under the broader heading of 'the
legal structure'.

One new area was added to the problems originally identified by the
SBC: the need for greater equality in the treatment of married women
in the scheme. The major factor in ensuring this was taken up was
a draft EEC directive published in December 1976 recommending that
member states should take steps to promote equal treatment between
men and women in their social security policies. In addition, members
of the review team said they were subject to 'persistent' pressure
from the SBC who 'pushed it very hard' and from 'young lionesses' in
the department. Nonetheless, the review team and the steering group
were less than enthusiastic about taking this issue on board because
it was such a complex subject which, they felt, took up a 'disproportionate'
amount of already limited time.

In practice, the review team found they were unable to keep to their
intention of considering all the areas raised by the Commission. The
main victim from this list was the examination of the scheme's
relationship with other benefits and services. The relationship between
the supplementary benefits scheme and social services departments was
deferred for further study; the overlap with employment services was
barely considered; the problem of the 'voluntary unemployed' was
deferred for further study; the overlap with education was discussed
only in relation to school leavers. One 'frontier problem', housing
costs, was given special attention, indeed it was discussed in a separate,
albeit brief, chapter. In the course of discussions with staff and
more importantly with David Donnison, the review team identified this

issue as being of particular importance, but also one of special difficulty and complexity. It was deferred for further consideration but the review team stressed in Social Assistance that reform of housing costs was crucial to a comprehensive review of the supplementary benefits scheme. A similar approach was used in the treatment of fuel costs. The fact that the review team kept fuel and heating costs on the agenda when other issues fell by the wayside is particularly significant because here they were pushing the boundaries of their remit, hinting at the need for policy changes outside the supplementary benefits scheme which would also have financial ramifications. That these issues survived owed much to the pressure from the SBC generally, and the personal commitment of David Donnison.

Whilst it is obvious that the SBC influenced the review team's analysis of the problems of the scheme, and the meetings between staff and members of the review team exposed difficulties within the administration, there is little evidence that any group outside the official circle had any significant impact on the review team's agenda, or their prognosis for change. The TUC, CPAG and the DHSS Staffside Unions all drew on the 1975 Annual Report when framing their written submissions to the review team. However, their interpretation of the problems and the issues they discussed differ radically from those of the civil servants. CPAG and the Staffside Unions, although looking at the scheme from opposite sides of the counter, were in agreement on the main thrust the review should take. Both stressed the need for an enquiry which considered supplementary benefit in the context of its interaction and inter-dependence with other parts of the taxation and social security systems. Both called for an increase in the level of the scale rates and a reduction in the numbers dependent on this means-tested benefit. The review team did not take on board such broader issues. With the exception of housing and fuel, discussed above, they stuck firmly to their remit and concentrated on incremental change within the existing framework.

At the other end of the spectrum, the review team did not take on board many of the smaller but significant problems faced by claimants which were included in the written evidence. For example, the out-of-hours and emergency service; the use of the Commission's discretionary powers to reduce benefit, and the impact of the closure of many local offices. Studies of claimants' attitudes to the scheme have found that claimants are very concerned with the procedure for claiming benefits: office interviews, home visiting, method and frequency of payment. Such aspects were not explored at this stage by the review team because they looked on them as technical aspects of the scheme: or 'a second stage operation which could be carried out after the structure was put right'. These issues were not, however, included in Social Assistance as an area for further consideration. (Appendix 2) Such 'technical' aspects are integral to the effective operation of any last resort assistance scheme and the way means-tested benefits are administered. The standard of service offered affects the image of the scheme in question and people's willingness to step forward and claim their entitlement. Attention to such aspects symbolises the true commitment of Government and its officers to provide an efficient and humane safety net to all those who need help.

Conclusion

The point at which different groups are granted access to the policy-making process and the significance attached to their viewpoint will affect the definition of a problem, the agenda which is set, and the outcome. The aim of the review became increasingly limited to finding answers to specific internal problems of the supplementary benefits scheme. To that end only those groups who could elucidate the most problematic areas of administration, or those whose opinions had to be taken into account in the implementation of new policy initiatives were involved in the first stage.

Thus, the SBC, local staff and representatives of all interested departments were consulted at the time when the review team were still formulating ideas for improving the scheme and could influence the content of Social Assistance. The views of claimants and pressure groups were sought only after the agenda had been set and the options for change narrowed by the constraints imposed on the review. Only at that stage was their participation considered functional. And then the importance of securing widespread involvement was not to influence or change the content of policy but was, as Long found, "linked solely to the need for changes in the operational efficiency and overall speed of the planning system". (1975, p. 125) As discussed earlier, the public discussion had a crucial part to play in building up impetus for Government action.

The fact that the review team did not take greater steps to obtain the claimants' perspective earlier was not the result of any lack of sympathy for the claimant. The negative attitude of one member towards discretion was greatly reinforced at a public meeting where claimants emotively described the humiliation they felt when being assessed for such help. However, there does seem to have been some lack of understanding of the problems claimants faced. One official admitted that, during the public discussion on Social Assistance, they had learned how 'finely pared' life on supplementary benefit was. Unfortunately, because of the way they organised their consultation, this crucial lesson was only learned after they had written their report.

The review team, however, concentrated on getting the views only of those who would be instrumental in getting changes accepted and implemented. In this respect, claimants had no influence or muscle whatsoever. Hence, as in many other enquiries before the review:

> "the needs of the customers were not forgotten,
> but they could in the short run be neglected
> with greater impunity".
> (Donnison, 1975, p. 312)

Notes

1. For a discussion of the role of research in Government enquiries see M. Bulmer, (ed), Social Research and Royal Commissions, London, George Allen and Unwin, 1980.

Chapter 6

Social Assistance: a review of the supplementary benefits scheme in
Great Britain

In July 1978, eighteen months after the review team had been set up,
their final report Social Assistance: a review of the supplementary
benefits scheme in Great Britain was published. (DHSS, 1978)
Publication of the report marked the end of only the first stage. The
authors presented it as "a realistic and practical basis for discussion,
in the light of which we hope it will be possible to draw up proposals
for helping to relieve the present serious strain on the supplementary
benefits scheme and adapting it to the task it now has to undertake".
(p. 104) In their foreword, David Ennals, then Secretary of State
for Social Services and Stanley Orme, Minister for Social Security,
requested "the comments of all concerned - interested organisations
and the public - before (we take) any decisions about the future shape
of the scheme". The purpose of this chapter is not to provide a
critical analysis of individual proposals in Social Assistance, a task
which has been comprehensively covered by other writers. (Lister, 1979;
Leaper, 1979) Its central aim is to consider how far the review team
succeeded in achieving their own limited objectives and the implications
of their models for reform for the future of the supplementary benefits
scheme. First, the main options for change which were raised in the
report are set out.

The limitations within which the review team worked became apparent
both in the range of options discussed and the tone of the report,
which is set in the introduction. The speed at which the review team's
analysis was completed was not without cost. Seventeen issues were
listed in an annex, which had been deferred for future consideration.
(Appendix 2)

The first dominant theme of Social Assistance became apparent in the
opening chapter. This included five references to the need for 'realism'
and other references to the exclusion of 'impractical' courses of
action. 'Reality' for the review team was recognition and acceptance
of the fact that no extra resources were likely to be made available
either outside the scheme to reduce the number of claimants dependent
on supplementary benefit, or for changes within the scheme. The review
team made clear that Social Assistance was produced with a firm eye on
the prevailing political and economic climate.

> "Against the background of continuing restraints
> on public expenditure and public service staff,
> there is no prospect of finding the massive sums
> for national insurance benefits or other services
> that would be needed to reduce the number of
> supplementary benefit claimants ... In our view
> the most realistic aim is to fit the scheme to
> its mass role of coping with millions of
> claimants in known and readily-defined
> categories for the foreseeable future".
> (my emphasis)   (p. 5)

In the opening chapter, the review team referred to the two
restrictions which governed their assessment of what constituted
realistic reform. First, the no-cost constraint:

> "it would be unrealistic to suppose that costly
> modifications to the scheme are likely to be
> feasible in present and prospective
> circumstances of economic constraint and
> pressure to reduce civil service staff numbers,
> and any question of devoting extra resources to
> the scheme raises issues of priority in social
> expenditure and in public expenditure at large
> which go well beyond our remit".
> (p. 2)

Secondly, the territorial boundary:

> "there is no prospect of finding the massive
> sums for national insurance benefits or other
> services that would be needed to reduce the
> number of supplementary benefit claimants ...
> with one important exception ... (housing
> costs) ... wider reforms outside the
> supplementary benefit scheme (such as in the
> national insurance system or in the tax
> system) have not been studied in depth ...
> but because supplementary benefit, as the
> scheme of last resort, affects and is
> affected by nearly every other Government
> programme in some way, we have taken account
> of how the changes will impinge on other
> programmes".
> (p. 5)

Thus, the framework of the report is set out. The review team are
restricted to "presenting choices for the better use of existing
resources within the supplementary benefit scheme itself". (my
emphasis) (p. 5): ie a no-cost, internal programme for reform. The
main tools used by the review team were simplification and a massive
reduction in the role of discretion in the scheme. The inevitable
adverse outcome of trying to simplify and of replacing individual
discretion with broad based rules on a no-cost basis was recognised
and accepted in the report.

> "This course is bound to involve some element
> of rough justice and some losers as well as
> gainers, as it would seem impracticable to
> expect that extra money would always be found
> for the process of always levelling up to
> ensure that nobody would ever be worse off
> than now. The question is how much loss, and
> how many, would be acceptable. Rough justice
> must not be too abrasive".
> (my emphasis) (p. 5)

'Realistic', 'mass role', 'nil-cost', 'rough justice': this was the
accepted vocabulary of Social Assistance.

The review team's options for change

It is not possible to include in this discussion all the many ideas which were raised in Social Assistance. Instead, this account concentrates only on the more significant options, and on the recommendations which were made. A difficulty arises when trying to draw out the most important issues featured in the report. As has been made clear, Social Assistance was published as a discussion document. It set out a number of possible options for change. However, not all the options received the same level of discussion or support from the review team. Some options were raised and eliminated in the same paragraph, perhaps because of their cost, or because they had ramifications for policy areas outside the supplementary benefits scheme. Other options were recommended by the review team and included in a package of possible changes. This package was constructed "as an aid to public discussion". (p. 103) However, the options which made up this package of "recommendations on how the scheme should develop" (p. 2) were not necessarily those considered to be the most important. They were merely one combination of proposals which could be implemented within existing resources. Two other changes "which would add substantially to the cost of the scheme, but which might be considered" were included alongside but separate from this package. (p. 104)

Discussion in Social Assistance centred on five main issues: simplification of the structure of the scheme; restriction of discretionary payments; a new legal structure; greater equality in the treatment of married women and arrangements for meeting housing costs. In this chapter, the last issue is considered alongside the more general area of simplification.

1. <u>Simplification of the main structure and assessment procedures</u>

The need for simplification was the "one common theme" underlying all the possible changes discussed by the review team. In addition, specific attention was paid to seeking ways of simplifying the main structure of the scheme and the rules governing assessment. Five chapters fell under the broad heading. These covered eligibility for benefit, the structure of the scale rates, the assessment of short-term claims, the treatment of resources, and the calculation of housing costs.

i) <u>Eligibility</u>: Supplementary benefit is payable to anyone over the age of 16, who is not in full-time work or on a full-time course of education, and whose resources fall below the supplementary benefit scale rates which are set and revised annually by Parliament. Married women and women living with a man "as husband and wife" are not allowed to claim in their own right.[1] The review team did not pursue the one major change which could be made in the eligibility rules - payment of benefit to all adults as individuals regardless of the needs or assets of any partner. Such a recommendation would have met the criticism of many women's groups that the existing scheme discriminated against, and imposed hardship upon those women who did not receive adequate financial support from their partner. It would have obviated the need for the cohabitation rule. The justification for not supporting this fundamental change was that it would bring

many more people on to benefit "many of whom would not be in need
of it because they would normally look to their spouse for support".
(DHSS, 1978, p. 32)

The review team then concentrated on more minor changes in the
eligibility rules. Two options extended eligibility. First the review
team suggested that pensioners should be able to continue receiving
benefit for up to two weeks when on holiday abroad. Secondly, the
review team suggested abandoning the practice of recovering benefit
paid between the fifteenth work day and pay day to claimants who
returned to monthly paid work. It was suggested that eligibility
should be restricted for two groups: immigrants and school-leavers.
The review team suggested that sponsored immigrants and visitors from
abroad should cease to be eligible for benefit. Under the terms of
the 1966 legislation, the SBC could use its discretionary powers to
pay benefit to such people in cases of urgent need. It was also
suggested that school-leavers be excluded from benefit until the end
of the holiday following the term they left school and that parents
continue to receive child benefit instead. [2] This proposal would
disbar school-leavers from claiming benefit for a possible 12-14 weeks.
The justification for this measure, which was recommended by the review
team, were largely administrative. School-leavers imposed a very
heavy burden on local supplementary benefit offices and careers offices
(with whom they had to register for work) during the staff holiday
period. It was also suggested that school-leavers artificially inflated
the number of unemployed as even those who did obtain jobs then
arranged to delay starting until September. Like the SBC, the review
team feared that the availability of benefit might tempt some to claim
even if they intended to return to school or higher education at the
end of the holiday. (See SBC, 1977, pp. 53-54)

ii)   The scale rates: As critics of Social Assistance
(Lister, 1979) have pointed out, only three of its 127 pages were
devoted to a discussion of the adequacy of the scale rates. What
discussion there was centred on the difficulty of deciding just what
is adequate. What is sufficient for some claimants, may be too little
for others. Benefit levels, it was argued, must be considered in relation
to other benefits and to the incomes of those in work. At what point,
if any, do benefits become a disincentive to work? Nonetheless, pointing
to evidence which has shown that, judged against a number of criteria,
the scale rates are inadequate, (DHSS/SBC, 1977) the report concluded
that "there can be no real doubt that many claimants, particularly
families with children, have little, if any, margin in managing their
financial affairs". (DHSS, 1978, p. 38) Nonetheless, the review
team felt unable to recommend an overall increase in the level of
benefits because of the financial implications. Furthermore, the
embarrassing question of what is the right level was left unanswered.
Discussion centred on "a range of other criteria, such as equity as
between claimants, costs, and administrative simplicity". (p. 38)
These options were concerned to redistribute and rationalise within
the scheme between groups of claimants, with the main shift of those
limited resources available being given to the review team's priority
group - families with children.

The review team discussed three aspects of the structure of the
scale rates: the number of rates payable, the relationship between
the supplementary benefit rates and national insurance rates and between
each other, and the rules governing eligibility for the long-term

rate of benefit. (See p. 90) The options for change offered in this
area were particularly limited, both by the cost constraint and
because it was feared increases might aggravate the work incentive
question. On the other hand, attempts to reduce the number of scale
rates by reducing some were limited if unacceptable hardship was not
to be inflicted on some groups.

TABLE 1: SUPPLEMENTARY BENEFIT SCALE RATES   (July 1978)

	Ordinary rate		Long-term rate	
	£	%	£	%
Married couple	23.55	(100)	28.35	(100)
Person living alone or single householder	14.50	(62)	17.90	(63)
Non-householder 18+ or 16-17 with children	11.60	(49)	14.35	(51)
Non-householder 16-17	8.90	(38)	-	-
Children's rates: 13-15	7.40	(31)	-	-
11-12	6.10	(26)	-	-
5-10	4.95	(21)	-	-
0-4	4.10	(17)	-	-

(note: there were also four separate rates, paid to blind claimants.

Three ways of simplifying the adult rates were discussed. First, the
abolition of the householder/non-householder distinction which some
argued could deter some families from caring for elderly dependent
relatives. (See Lister, 1979; DHSS, 1978, p. 40) This option was
rejected because it was considered too expensive in terms of both
staff and benefit costs. The review team discussed the possibility
of paying the same rate to all adults, doubled for married couples
plus, where appropriate, a householder's allowance. This change,
which would have had the advantage of realigning the rates paid to
single persons and couples, (see Table 1) was rejected because it
did not offer any significant simplification or staff saving and would
have penalised non-householders disproportionately if introduced on
a no-cost basis. The review team recommended a third option which,
they argued, offered the only "practicable prospect of clarifying
the benefit structure. (DHSS, 1978, p. 43) It was proposed that
the national insurance benefit rates and supplementary benefit rates
be aligned. At 1978 benefit levels, this involved an increase of
25p in the short-term rate and a drop of 35p in the long-term rate.
Whilst this change appears on the surface to be inconsequential, and
indeed, as the review team pointed out, had the advantage of providing
a once and for all reduction in the differential between the short-term

and long-term rates, it was one of the most significant proposals in
the report. First, if implemented, it would generate a net benefit
saving of £30m which could then be redistributed within the scheme.
Secondly, it would erode further an important point of principle
established by Beveridge and supported in theory if not in practice
by successive Governments that national insurance rates should
be higher than assistance rates. Furthermore, as the review team
recognised, such a change would be more of a tidying up exercise
than a real simplification because the total levels of benefit
received by families would still be different because the two
schemes paid different rates for children and only supplementary
benefit recipients received help with housing costs.

The review team also looked at the possibility of simplifying the
children's rates by reducing the age bands from five to three. Again
the discussion centred, not on the level of the rates, but on the
structure. [3] The option to reduce the number of age bands was dropped,
but reluctantly. Although it was regarded by the review team as a
desirable simplification, if introduced within the no-cost framework
it would lead to unacceptable losses to families with children who
had been identified earlier in the report as being in need of extra
help.

The review team went on to identify a number of problems concerning
the different scale rates and the uprating policy. In particular,
consideration was given to several anomolies which had arisen since
the introduction of the long-term rate of benefit in 1973. As the
review team pointed out, the long-term rate consolidated the long-
term addition which had been introduced in 1966 to curb the prolific
use of discretionary additions. First, it was argued, the rationale
for the existence of two levels of benefit had been undermined as
the number of discretionary payments had risen once again. Secondly,
the differential between the two rates had widened from 1974 onwards
as long-term rates were uprated more generously than the short-term
rates. [4] By 1979, a married couple on the long-term rate was
receiving 25 per cent more than a similar couple in receipt of the
short-term rate. The review team were unable to resolve this
difficulty. To recommend a more favourable uprating policy for
short-term benefits would have cost an additional £16.5 million
for each one per cent increase and, if it was not extended to the
national insurance scheme would have brought more people on to
supplementary benefit. The review team even felt unable to recommend
that, like the long-term scale rates, children's rates might be
increased in line with earnings, or prices, whichever was the higher.

The review team rejected the possibility of abolishing the short-
term rate of benefit and paying all claimants the higher rate because,
although it would lead to a "real simplification" and staff savings,
it would be too expensive. (p. 47) Two more limited options were
listed which would assist some claimants in receipt of the short-
term rate. First, it was proposed that the higher rate be paid
after one year instead of two and secondly that the long-term
unemployed should receive the higher rate on the same conditions
as other supplementary allowance recipients. These were amongst
the main expenditure proposals in Social Assistance. The latter
proposal, which would have put an end to the discrimination against
the unemployed and therefore was a policy change of great significance,
was given high priority by the review team, who argued that the

exclusion of one of the poorest groups of claimants could no longer
be justified. The reduction in the qualifying period was a less
important option, which they recommended only "if it could be afforded".
(p. 48)

iii)   Short-term claims: A third chapter which stemmed from
the objective of simplifying assessment considered the possibility
of introducing a short-term scheme which would involve a less
complicated initial assessment procedure. As discussed in Chapter
3 the increase in the number of supplementary allowance claimants
in recent years led to a disproportionate increase in the number
of new claims, one-third of which ended within four weeks and half
within 13 weeks. The aim of the proposed short-term scheme was to
reduce the large proportion of staff time which was spent on
"unnecessarily elaborate and time consuming (procedures) for those
claimants who simply need a payment quickly to tide them over for a
while". (p. 53) It was envisaged that a short-term scheme would
involve a much less rigorous test of means, with fewer and simpler
scale rates. Benefit would be assessed according to the prevailing
adults' rates, one children's rate regardless of age, no income or
earnings' disregards, a fixed cut off point for capital, no
discretionary additions (though deductions would be made where
applicable), and a standard rent addition. The scheme would run for
the first eight weeks of a claim, or preferably, for thirteen weeks,
if responsibility for meeting housing costs could be removed entirely
from the scheme.

In Social Assistance the introduction of a short-term scheme was
regarded as "one of the most important possibilities for consideration"
(p. 53) and the review team put forward a model scheme which, they
argued, showed "there is certainly room for manoeuvre in setting
benefit rates which are high enough not to leave many people
significantly worse off and low enough not to lead to extra costs
or to too many being significantly better off". (p. 57) Under the
model scheme, more claimants would gain than would lose, but
approximately 30,000 would lose over £7 per week. The review team
estimated that the new assessment procedure would bring staff savings
of 640, if run for up to eight weeks, or 1000 if run for the first
thirteen weeks of a claim.

TABLE 2:   EFFECT OF THE MODEL SHORT-TERM SCHEME

Losses			Gains		
£7+	£1.51-£7.00	£0.01-£1.50	£0-£1.49	£1.50-£6.99	£7+
3%	11%	8%	63%	14%	1%

Source: Social Assistance, p. 57

iv)   Resources: Calculation of benefit entitlement is based
on the claimant's requirements, less any income from part-time
earnings, other benefits or savings. Both the supplementary benefits
scheme and before it national assistance always included elaborate
provisions to enable claimants to keep some additional resources
without benefit entitlement being affected. The rules governing
these 'disregards' in 1978 were extremely complex and varied between
different groups of claimants and according to the source of the
additional income. The review team suggested various ways of
simplifying these rules. First, a fixed cut off point for savings
above which there would be no entitlement to benefit. This would
replace the system of assuming a tariff income of 25p for every £50
savings held over £1,200, which was extremely complicated to understand
and administer. Next the review team considered simplifying the
rules on part-time earnings. In doing so, however, they confronted
the dilemma that to improve the disregards on part-time earnings to a
level high enough to encourage participation in the labour market
might prove a disincentive to seeking full-time employment. No
meaningful improvements in the level of earnings' disregards for
those claimants who had to register for work were considered. Instead,
lone parents were singled out for special attention. Even here, the
possibility of introducing a tapered disregard, to increase gradually
in line with earnings, was ultimately rejected because of its complexity.
To provide some simplification, the review team suggested reducing
the three different levels at which earnings disregards operated to
two: a single earnings disregard of £4 for all adults except lone
parents who would be allowed to keep the first £6 of their earnings.

Thirdly, the review team considered ways of simplifying the various
levels of disregards allowed on other benefits paid to claimants. It
was suggested that, apart from benefits for special expenses, which
should continue to be disregarded in full, and national insurance
and child benefits which should have no disregard, all other benefits
should be aggregated and a single £4 disregard be applied to the
total. It was suggested that recipients of occupational pensions
and sickness benefits should no longer be allowed to keep the first
£1.

v)   Housing costs: Under the Supplementary Benefits Act 1966,
all claimants were entitled to an amount to cover rent or mortgage
interest payments on top of the appropriate scale rates. In the
chapter in Social Assistance devoted to an examination of this aspect
of benefit assessment, the review team set out a number of arguments
against the prevailing arrangements, most of which had already been
set out by the SBC in its 1976 Annual Report. These included the
'better-off' problem which made it difficult for pensioners in particular
to decide whether they should claim supplementary benefit or rent and
rate rebates and the high proportion of errors which resulted from the
complex calculations involved in working out housing costs - "It
is clear", said the review team, "that any comprehensive review of the
supplementary benefits system must deal with the problem of housing
benefits". (p. 59) In this case, no minor administrative reforms
were discussed for immediate implementation because, by the time
Social Assistance was published, the Department of the Environment was
actively engaged in discussions on the restructuring of all the
existing means-tested housing benefits.

2. Reducing discretion

Given the enormous growth in the use of its discretionary powers over the lifetime of the SBC, this area offered the review team considerable scope for simplifying the scheme. The review team discussed in detail the Commission's power to increase benefit by way of lump sum exceptional needs payments (ENPs) or by a weekly addition to benefit to meet continuing special needs called an exceptional circumstances addition (ECA). The administratively much smaller area, but of great concern to those claimants affected, of discretionary deductions was discussed only briefly and no changes were proposed except that the criteria relating to deductions should be enshrined in legislation and not be left to the SBC's discretion. There was no discussion of the circumstances in which benefit could be reduced, the level of deduction made or the growing practice of payments of fuel and rent direct and 'voluntary' savings, for items such as clothing.

The nub of the review team's answer to the problem of an over-reliance on discretion was to find ways of concentrating "discretionary lump-sum payments on the sphere for which they are really appropriate ... (ie major unforeseen disasters, like fire and flood and truly . exceptional cases) phasing out of discretionary weekly payments, with new arrangements for help with heating costs, special help for the very small minority with unusual and continuing difficulties". (p. 2)

   i)   Exceptional needs payments (ENPs) In looking for ways of reducing the number of lump sum payments, the review team drew a distinction between those expenditures which were supposed to be covered by the scale rates, such as clothing and fuel bills, and those occasional additional expenses for which a claimant could not be expected to make provision, such as removal expenses or the purchase of essential items of furniture. It was proposed that ENPs should not be made for items in the former category. At the same time, however, it was argued that it would be "inappropriate" to lay down in any more than general terms in the legislation the precise expenses covered by the scale rates. (p. 74)⁵ To avoid the considerable hardship which a total withdrawal of ENPs for scale rate items would cause (over half the ENPs made at the time were for expenses supposedly covered by weekly benefit), the review team recommended the introduction of regular lump sum payments to all claimants, say, every six months. Such a proposal, it was argued, would lead to greater equity between claimants, and overcome the existing problem that ENPs were distributed according to local custom and individual claimant demands not necessarily according to need. This option was recommended, despite the additional work and costs involved, to offset the hardship which would result from the loss of flexibility to meet individual need. The review team suggested that non-scale rate expenses should continue to be met by lump sum payments when the need arose, but according to criteria laid down in regulations, and not according to SBC policy.

   ii)   Heating additions: The rising cost of all types of fuel since the early 1970s presented difficulties for all poor consumers. The Supplementary Benefits Commission provided some extra help to claimants by increasing the availability of heating additions to those with health problems, to those living in accommodation which was difficult or expensive to heat, and to those with central heating. In this case, the review team explicitly referred to the lack of scope for change available to them in the light of the financial and departmental boundaries within which they were working. They did, however, allow themselves a vague reference to a comprehensive fuel allowance scheme covering all poor consumers, which had been widely canvassed by the SBC.

> "We have found little room for manoeuvre within the supplementary benefits scheme itself to alleviate the difficulties created by rising fuel costs, and supplementary benefit alone cannot protect all consumers. In our view the solutions must lie in measures having wider application".
> (p. 80)

The main thrust of the recommendations, which the team did make, concentrated on a rationalisation and standardisation of provision within the scheme. It was suggested that some of the savings made from other reforms elsewhere in the report should be used either to consolidate all heating additions into the scale rates or, the more limited option of paying them automatically to the two main groups of beneficiaries, namely pensioners and families with a child under 5. In case neither of these expenditure options was accepted, the review team suggested possible reforms to the availability of heating additions. These included changes in the qualifying criteria by, for example, a stricter definition of difficult to heat accommodation, additions for central heating confined to electric systems only, and reducing the three levels of heating addition down to two.

iii)   Other exceptional circumstances additions (ECAs): After heating costs, special diets and extra laundry expenses were the two main categories of need for which ECAs were paid in 1978. The review team's recommendations on these items particularly reflected a pre-occupation with simplification on administrative grounds, rather than with the needs of claimants. They recommended that consideration be given to phasing out additions for special diets, which were paid only if there was medical support, because: "There are differences of opinion among doctors on the need for, and the use of special diets, but the point is that there is a body of opinion which sees no place for special diets at all". (p. 81) No evidence was given either in Social Assistance or in the background papers to support this statement. The decision to cut back ECAs for laundry expenses was recommended also for the administrative simplification which would follow.

iv)   Cases needing special attention: The review team recognised that the movement away from individualised discretion to more general and less flexible rules, would cause difficulty for some families. Their recommendations in this area led the authors to stress the importance of creating posts for 'Special Welfare Officers' who would help with the "minority of difficult cases" which would arise. (p. 91)

3. A revised legal structure

At the start of their enquiry, the review team looked on changes to the
legal structure as a largely peripheral issue which needed to be taken
on board mainly to meet the consequences of the increasing judicialisation
of the appeals procedure. During the first stage, the need to devise
"a new legal structure, with clearer and more public rules" (p. 5) came
to be seen as crucial to adapting the scheme to its mass role. The
skeletal legislative framework, supported by wide discretionary powers,
was unpopular with lawyers in the DHSS and with some officials because
it allowed "the scheme (to) be stretched to cover practically any case
if persuasive enough arguments can be found". (p. 23) And the review
team mindful of previous failed attempts to find permanent solutions to
many of the supplementary benefits scheme's difficulties wanted to ensure
this new attempt would not suffer a similar fate.

> "Which choices offer the best prospect of laying
> down broad and simple rules centrally in
> legislation to ensure fair treatment for all, while
> leaving sufficient scope for sensible variations of
> judgement to meet proven cases of exceptional
> individual need, without leaving the door open to
> further pressures for complication and extension
> of the scheme which would quickly get it back to
> its present unsatisfactory state".
> (p. 5)

The review team recommended a more detailed Act, supported either by
a set of regulations, which would set out precisely the basic rules
of entitlement and the circumstances in which additional help might be
provided, or by a code of practice which contained similar information.
In either case, the Commission's existing discretionary powers would
have to be put on a legal basis, which would be binding on staff,
claimants, and appeals tribunals. In Social Assistance, the review
team favoured the code of practice option as it retained a greater
degree of flexibility.

4. Equal treatment between men and women

As discussed in the previous chapter, equal treatment did not fit
easily into the review team's framework. It was an extremely complex
subject which took up a considerable amount of the limited time
available, and any measures implemented would be bound to make extra
demands on staff and would probably increase benefit costs. The
discussion in Social Assistance reveals the ambivalence with which the
issue was taken on board, and the limitations of what could be achieved
within the remit. The options presented represent only very limited
advances in promoting the interests of women. The review team's
primary concern was "the practical one of how equality can be achieved
in an acceptable way without either massive increases in benefit cost,
additional manpower or further complications to a scheme which we are
seeking to simplify in every way possible". (p. 93) Thus the two
solutions most favoured by feminist and other pressure groups, individual
assessment and joint claims, were not put forward for discussion. The
first discussed earlier, was rejected on cost grounds. The second was
judged to be administratively too complicated. Three ways of pursuing

the objective of equal treatment were explored:

    a)   a 'free choice': the couple would decide which
           partner would make the claim;

    b)   'main breadwinner': whichever partner had earned
           more than half the family income over a specified
           period prior to the claim would be regarded as
           the claimant;

    c)   'nominated breadwinner': either partner who had
           been in full-time work for a specified period would
           be allowed to claim.

The nominated breadwinner option was considered "on balance" by the review team to be the best course. It was argued option a) would lead to considerable complication because, in order to minimise the risk of men using this provision as a way of avoiding work, both husband and wife would be subject to the full-time work exclusion clause, and the application of the voluntary employment rules. The main breadwinner option was rejected because it would affect very few couples and would allow the couple no choice about who should claim. The nominated breadwinner option was considered the most appropriate first step on the road to equal treatment. This left the couple the right to decide, and kept the number of extra staff required within acceptable proportions, approximately 400.

Discussion

This brief resumé shows that the scope for change and the nature of the reforms discussed in Social Assistance were restricted by the limitations which were imposed. It also shows that, for the large part, the review team stayed well within their guidelines even when it became clear that the options for effective change on such a basis were few or non-existent. Only occasionally did the review team go beyond the strict boundaries of their remit. In the second chapter of Social Assistance the main reasons for the growing dependence on means-tested assistance were spelled out and, although there was no call for steps to be taken to rectify the situation, the discussion at least pointed up the problem. Such a chapter would not have been included in a more typical civil service report. The report also included references to the need for more comprehensive solutions to the problems of fuel and housing costs than could be found within the supplementary benefits scheme itself. Solutions which, if implemented, would have had implications for other Government departments and policy and would have been expensive to administer. Why the review team felt able to ignore the cost and departmental considerations on these issues but not others remains a matter for argument. It is clear, however, that the Commission was extremely committed to getting new arrangements for fuel and housing costs and that their arguments were beginning to hold sway in the Department of Environment and the Department of Energy. Those suggestions for external reform therefore might have seemed a 'realistic' possibility.

Elsewhere in the report, the review team was constantly preoccupied by the no- cost and departmental limitations. Their discussion throughout not be the starting point for their deliberations.

   As officials, working within such strict departmental and
financial boundaries, it is hardly surprising that the review team
would concentrate on the search for incremental change building on the
existing framework and trying to find improvements within. More
fundamental structural change was unlikely in this context. An
independent enquiry, such as a Royal Commission might have examined
such broader problems, and considered the role of the supplementary
benefits scheme. The aim of the review was much more modest: to relieve
an intolerable and worsening administrative burden .   Thus the purpose
of the review was not to tackle the underlying causes of the scheme's
problems, but only their symptoms. And that is the very reason that
enabled a review to be created in the first place.

Notes

1.   Donnison had served on the Plowden Council on Children & Their Primary Schools,
       1967, and had been Director of the Centre for Environmental Studies before his
       appointment as Chairman of the SBC.

2.   This term was coined by Tony Lynes in "A Watchdog for the Poor", New Society,
       27 September 1976.

3.   The Conservative Government introduced changes to the supplementary benefits
       scheme in the Social Security Act 1980 and new arrangements for meeting
       housing costs in the Social Security and Housing Benefits Act 1982. Both
       were on a no-cost basis. Green Papers were produced on ways of reforming
       the death grant and maternity pay and allowances. Again both involved no
       extra cost.

4.   For an account of the steps taken by Seebohm to stimulate debate and push
       the report after publication, see P. Hall, 1976.

5.   For a discussion of the failure of the Labour Government to introduce its
       plans for a new pension scheme see R. Crossman, 1972.

6.   For a fuller explanation see "The Role of the Central Policy Review Staff in
       Whitehall", Memorandum submitted by the CPRS to the Expenditure Committee
       (General Sub Committee) in the Eleventh Report from the Expenditure Committee:
       The Civil Service, 1976-77, Cmnd 535, July 1977.

It was the need to confine their proposals to within existing resources which placed the greatest limitation on the review team's proposals as a whole and often came into conflict with the search for simplifications. Some of the most effective and sweeping ways of reducing complexity had to be dropped because of their cost. This conflict becomes most obvious in the discussion on the scale rate structure. For example, a reduction in the number of children's rates was regarded as an effective way of simplifying the structure of the scale rates but was dropped because "it would (not) be justifiable to cause losses in real terms ... Equally, we doubt whether the simplification is of itself important enough to justify expenditure on the scale of £25m or more in order to avoid losses". (p. 45) The dilemma emerged again when the review team examined ways of simplifying the eligibility rules. Allowing married women to claim as individuals would simplify administration but would lead to a massive increase in costs. Extending aggregation to other members of the household, apart from being less acceptable on principle, would decrease costs but increase complexity. In the context of controlling expenditure, the review team were also careful to avoid recommendations which would bring more people onto supplementary benefit. Changes in the uprating rules, the proposal to pay the same rate to all adults and an improvement in the earnings disregard for pensioners were all dropped because they would have led to an increase in claimants.

Some of the proposals in Social Assistance aimed to simplify one part of the scheme would, in fact, lead to complications elsewhere. The establishment of a short-term scheme, for example, would simplify the initial assessment for both staff and claimants. However, the 50 per cent of new claimants who did not go off benefit within 13 weeks would have to undergo a second assessment. Such a change might be confusing for those claimants who might not have been eligible under the short-term scheme but would qualify under the main scheme. Such claimants could well be deterred from making a second claim. The proposed reduction in the availability of ENPs represented a significant simplification, but offset against this proposal was the suggestion that all claimants should receive regular lump sum payments, which might vary according to the size of the family, and the creation of special welfare officers to help those claimants who got into difficulty.

Throughout Social Assistance the review team's first concern was with solving administrative and operational difficulties. That, after all, was the objective of the exercise. However, the problems and needs of claimants not only took second place, in many cases the implications of some policy options on the individuals affected seems to have been completely overlooked. The review team argued that all claimants would benefit from the emphasis on rules which would be published and uniformly applied and the reduction in the arbitrariness which can arise in a discretionary system. Claimants would know, for example, in what circumstances lump sum payments could be made, and in what circumstances they would not be available. Greater clarity, it was assumed, would increase take-up and confidence. Replacing discretion with published rules was expected also to remove one of the main areas of conflict between staff and claimants, and between different groups of claimants. However, the creation of rules does not, of itself, improve the position of claimants. Many

In the past two decades, two interconnected concerns have dominated all policy considerations: the effect on staff and the cost implications. The range of policy initiated within the civil service is limited by these two constraints, unless a Minister dictates otherwise, and he has the support of his colleagues. Throughout the civil service, and especially in the DHSS and the Inland Revenue, there has been a "general awareness of the need for simplification" with the result that "all new work proposals are examined to assess their operational consequences (and) ... introduced in a way that avoids overloading the staff with new procedures".(DHSS memo to the Expenditure Committee,1977, vol. III, p. 953)   In 1971, research was carried out into ways of simplifying the pay-as-you-earn tax system in order to make staff savinqs. In 1972 a joint working party was set up in the DHSS to explore ways of simplifying administrative procedures, a concession made to resolve the industrial dispute which occurred in that year. (See chapter 3)

Officials cannot ignore cost constraints. The Treasury is the most pervasive of all Government departments, influencing policy in the spending departments in three ways. (See Heclo & Wildavsky, 1974, Ch. 2) First, it controls day to day expenditure. The great proportion of expenditure made by all departments is fixed and unavoidable, and it is only on the margin that adjustments can be made. Sir William Armstrong (formerly Permanent Secretary of the Treasury and later official head of the Civil Service Department), for example, estimated that only about 2½ per cent of total public spending is open to variation. (Heclo & Wildavsky, 1974, p. 24) In the DHSS, cash limits, the favourite tool in expenditure control, cannot be applied to benefit costs. Savings could only be made on marginal areas, like discretionary payments (5 per cent of total benefit expenditure). Cash limits could, however, be imposed on administrative costs, which on a staff intensive service like supplementary benefits could have a dramatic impact. Any constraint on staffing levels, including just the failure to allow the numbers of staff to rise in line with the increased clientele and workload, would have a significant effect on the way the scheme could be administered.

The Treasury are continuously involved in all policy developments in the spending departments.   Although Treasury officials have no formal role to play in shaping departmental policy, they inevitably play a key part in its direction because it is they who control the purse strings. "Any consideration of substantive policy - be it a Cabinet official committee, working party or Treasury/departmental study group - is bound to involve questions of allowable spending, and any consideration of major expenditure is bound to involve vital questions of substantive policy". (Heclo & Wildavsky, 1974) Thirdly, it is the Chancellor of the Exchequer and the Treasury who "manage the economy" and it is within the overall climate which they create that decisions are reached on areas for expansion and retrenchment. Thus, apart from any direct pressure which the Treasury may apply, for example at meetings of a steering group, or through the department's Principal Finance Officer, officials in the spending departments will always take into account the expectations of Treasury officials when putting forward policy options. Members of the review team have said that some possible policy options were not even considered and others were not included in Social Assistance because of their cost implications.

man to avoid work. The proposal to defer payment of benefit to
school-leavers was also justified in part because of the review
team's fears that claims might be made for benefit even when the
person concerned intended to return to school or higher education
at the end of the holiday. In fact this area of abuse had already
been discounted by the DHSS Co-ordinating Committee on Abuse.
(DHSS, 1976)

Conclusion

Social Assistance represented the results of a thorough internal
analysis of the structure and operation of the supplementary benefits
scheme. The findings inevitably reflected the views and concerns of
those consulted: staff, the SBC and other Government departments.
Thus, the reforms put forward were designed to overcome the increasing
administrative and operational pressures of an overburdened scheme.
Pressures which were likely only to get worse in the future. The
report assumed, and did not challenge, that the scheme would continue
to play a mass role. Originally, the protagonists for the review had
hoped to slip expenditure proposals past the Treasury, but this was
ruled out when the review team took the decision to produce a final
package of recommendations which had to be a no-cost package.

For the most part, the review team obeyed the confines of their remit,
and used it as a justification for not taking a broader approach.
However, on some issues they did not feel so constrained. Thus, their
discussion on heating and housing costs had implications for other
departments. Their proposals on school-leavers also involved an increase
in expenditure on child benefit. Would it really have been impossible
for civil servants to produce more than one package of reforms: one
no-cost and one assuming, say, a 5 per cent increase in expenditure?
Such a course would at least have suggested that there might be better
and more efficient ways of reforming supplementary benefit if even
limited extra resources were made available. As it was the review team
gave the Treasury and Ministers a justification for not giving extra
resources: Social Assistance showed that no-cost reform was possible.

It was at this stage that the supplementary benefits review was
opened to all-comers. But both the agenda and the framework for
the discussion had been set. Those critics who had been looking
for real monetary improvements for claimants found themselves trying
to protect the existing provision. Such was their disappointment
that much of the emphasis in the early public debate rested on the
remit and what was not in Social Assistance, rather than on its
precise contents.

Notes

1. For a discussion of the cohabitation rule see "Living together as husband and wife", HMSO, 1976.

2. The SB scale rate for school-leavers far exceeded the level of child benefit. £13.10 or £17.05, depending on age, versus £4.75 child benefit, November 1980 rates.

3. For a discussion of the adequacy of the SB scale rates for children see D. Piachaud, The Cost of a Child, CPAG, Poverty Pamphlet 43, 1979.

4. In July 1974, long-term benefits were increased by 29% and short-term by 17%. In 1975, the Social Security Act 1975 provided that national insurance long-term benefits be increased in line with the rise in prices or earnings, whichever was the greater. The Social Security Act 1980 ended the more generous uprating for long-term rates, and all rates are only increased in line with prices. By convention, the SB rates are increased in line with the national insurance rates.

5. According to the Supplementary Benefits Act 1976, the scale rates are expected to cover all normal requirements. These have been defined by the SBC as "all normal needs which can be foreseen, including food, fuel and light, the normal repair and replacement of clothing, household sundries ... and provision for amenities such as newspapers, entertainments and television licences", DHSS/SBC, 1977, para 43.

6. It was proposed that the changes should be introduced at the same time as the annual uprating so that claimants would not suffer a money loss in their benefit.

Chapter 7

The Public Debate

Publication of Social Assistance in July 1978 marked the end of only
the first stage of the review. The public discussion which was to
follow was an integral part of the review process. In the foreword
to the report, David Ennals, Secretary of State for Social Services
and Stanley Orme, the Minister for Social Security, reiterated that
neither they nor the Supplementary Benefits Commission were committed
to any of the proposals. They wrote: "We are publishing the report
in accordance with the Government's pledge of more open government,
and as a focus for wider public discussion of the type of provision
which the community is prepared to make for its poorest members".
(DHSS, 1978) When introducing the report to the House of Commons,
the Minister for Social Security told members that the Government
would be taking account of "an informal, public discussion on the
issues involved, before firm decisions are taken about the future
shape of the supplementary benefits scheme". (Hansard, vol. 638,
col. 952, 12 July 1978) Commentators were given until the end of
1978 to send their views. Eventually the response was so great that
this time limit was extended. The purpose of this chapter is to
explore the extent of participation in this public debate and examine
the response to Social Assistance. The next chapter considers what
impact this wider discussion had on the subsequent reform of
supplementary benefit.

The process of participation

The 'open government' strategy adopted in the review was a completely
new departure in this sphere of policy-making. Whilst considerable
attention has been paid to the methods of involving the public in
planning policies (see The Skeffington Report, 1969) and tentative
steps have been taken to involve the public in some social services
such as housing and education, similar steps have not been taken with
those services provided for the "more vulnerable deviant groups".
(Donnison, 1975, p. 315) Social security policy has evolved normally
within the administrative structure and as such has rarely been exposed
to public discussion. Neither the reforms of 1948 nor 1966 arose from,
or led to, a wide public debate. Only the Conservative Government
green paper on tax credits had offered an opportunity for public comment.
(HMSO, 1972) [1] As discussed earlier, it had been decided when the
review was announced that its findings would be published and open
for public discussion. (See Ch. 4) But the actual form and extent
of the 'open government' strategy emerged only over time, and developed
most significantly only during the public debate itself, between July
and December 1978.

Commitment to more 'open government' was fashionable in the mid 1970s,
it seemed a natural successor to the equally popular concept of the
1960s, 'participation'. Neither term can be simply defined, both mean
different things to the policy-maker and to the participant. (Rose,
1976, p. 60) 'Open government' for example, might mean, at one end
of the continuum, the disclosure of hitherto confidential material,
such as the SBC policy codes, to, at the other extreme, the granting

of access to the policy-making process and participation in the formulation of policy. In any particular case, its definition will be determined by the aims of the exercise which in their turn will determine the substance of information to be released, the groups whose participation will be invited and the timing and effect of their involvement.

In Chapter 4, a number of reasons were put forward to explain the decision to adopt the 'open government' strategy for the supplementary benefits review. This discussion concluded that the aim of the second stage, the period of public debate, was not to allow a wider range of groups <u>participation</u> in the policy-making process but to use the period of <u>consultation</u> to keep the review high on the political agenda. (See also <u>Walker, 1982</u>) It was primarily a public relations exercise designed to educate a diverse public, including claimants, pressure groups, staff, Government departments and politicians into the need for and urgency of, change; to educate this public on the scope of reform likely to be implemented and the review team on how far such reform would be accepted. The public debate allowed the policy-makers to highlight the many complexities of this issue and for areas of potential conflict to be confronted, if not generally resolved, before the introduction of legislation. As Fagence has argued: "most if not all proposed actions and policies need to be publicly aired to generate a response before they are resolved, to obviate the likelihood of unsuspected opposition at a subsequent time. Thus, if for no positive reason, it seems desirable that the public is consulted on planning matters before the stage of resolution is reached". (1977, p. 202)

Although it was not only, nor even primarily, altruistic motives that had given rise to the open government strategy, the very publication of <u>Social Assistance</u> was the first concession to less secrecy and more involvement in this area of policy-making. However, by the time the consultation process was thrown open to <u>all</u> interested parties the agenda had been set. In the subsequent debate participants were forced to respond to a framework of discussion laid down by the officials. In this instance then, the open government strategy conferred "no new rights to the consumer ... (nor did it wrest) responsibility for the policy-making process from the elite, it (was) merely an extra stage grafted on to the existing structure". (Long, 1975)

There is no easy answer to just what is the most appropriate point at which to invite wider participation in the planning process. If the public is drawn in too early then discussion may be too diffuse to be meaningful. One writer has argued that: "Participation must wait until the experts have assessed the need to be accommodated, ascertained the operative constraints, worked out feasible alternative ways of meeting the needs within the constraints". (Senior, 1971, p. 95) Skeffington argued that the public should not be involved in drawing up a plan but should be involved at the formative stage of development. How far did those associated with the review recognise the difficulties? There is no indication that either the review team, their senior officials or the Commission saw the production of <u>Social Assistance</u> as in any way constraining the public discussion. In public, members of the review team and David Donnison argued that commentators need not be tied either to the proposals or to the parameters within which they had been drawn up. (Partridge, (1979a) In practice, as will be seen later, respondents found it difficult to widen the debate.

It was only with hindsight that some of those who had been involved
regretted the decision to include a package of options for change.
This attempt by the review team to give structure to the public debate
was interpreted cynically by many outsiders. One commentator was not
alone when he wrote to the review team that the final package led him
to suspect that 'the consultative exercise may be something of a
formality, and that the options to be followed have already been
identified'.

Two difficulties faced commentators who wished to enter the public
debate. The first stemmed from the lack of clarity about the review
team's terms of reference. Participants were anxious to establish
why the general remit announced by Ministers had been narrowed, and
by whom. Thus, as Bull has pointed out, "gatherings that should have
been the occasion for discussion and debate about the content of Social
Assistance were liable to be side-tracked into a whodunit about the
responsibility for the no-cost approach". (Bull, 1979) The officials
were unable to clarify questions on the remit because to have done
so would have meant attributing responsibility to other Government
departments or Ministers which would have been a breach of Whitehall
etiquette. Similarly the officials could not enter into a dialogue
on, or defence of, specific proposals without apportioning at least
some responsibility to other departments or embarrassing Ministers
by appearing to commit them to future action. The officials could
only "take delivery", (Burgess, 1978) of comments without entering
into a dialogue.

It was largely because commentators were asked to comment on
proposals for reform which were themselves based on criteria
unacceptable to many, that the second stage of the review almost
foundered before it began. Some critics argued that the review should
be rejected outright and urged others not to dignify the report by
responding in the public debate. The most influential of this group
were the Welfare Rights Officers Group (WROG) which retained this
position throughout, and the National Campaign against the SB
Review, which as the name suggests was set up specifically to
co-ordinate opposition to Social Assistance. This group eventually
did respond to the report. Alan Palmer, Leader of the review team
urged critics not to take this stance:

> "If commentators do not go along with options
> in the report, they should use this information
> constructively to put forward their own
> proposals for change. The scheme will only be
> improved if there is sufficient public interest
> and pressure for reform. A negative rejection
> of the whole review will do nothing to help
> improve the scheme, and will waste a unique
> opportunity to contribute to future change".
> (Community Care, 15 November 1978, p. 14)

Despite widespread reservations and in some pressure groups long
debate on whether to participate, most commentators chose, eventually,
to respond with "reasoned opposition". (Bull, 1978) These groups
commented on individual proposals in Social Assistance, but prefaced
their remarks with criticism of the scope of the document and the terms
of reference. For example, the response most highly regarded by the

review team, after only that of the SBC, came from the Child Poverty
Action Group. Ruth Lister's pamphlet, The No-Cost No-Benefit Review,
analysed step by step, all the major proposals in Social Assistance.
(1979) In her introduction, the author stressed the context in which
these comments had to be considered: ie "... against the background
of our rejection of the review's aims: 'to fit the scheme to its mass
role of coping with millions of claimants' ". (p. 5) In fact, this
pamphlet was the second to be produced by CPAG in response to the
review team's report. An earlier pamphlet was devoted entirely to
criticising the no-cost and mass role assumptions of the report and
setting out the Group's analysis of the fundamental problems of the
supplementary benefits scheme. (Lister, 1978) Other major pressure
groups were similarly cautious in their responses. Help the Aged
stressed their "continued opposition to various aspects of the
supplementary benefits concept, and indeed the entire system of employing
the supplementary benefits for topping up the retirement pension".
(1978, p. 1) The Disablement Income Group found itself" ... forced
into a paradoxical position. We are forced to argue for improvements
in the Supplementary Benefits Scheme which can only make more
chronically sick and disabled people more dependent on it". (1979,
para. 1.6)

Despite adding forceful riders to their comments on the proposals
in Social Assistance, commentators were confronted with a dilemma which
stemmed from the restricted remit. Reform on a no-cost basis
necessitates a redistribution of resources amongst the poor: one group
of claimants must finance another group's benefits. Commenting on
proposals based on this premise inevitably led to conflict even between
those groups which shared a common dislike of the review. Although
virtually all the national pressure groups rejected the limited terms
of reference, as soon as they entered the discussion arena they
inevitably sought to protect the interests of their own constituent
group, and to make the case for priority attention. The dilemma was
noted by Age Concern: "One unhealthy and unfortunate result of seeking
to balance out losses and gains is that different beneficiaries, directly
or through those who represent them, would inevitably compete to ensure
that they were not among the losers". (1978, p. 1) The following
extracts from submissions to the review team illustrate the difficulty:

> "Help the Aged would be failing in its duty
> to the permanently underprivileged generation
> above the retirement age, if it did not
> oppose any proposal to tilt resources away
> towards families with children".
> (1978, p. 1)

> DIG rejects the idea that families with
> children should be the group to benefit from
> any shift in resources: "the presence of
> chronic sickness or severe disability creates
> the greatest need of all".
> (1978, para. 1.7)

> "We (CPAG) believe the first priority must be
> improvements in the children's rates".
> (Lister, 1979, p. 38)

Despite such difficulties, few did reject the review outright. Most took part in the public debate. The success of that debate can be judged against two yardsticks. First, the level of response generated, which, together with an analysis of the comments made, is the subject of this chapter. The second is the impact which that public debate had on the outcome, a topic which is discussed in the next chapter.

The level of response

Social Assistance undoubtedly generated the most informed debate since the war on the British system of last resort assistance for the poor. Much of the success is due to the considerable effort and enthusiasm which members of the review team and others closely associated with them, especially David Donnison, put into the exercise. Over 65,000 copies of the full or abridged version of the report were distributed free of charge. Such availability far exceeded that permitted to other Government publications, especially in recent years.[2] The review team sought views and comments in three ways:

- through a series of meetings, most with specific interested groups, but also 37 'public' meetings held throughout the country;

- an invitation for written responses made in the Ministers' foreword to Social Assistance;

- a specially commissioned survey of claimants.

Meeting the public

Between August and December 1978, members of the review team held over one hundred meetings which took place all over the country. Most of these meetings were in fact held with specific groups such as local office staff, SB tribunal chairmen and Directors of Social Services. However, 37 were held in 'public' and it was these that attracted most attention. Though in other policy areas "the holding of public meetings or hearings" could rightly be described "as traditional" (Fagence, 1977, p. 278), it was a totally new phenomenon to social security and to the officials involved. The public meetings on the SB review always provoked a lively discussion between the audience and the panel, which normally included a civil servant who had worked on the review. David Donnison and Tony Lynes took their places on a few occasions.

The public meetings often provided a catalyst for further local action either in the form of written submissions to the review team or to the creation of local umbrella groups to carry on the debate. It was because of the considerable interest generated at the public meetings that the period for sending in comments was extended beyond December 1978.

TABLE 1:   REVIEW TEAM'S PROGRAMME OF MEETINGS:
                AUGUST - DECEMBER 1978

	Number of meetings
DHSS policy units, headquarters' staff	5
Social work service: including Directors of Social Services and the British Association of Social Work (BASW)	11
Local and regional management	31
Supplementary benefit appeals tribunal (SBAT) chairmen	7
Supplementary benefit office staff	3
Public meetings and seminars	37
Other: including careers officers, welfare rights officers' group, claimants' union	10
TOTAL	104

Although the public meetings were widely welcomed and well attended,
they were the subject of some criticism, mainly because of the way
they were organised and because of their agenda. (Bull, 1978) The
first public meeting was suggested by a local newspaper; further approaches
by various local groups encouraged the review team to try to organise
others throughout the country. The meetings were not conducted according
to a formula laid down by the review team but were organised in an
ad hoc way by the initiators or later by regional DHSS offices who
sometimes approached a local academic or other outsider to make the
necessary arrangements. Access to the meetings varied and whilst a
great deal of hostility was generated against what was regarded as
controlled entry (often admission tickets were issued), admission was
generally confined only by what was considered locally to be an
appropriate size of meeting and the size of the accommodation.
Those who did manage to learn about the meetings - and publicity varied
greatly between areas - and who did manage to attend were most concerned
with the format. In several cases, an agenda was circulated which
bore close resemblance to the contents page of Social Assistance.
(This approach was later dropped but not until two-thirds of the way
through the period of public discussion.) Such an approach did little
to maintain confidence in the review team's contention that they hoped
for a wide-ranging debate. Participants who objected to this approach
had difficulty in broadening the discussion:

"It was necessary to insist from the floor
that the introductory speech itself be
discussed, thus pointing the spotlight at
awkward questions about the desirability
of a 'no-cost' review and a mass role for
the supplementary benefits scheme. How
many of these consultative meetings have
been held on an artificially structured
debate of that framework itself. Excessive
stage management is not conducive to 'open
government' ".
(Fimister, 1978)

A similar objection was made in a report of a seminar arranged to discuss
Social Assistance and attended by local voluntary groups, which was sent
in to the review team:

'Several participants of the meeting felt
that the scope and emphasis of the review put
them in the position of responding to
proposals rather than discussing the
strategies and assumptions on which those
proposals were based'.

Where the broader issues relating to the remit were raised, the
ambiguity of a civil servant addressing a public meeting became clear.
As discussed above, considerable time was spent trying to clarify why
the comprehensive remit announced by Ministers had been narrowed to
exclude the possibility of extra expenditure or an examination of the
interaction between other policies and supplementary benefit. However,
for the officials on the platform to have answered such questions would
have meant attributing responsibility to other departments and/or
Ministers which would have contravened civil service mores. Similarly,
the officials refrained from entering into any dialogue on or defence of
specific proposals, they merely noted the comments made. It could well
have been the frustration caused by such a passive response to what was
frequently a very highly charged and emotional atmosphere that led some
people in the audience to lose their tempers and for some meetings to
end up, as one member of the review team described them, 'as slanging
matches'.

The written response

A total of 1055 written submissions were sent in to the review team, in
response to the invitation for comments made in the foreword of Social
Assistance. Many of these had several signatories. The volume of letters
and comments sent in indicates a very high level of response overall.
However, more detailed examination reveals a very great disparity in the
degree of participation between groups. In the Analysis of Views and
Comments, (DHSS, 1979) conducted by the review team on all the written
responses sent in the respondents were divided into twelve groups: (see
Table 2)

TABLE 2:   NO. OF WRITTEN RESPONSES BY GROUP

National organisations	65
Local organisations and branches of national groups	201
Claimants	31
Members of the public	239
Regional and national DHSS staff	21
DHSS staff: individuals and small groups	105
Trade unions	47
SBAT members	22
Local authority social services departments	31
Social workers, probation officers, welfare rights officers	201
Other local authority departments	67
Universities and polytechnics	25
	1055

The differing level of participation amongst the various groups reflects several factors: the ease with which information could be passed on, the degree to which responses could be co-ordinated and the proclivity of each group to put forward their views. Many groups could be contacted easily by the review team. Copies of the abridged version of Social Assistance were sent to staff in the local and regional offices, supplementary benefit appeal tribunal (SBAT) chairmen and members, and 'other interested organisations'. As might be expected, response from the last group was high, with most national pressure groups, interested professional associations and other national organisations like the Equal Opportunities Commission, the Commission for Racial Equality and the SBC itself commenting in detail. At the review team's request, many local regional supplementary benefit offices held meetings and seminars to discuss the report and the majority of the 21 regional and national staff responses were composite reports from each of the DHSS regions on the views expressed at these meetings.

The relatively high response from Careers Officers, which comprised over two-thirds of the responses from the local authority departments, other than social services, followed a letter to all Chief Careers Officers asking for comments on the proposal to defer payment of benefit to school-leavers. A substantial response might have been expected from these groups, as well as social workers and social services departments, because they were all relatively easy to inform and are part of an articulate middle class group prepared to make their views

known. The one group which proved not to conform to this thesis was
that comprising the members of tribunals. In 1978, there were 314
SBAT chairmen and 2,423 members, all of whom were sent a copy of the
abridged version of Social Assistance. Only 22 responded. Chairmen
were able to express their views at a series of special meetings;
members were offered no such opportunity. Whilst some trades council
delegates might have raised the issue through their unions, it is
unlikely that this happened often (there were only 47 responses from
trade unions). There is no obvious explanation for the apparent apathy,
though it could be seen partially as a reflection of members lack of
involvement with and knowledge of the scheme. Despite their position,
Tribunal members at that time were not briefed about their own role
and function or indeed about the supplementary benefits scheme.

  The second criterion which determines the level of participation
is the extent to which activity can be co-ordinated. The high response
from locally based groups reflects the effectiveness of some national
organisations to mobilise their local branches, and of local activists
to stimulate participation (see Table 3). CPAG, Gingerbread, the
National Federation of Advice Centres and the National Association
of Citizens' Advice Bureaux were, amongst others, successful in getting
several local branches to respond.

TABLE 3:   WRITTEN RESPONSES FROM LOCAL ORGANISATIONS AND
            LOCAL BRANCHES OF NATIONAL ORGANISATIONS

	Number of Responses
Advice centres	26
Women's groups	26
Housing associations and groups	19
Local social services groups, including BASW, Council for Voluntary Service, Family Service Units	18
Political parties (all Labour except 2 communist)	17
Local war pensioners' committees	15
Lone parent groups	10
Community associations	10
Umbrella organisations	9
Groups for the elderly	8
Citizen's Advice Bureaux	8
Religious groups	6
Local CPAG branches	5
Groups for people with disabilities	4
Community relations councils	4
Other	16
TOTAL	201

Fifteen local war pensioners' committees responded, the majority on
one issue: the proposal to reduce the value of the war pensions disregard.
The National Campaign against the Supplementary Benefits Review (NCASBR)
which was set up in November 1978 and held its first annual conference
in December that year, circulated a standard letter opposing the review
which many local groups, as well as respondents in the 'general public'
and the claimants groups, sent in. Local activity was well organised
in several areas. Umbrella groups were set up in Manchester, Liverpool,
Islington, Lambeth and Wandsworth and in others a joint response compiled
by a number of groups was submitted. In some cities, such as Bristol,
Leicester, Coventry and on Tyneside, concerted action was taken to
encourage local voluntary groups and political parties to respond and
several submissions were received from these areas, many of which were
obviously co-ordinated.

The response from three other groups warrants closer examination:
individual members of staff, the 'general public' and claimants. The
105 responses from individual or small groups of staff, whilst representing
the fourth largest group of respondents, is small when compared to
the more than 30,000 staff employed on supplementary benefit, especially
given the very considerable efforts made by the review team to
stimulate debate. Part of the explanation may be that staff felt that
their views were represented already in the local office submissions
or official Staffside unions response. Some members of the review
team reported that, when visiting local offices, they found many more were
in favour of Social Assistance than the written responses from this
group indicated. A second explanation is the very considerable
scepticism felt by many staff on the review itself and on the
'participation' element in particular. It must be remembered that
staff had been consulted about simplifications of the scheme on several
occasions, most recently by the joint working party set up after the
industrial action of 1972, and yet had seen their workload increase.
This scepticism was evident in one of the regional reports: 'The
initial interest generated by the Report soon waned when it was realised
that its proposals, if implemented, would not achieve the main aims
of the review'. The scepticism of the participation process, shared
by other groups, could be found in some individual staff submissions,
as well as the regional reports. One of the latter noted a 'worrying
reluctance amongst staff to accept that their views and a rational
approach to a better and simpler scheme, will carry sufficient weight
against the needs of political expediency and voluntary sector lobbying'.
Other staff respondents assumed that the views of the 'voluble and
often politically motivated pressure groups' would carry more weight
than the views of staff.

The problems implicit in trying to obtain the views of the 'general
public' are more complex. The low response in this group reflects,
first, the difficulty of transmitting information on a very technical
subject to a wide, diverse audience, most of whom do not relate to
the topic under discussion. In their comment on Social Assistance,
several respondents complained that it had been difficult to find out
about the review. One respondent in this group wrote: '... as an
exercise in open government, this has been far from successful. To
find out anything about this review, obtain the literature and understand
the important points has taken the utmost in perseverence'. A second

explanation for the disappointing response is that "It is unlikely
that the public en masse has a satisfactory grasp of pertinent issues",
(Fagence, 1977, p. 144) a point particularly relevant to a topic as
complex as supplementary benefit and a report as technical and detailed
as Social Assistance. Finally, whilst many people might hold strong
views on social security policy in private, they are unlikely to become
actively involved because they do not generally feel that they have
a personal stake in the outcome.

The most disappointing response has to be that from claimants. Of
the nearly 3 million claimants in receipt of benefit in November 1978,
31 responded, half of whom sent in a standard letter circulated by
a local pressure group. A poster was sent to local offices for display
(see Appendix 3). The limited impact of this medium as a way of
conveying information or stimulating participation, which has been
spelt out elsewhere, (Fagence, 1977, Ch. 7) was exacerbated in this
case by a number of organisational factors. The posters were not
distributed until some months after publication of Social Assistance;
many offices did not display the poster; where they did it was often
not in the public waiting room. A claimants' union in Scotland
reported that none of the offices in one major city had displayed the
poster and said that some 'don't even have noticeboards'. Even when
the poster was displayed the difficulties were not over. One
respondent complained that 'It took me over an hour to get the address
of the place to write and to get a copy of the report ... no one had
heard of it and I was shunted from queue to queue'.

Some claimants' views were represented in the responses sent in by
local branches of organisations like Gingerbread and women's aid groups,
as well as some by local claimants' unions. The isolation and alienation
of the vast majority of claimants, however, who belong to no organisation,
meant that their views were not put forward. This problem has been
noted in numerous other studies of participation:

> "The simple extention of the opportunity
> to participate does not equalise participation
> rates; despite the equal availability of
> participation, the fact that the acceptance of
> the invitation generally remains a matter for
> voluntary initiative will ensure that some will
> take more advantage than others of the
> opportunity presented".
> (Fagence, 1977, p. 204)

Supplementary benefit claimants, like other consumers of social services
and the poor in general, are a divided and isolated group; they hold
a low status in the scheme, lack knowledge, skill and confidence to
participate, and feel a sense of powerlessness and futility which
prevents them trying to influence change. (Forder, 1974,; Jones et al,
1978)

A survey of claimants' attitudes

In anticipation of a low response from claimants, the review team commissioned a survey of claimants' attitudes to some of the "central issues" of the review. (DHSS, 1979a) There are at least two difficulties in comparing the survey findings with the spontaneous views expressed by claimants, or the other respondents. First, on the survey, answers were, by definition, restricted to the questions asked. The survey raised only four of the eight issues most frequently raised by claimants. Secondly, survey respondents were given less information than had been available to those who had read Social Assistance and it would appear that, if they had been presented with fuller information, some answers would have been different. On two of the four issues where comparison could be made between the survey results and the written responses, there was a noticeable difference. The short-term scheme proposed in Social Assistance, which would have left 22 per cent of claimants worse off and 3 per cent over £7 per week worse off, was rejected by half the claimants who wrote in. To ascertain views on this issue on the survey, respondents were asked, first, whether they thought claimants should be assessed individually when applying for benefit or whether it should be standardised (question 1 below). They were then asked (question 2 below):

> "they are in fact thinking of making the
> calculation for benefit much simpler when
> you first ask for help, that is for the
> first 8 weeks. There would be standard
> payments, including the rent allowance
> for everybody. Claiming would be easier,
> and they would not need to ask so many
> questions unless you needed to go on
> benefit after that time. Would you be
> in favour of this change, or against it?"
> (DHSS, 1979a, p. 6)

The answers were as follows:

	Pensioners %	Sick and Disabled %	Lone Parents %	Unemployed %
Question 1				
Individual assessment	91	94	92	60
Standard payments	7	6	6	33
Question 2				
For standardisation	58	53	53	70
Against standardisation	30	32	42	20

Even after the interviewers pointed out that standardisation would lead to losses for some claimants, few changed their minds. "Most ... said either that it would work out fairer overall, or that this unfairness did not matter for 8 weeks, provided there was the advantage of speedy payment". (p. 48) One unemployed respondent who was in favour of such a standardisation said: "I wouldn't like (it) if the money they give us is too low to manage on". (p. 48) Clearly, at least some survey respondents would not have been in favour of the model short-term scheme put forward in Social Assistance.

The second issue on which there was a disparity between the survey findings and claimants' written responses was the deferment of payment of benefit to school-leavers. Nearly half the claimants who wrote in rejected this proposal; no comments were made in its favour. On the survey, the following question was asked:

> "At present children can get supplementary benefits as soon as their last term at school ends but the mother no longer gets a child benefit. Do you think this is the right way to do it, or should the parents be responsible for the children until the end of the school holidays with the child benefit continuing until that time?"
> (Appendix p. 10, Q. 10 d)

The researchers themselves doubted that many respondents were aware of the large difference between the rates of child benefit and supplementary benefit. Sixty-one per cent were in favour of "parents being responsible for the children until the end of the school holidays". Had the question asked instead "are you in favour of excluding children from benefit for up to eight weeks?" the result might have been different.

Other questions were similarly loaded. Sometimes interviewees were told about current policy and then asked if they thought it was right. For example, respondents were told that the long-term rate of benefit was not paid to those claimants who have to register for work. Two questions later they were asked which groups should or should not get the long-term rate. In such cases a significant number automatically accepted the status quo.

The response to Social Assistance

The review team made an ambitious attempt to draw together the many views expressed during the period of public debate in an Analysis of Views and Comments. (DHSS, 1979) The vast majority of comment was derived from the 1055 written responses, and it is on these that the following discussion is mainly based. [3] Whilst information is provided in the Analysis on the views expressed at the 100 meetings held by the review team, this is not comparable to the analysis of the written submissions as it is not possible to distinguish between the comments made by different groups of respondents.

A number of difficulties emerge when trying to examine the composite picture presented in the Analysis, first in a commentary and then in a series of charts which were designed to show, at a glance, the main issues raised by different groups of respondents. Some of these problems arise from the diversity of response and some from the way in which the data are presented. First, it was decided that it would not be practicable to weight views; thus, in the charts, the views of an established, well-informed organisation with a large membership, a petition of 600 signatures and the views of one individual were given equal weight: each counted as one response.

Secondly, the responses were as good as the information on which they were based. The agenda for many respondents' comments was Social Assistance but even where this was the case the views expressed related to only part of that agenda. Most respondents concentrated on the issues of most concern to them or their members. Respondents representing the old, or people with disabilities tended to confine, or at least concentrate, their reaction to the issues which most affected their constituent group. As discussed above the careers officers and war pensioners tended to comment on the one specific issue that had a direct impact on them. Other respondents sent in comments based not on Social Assistance but on information obtained from the press. As Fagence has argued, such coverage inevitably centres on "the editor's interpretation of what constitutes his public's interest" (1977, p. 285) and as such provided a doubtful basis for informed comment. Many of the responses in the social worker group seem to have been influenced by an article in Social Work Today which drew attention to four specific issues and their comments are clustered around these. (Jordan, 1978) [4] For example, of the 141 responses rejecting any restriction of urgent needs payments, 103 were made by respondents in this group. Over half the respondents in the 'general public' group were in fact replying to an emotive article in a local evening newspaper. Under the headline "Where is the Welfare State going wrong: the DHSS wants to know your views on the SB scheme", readers were asked:

"Is it (the welfare state) too mean with the old, sick and single parents?"

"Is it too generous with layabouts?"

"Does it have too many bureaucratic regulations?"

"Does it positively discourage people from looking for work?"

The questions appeared in the last article in a series which had discussed the effect on pensioners of the proposal to introduce a £2,000 savings cut-off; had analysed the 'better off' problem and drew attention to significant numbers of school-leavers alleged to be claiming supplementary benefit in the summer even though they intended to return to school. Inevitably the very considerable number of readers' letters which the series generated, only about half of which were forwarded to the review team, were overwhelmingly sympathetic to pensioners but largely hostile to other groups of claimants.

The third and most fundamental difficulty faced by the review team in compiling their analysis of the response to <u>Social Assistance</u> arose out of the complexity of the subject under discussion. It was not possible in the brief commentary on each issue included in the <u>Analysis</u> to cover at length or in any detail the diverse range of views expressed on the many options raised in the report. Whilst the charts could record <u>all</u> the views, they could not register the qualifications attached to respondents' acceptance or rejection of options. It is important to keep this in mind when looking at the comments on specific options.

The most frequent qualification made to responses in general related to the parameters within which the review team's proposals had been drawn up; nearly one-fifth objected to a review of the supplementary benefits scheme in isolation from other income maintenance policies. Acceptance of some specific proposals was on the understanding that no claimant would be left worse off, or, as the Commission said in its response, that any losses would be measured in 'pence rather than pounds'. (DHSS/SBC 1979, p. 26) The Commission emphasised in its conclusions that "our proposals must not be regarded as isolated recommendations to be adopted selectively and implemented haphazardly. In the main, they represent 'packages' of closely related measures for the reform of the SB scheme" (p. 34). [5] The staff respondents tended not to put forward such a clear-cut criticism or qualification and the charts representing staff views suggest considerable agreement with the review team's proposals. However, a closer examination of the text of their responses shows that a significant proportion felt that the review team had not been 'radical' enough. Whilst many agreed with individual proposals, they did not feel the review tackled the underlying problems of the scheme.

The series of charts do not reflect the different reasons which might be given for the acceptance or rejection of a proposal. As is discussed below, the staff response was very different from that of most other groups. Where, on some issues, they reached the same conclusions, they tended to give very different reasons. For example, staff rejected the proposal to pay regular lump-sum payments to compensate for a reduction in discretion because they thought it would complicate administration. The reasons for other groups' opposition to the proposal were the low levels at which these grants were set or that they were an unsatisfactory substitute for adequate scale rates. On the one issue overwhelmingly rejected by <u>all</u> groups, the short-term scheme, staff felt that it was an added complication; other critics thought it meant an unacceptable drop in benefit for many new claimants.

When these important shortcomings are taken into account, the <u>Analysis</u>, considered alongside individual submissions, provides a useful picture of those issues which caused greatest concern and interest. Taken alone, it provides a more limited picture of the different reactions of the various groups of respondents. Analysis of the issues most frequently raised by respondents shows that on only five of the eighteen issues raised by more than 10 per cent of respondents did the majority agree with the review team (see Table 4): payment of the long-term rate of benefit to the unemployed, the alignment of the national insurance and supplementary benefit scale rates, the introduction of a unified housing benefit, the introduction of a more specific Act and code of practice and the need for simplification. In the <u>Analysis</u>, it is argued that this occurs because many respondents commented only on those issues with which they disagreed. It was also suggested by members of the

TABLE 4:   ISSUES MOST FREQUENTLY RAISED IN THE WRITTEN RESPONSES [1]

Option	For		Against		Total	
	No.	%	No.	%	No.	%
Limit right of appeal	25	2.4	356	33.7	381	36.1
Short term scheme - in principle	45	4.3	326	30.9	371	35.2
Defer benefit to school-leavers	83	7.9	211	20.0	294	27.9
No-cost remit	-	-	246	23.3	246	23.3
Regular lump-sum ENPs	92	8.7	154	14.6	246	23.3
Review in isolation from wider income maintenance	-	-	200	19.0	200	19.0
Abolish diet ECAs	28	2.6	151	14.3	179	17.0
Nominated breadwinner	62	5.9	101	9.6	163	15.5
No restriction of discretionary payments	203	19.2	-	-	203	19.2
Pay long-term rate to the unemployed	133	12.6	46	4.4	179	17.0
Increase benefit rates	152	14.4	-	-	152	14.4
Short-term model scheme	3	0.3	138	13.1	141	13.4
Restrict laundry ECAs	39	3.7	100	9.5	139	13.2
Align NI/SB scale rates	87	8.2	42	4.0	129	12.2
Unified housing benefit	81	7.7	27	2.6	108	10.3
More specific Act and code of practice	92	8.7	19	1.8	111	10.5
No restriction of urgent needs payments	141	13.4	-	-	141	13.4
Need for simplification	133	12.6	-	-	133	12.6

1   Table includes all issues raised by 10 per cent or more respondents

Source: Compiled from diagrams 1 - 12 in the Analysis of Views and Comments
         on the review of the supplementary benefits scheme

review team that the written was more negative than the general
response because critics are more likely to make their views known
than supporters. However, comprehensive analysis of the individual
responses shows that respondents were not entirely negative, and were
as likely to comment when they were in agreement. (See Table 5) Most
respondents confined their comments not to those issues with which
they disagreed, but to those aspects which affected them or those they
represented. Furthermore, the two staff groups of respondents, who
were the groups most frequently in agreement with individual proposals,
also commented on a larger number of issues. The average number of
issues covered by each respondent in the staff groups was 11.1 for
the options included in the final chapter and 26 for all issues
discussed. Other groups commented on between 0.6 and 5.1 issues for
the former and 2 and 12.6 for the latter.

The proposals which attracted most comment were those recommended
by the review team rather than merely raised for discussion, or those
that related to the terms of reference. Of the 18 issues most frequently
raised, 12 were included in the final package: 2 related to the terms
of reference, and 3 to the review team's main tools for changing the
scheme - the decrease in the use of discretion and simplification.
The final issue in this list, the need for an increase in the scale
rates, was put forward spontaneously by 14 per cent of respondents as
an alternative to the review team's redistribution of resources
between claimants. The level of the scale rates was also of great
concern to those interviewed for the claimants' survey. Whilst
they were not asked their opinion of the adult rates, lone parents
and the unemployed indicated in supplementary answers that the
children's rates were too low. The authors concluded: "There was
a strong feeling among all groups that the supplementary benefit
covered only the most basic needs, and that there was always the need
for more..." (DHSS, 1979a, p. 38)

The concentration of respondents on those issues given greatest
prominence in Social Assistance led to some misleading conclusions
in the Analysis. On the issue of equal treatment, for example, it
is concluded that "of those who express a preference between the
alternatives put forward in Social Assistance, most favour the 'nominated
breadwinner approach'". (DHSS, 1979, p. 7) However, this option,
which was the one favoured by the review team, attracted most comment
overall and more were against the proposal (101 respondents) than were
in favour (65).

The reactions to the review team's proposals were not uniform across
the different groups of respondents (see Table 5). The two staff groups,
followed by tribunal respondents, were both significantly more likely
than any other group to agree to a cost-saving proposal and less likely
to agree to proposals necessitating an increase in resources. The
individual staff responses were considerably more sympathetic to the
review than the official response from the Staffside unions. Although
concerned with the effect of the changes on staff numbers and workload,
Staffside also displayed concern for the effect on claimants. (BG 37)
The staff respondents were the only groups to agree that exceptional
circumstances additions (ECAs) for special diets should be abolished
and ECAs for laundry expenses should be cut back. Only the staff and
SBAT respondents agreed with the proposal to defer payments cf benefit
to school-leavers, or to make sponsored immigrants ineligible for
benefit. The obvious reason for the disparity of views between staff

TABLE 5:   OVERALL RESPONSE TO 20 ISSUES LISTED IN THE FINAL CHAPTER OF SOCIAL ASSISTANCE BY GROUP OF RESPONDENTS [1]

	Agree with a cost saving proposal (maximum 10)	Agree with a neutral or an expenditure proposal (maximum 10)	Disagree with a cost saving proposal	Disagree with a neutral or an expenditure proposal	Group evenly divided	Total no. of proposals commented on
National organisations	2	9	7	1	1	20
Local organisations	2	9	8	1	-	20
Claimants	1	2	3	1	-	7
Members of the public	1	5	7	2	3	18
Staff I	8	7	2	3	-	20
Staff II	8	7	2	3	-	20
Trade unions etc	2	8	7	1	2	20
SBAT members	6	6	4	1	1	18
Social Services Depts	2	9	7	1	-	19
Social Workers etc	1	9	9	1	-	20
Other local authority depts	1	7	7	1	1	17
Academics	1	4	9	5	-	19
Maximum no. of proposals	10	10	10	10	10	20

1 See Appendix 6

Source: compiled from charts in Analysis of Views and Comments

and other groups is that the former's first concern was not with the
effect of changes on claimants but on their own workload. The staff
groups, who on this, as on some other issues, disagreed with the
official Staffside response, were the only respondents opposed to the
proposal to pay the long-term rate of benefit to the unemployed. As
such a change would simplify administration, their view seems to confirm
that local office staff share the less sympathetic attitude to this
particular group of claimants reflected in much of the popular press
and held by sections of the general public.

Other groups were more likely to agree with the review team where
the proposal improved the position of some claimants, without adversely
affecting others. Thus on the issues which fitted this criterion
- paying of benefit to pensioners when abroad, an increase in the earnings
disregard, payment of long-term benefit to the unemployed, abolition
of the 50p offset, and consolidation of the heating addition to the
under 5s - national organisations, local organisations, members of
the public, trade unions, the social services departments and the group
of social workers and welfare rights workers were in favour of all
five. The cost-saving proposals most frequently supported by these
groups were the alignment of the national insurance and supplementary
benefit adult scale rates and the fixed cut-off point for capital.
However, the percentage of respondents in each group who actually
commented on the latter proposal was less than 7 per cent except for
staff (50 per cent and 32 per cent) and SBAT members (22 per cent).

Conclusion

The review of the supplementary benefits scheme offered a wide range
of interested groups a unique opportunity to take part in the social
security policy-making process. Because it was a new experiment in
this area of policy and a new experience for those involved, particularly
the civil servants, it is not surprising that a number of difficulties
and shortcomings emerged as the process and practice of open government
unfolded.

Some of these problems arose out of the lack of any coherent plan
to promote public discussion. In organisational terms, this meant
that the arrangements made for some public meetings were unsatisfactory,
either because of the size of the accommodation or the freedom of access
given. It also meant that they did not get fully under way until the
end of October, over half way through the time allowed for public
comment. This in itself provoked criticism until the deadline for
accepting written comments was extended. More serious problems which
arose at the public meetings stemmed from the unusual status of the
report and the lack of clear published terms of reference. Much time
was wasted while commentators tried to establish the reasons for the
restricted scope of the enquiry and considerable antagonism built up
amongst some participants as the officials, who admitted responsibility
for the content of the report, desisted from clarifying questions on
the terms of reference. To have done so would have implicated Ministers
or other Government departments, which was contrary to Whitehall
convention.

Although the review team was successful in generating a large number of written responses, these came mainly from predictable groups, such as those forming the welfare rights lobby. Little response came from claimants, the group most affected by any reforms, or from the general public, whose views the review team felt provided the context within which social security reform must be considered. Such shortcomings could only partly be compensated for by the two surveys which were commissioned. However, the review team lacked the time and the resources to take more positive steps to seek out views, for example by advertising or sending information direct to claimants, the success of which would have been doubtful anyway. As a result of the uneven response, the debate was dominated by those groups which were the best organised and most easily informed. The overall response was skewed, therefore, either as a result of initiatives taken by the review team, for example in contacting the War Pensioners Committees, or by articles in the press which stimulated a considerable response but on a narrow range of issues. The existence of such distortions in the overall response enabled the review team, and later the Conservative Government, to play down the significance of the response as being unrepresentative or unduly negative. As one official commented, the largely negative response did not surprise anyone: 'people are always more willing to criticise than to write in and support you'.

The complex and technical format of Social Assistance presented a further difficulty with relation to the extent that public comments could be effective in influencing the content of policy. The report attracted many diverse views on a very large number of issues, some of which were relatively insignificant for the majority of claimants, and others, such as the proposed reduction in discretion, representing a major change of direction in policy. The spread of views was very thin; on many issues only a few comments were received, sometimes with only one or two being for and against. Even those issues which were most frequently raised occurred in only just over one-third of responses.

The wider the potential groups of participants, the greater the degree of diversity and conflict will be. In the case of the review, the range of opinions held on social security in general was expressed in relation to Social Assistance. However, the perhaps predictable conflict between staff and claimants, or between pressure groups compaigning on behalf of the poor and others hostile to the welfare state, was accompanied by the additional conflict which arose between groups, who might have been expected to unite. Despite their awareness of the dilemma with which they were faced, groups who entered the debate had to set their own priorities and inevitably sought to protect the interests of their own constituent group. The result was that views were expressed which would support an infinite variety of policy options.

How 'successful' the review was as an exercise in 'open government' is a matter of judgement. The publication of Social Assistance and the open government approach did result in one of the most comprehensive debates on any aspect of social security policy since the war, and lifted the debate above the level of the more usual popular media concern with 'scrounging' to a more informed discussion of fundamental issues. Despite its faults, the Analysis made an attempt to provide a picture of the response made, and its publication, despite the fact that it showed fundamental disagreement both with the remit and with many of the specific recommendations, was a significant step forward and an achievement for the officials who persuaded the new Conservative Ministers to publish. However, the aim of these who took part in the public debate was to influence the direction and content of the changes to the supplementary benefits scheme. How far they succeeded is the subject of the next chapter.

Notes

1. The 1979 Conservative Government issued Green Papers on the reform of maternity benefits, the death grant and new sick pay arrangements, as well as a discussion document on the industrial injuries scheme.

2. For example, the review team's analysis of the response to Social Assistance, (DHSS, 1979) received very little publicity, was more complicated to get hold of and cost £4:75. The Report of the Working Group on Inequalities in Health (The Black Report) fared even worse. 260 duplicated copies of the typescript were produced. See Townsend P & Davidson N (1982), Inequalities in Health, Penguin p. 11.

3. The Analysis included charts on the views recorded at the meetings and the claimants' survey. These were not included in the tables below because they are not comparable to the written responses and are less reliable. In this chapter I have drawn mainly on the written responses sent into the review team, to which I was kindly given access.

4. November 1978. The four issues were: the abolition of discretion during the first 8 weeks of a claim; fixed rent payments during this period; limitations on the right of appeal; restrictions in the availability of urgent needs payments.

5. One example of a 'package'. "We would not reduce reliance on discretionary benefits without first ensuring that the scale rates, together with sufficiently generous lump sum payments at regular intervals, are adequate, all rights to appeal are preserved, and each local office is capable of giving closer attention to the minority of claimants who will have difficulty in managing on the income provided". (DHSS/SBC, 1979, p. 34)

Chapter 8

The Outcome

The purpose of the supplementary benefits review was literally to
reform the administrative and legislative structure of social
assistance in Britain. (Chapter 1) The review itself was structured
in a new and unique way, as a two-stage process, to ensure that
momentum would be maintained and action taken regardless of changes
in Government policy, or even a change of Government. (See Chapter 4)
Social Assistance was produced by officials, without any party political
underpinning, and was framed in politically neutral terms, in order
that its findings could appeal to both major political parties. The
period of consultation which took place after publication of the report,
though eliciting comments often not in agreement with the review team's
conclusions, nevertheless reinforced the already perceived need for
fundamental reform and created a climate in which major change was
expected.

The success or failure of the review can be judged against two
criteria. First, how far the review process per se was instrumental
in ensuring the eventual reform of the supplementary benefits scheme.
In the longer term, it will be judged on how far the changes which
followed provided permanent solutions to the problems confronting the
scheme; and their impact on the administration, on staff and on
claimants. Any assessment of the significance of the review to the
reforms which were included in the Social Security Act 1980 must take
into account the whole review process, namely the proposals contained
in Social Assistance and the views and comments made during the public
debate.

Social Assistance and the Labour Government

At no time did the Labour Ministers to whom the review team reported
in 1978 make any formal public statement of their views on the
proposals in Social Assistance or on what their future policy would
be on the reform of the supplementary benefits scheme. Instead comment
was deferred pending the outcome of the public discussion. By the
time this debate drew to a close in the early months of 1979, a general
election had been announced. Given the sensitive and electorally
unrewarding nature of supplementary benefit, no further action was
taken, and in fact, publication of the Supplementary Benefits
Commission's critical response to the review team's report was
deliberately delayed. No reference was made to this aspect of social
security in the 1979 Labour Party manifesto.

Though no official pronouncements were made, it is clear that Labour
Ministers did have considerable sympathy with the main tenor of the
report and did see it as a way forward, though this view was not
shared by some backbenchers. Between July 1978 and the end of the
Labour Administration, Ministers often referred to the need "to move
towards simplification so that those who are entitled to benefit can
claim and receive that benefit". (Stanley Orme, Hansard, vol. 957,
col. 665, 7 Nov. 1978) On other occasions, allusions were made to the need
for financial stringency. With regard to the payment of the long-term

rate of benefit to the unemployed, for example, Stanley Orme,
Minister for Social Security, told the House of Commons that "It is
a matter of resources, but dealing with this problem is high priority".
(Hansard, vol. 957, col. 665, 7 Nov. 1978) With regard to the review
team's recommendation that each claimant should receive automatically
a written statement of how benefit entitlement had been worked out,
he said that the desirability of such a policy had to be weighed
against the implications for staff costs.

Social Assistance and the Conservative Government

If the Labour Government's attitude towards the kind of reform
recommended in Social Assistance was not spelt out officially, the
same cannot be said either of the Conservative Party in Opposition
in 1978 or of the Conservative Administration which took office in
May 1979. When he was Opposition Spokesman for Social Services,
Patrick Jenkin, told the House of Commons that:

> "We on the Opposition benches accept
> the main message of the review, namely
> that substantial changes are needed if
> the system is not to break down
> utterly ... We accept that a major
> simplification is necessary. We
> accept that we have to reduce
> substantially the areas of discretion".
> (Hansard, vol. 958, col. 1188, 21 Dec. 1978)

The 1979 Conservative Party manifesto contained no reference to
supplementary benefit but it was clear that its policy proposals for
the social security system as a whole, which was said to be so
complicated that "even some Ministerial officials do not understand
it", had implications for the scheme. (Conservative Central Office,
1979, p. 27) The party's long term aim was to move slowly towards
a system of tax credits, but there was also a short term objective:
"We shall do all we can to find other ways to simplify the system,
restore the incentive to work, reduce the poverty trap and bring more
effective help to those in greatest need". (p. 27) The reform of
supplementary benefits was to be the first step to 'simplify' the
system. Radical changes to unemployment and sickness benefits, and to
the range of help with housing costs followed.

The Conservative Government and Social Security

The Conservative Government began its programme of reform of the
social security system in its first year of office. It was announced
in the Queen's Speech which opened a hectic first session of
Parliament under the new Conservative Administration in May 1979 that
"Ways will be sought to simplify the operations of the social security
system". (Hansard, vol. 967, col. 51, 15 May 1979) On November 1979,
the Government published its first Social Security Bill, to become
the Social Security Act 1980, the main part of which was devoted to
reforming the supplementary benefits scheme. The proposals for change

were set out in a White Paper which was published on the same day as
the Bill. (HMSO, 1979) These proposals, and more importantly Clause
1 of the Bill, which broke the link between upratings of long-term
benefits and the increase in earnings, provided a foretaste of the
new Government's very different approach to social security policy.

Since the cuts in unemployment assistance in the 1930s, successive
Governments of both political parties have regarded the level of
social security benefits as inviolable. Though the value of some,
most notably family allowances and later child benefit, fell because
they were not tied to any formal regular uprating policy, all the other
major benefits have been protected from any cuts. Changes in the level
of benefits are called 'upratings' for the very reason that they have
only been revised upwards either to compensate for rises in the cost
of living or to allow recipients to share in the general rise in the
standard of living enjoyed by the rest of the community. Under the
new Government, social security expenditure was not sacrosanct. The
first indication of this new attitude was made by Patrick Jenkin, the
new Secretary of State for Social Services. In the debate on the
Second Reading of the first Social Security Bill, he said that these
measures were the first part of a wider package of changes in the
social security programme which "faces up to some of the problems
confronting the nation from the rising share of the national income
absorbed by social security". (Hansard, vol. 976, col. 897, 10 Dec.
1979) The first Social Security Bill delayed the payment of the
November 1981 uprating by two weeks, saving £125 million. The
Government also refused to make good the 1.7 per cent shortfall in
the November 1979 uprating which provided a further saving of £195
million. By the time of the Government's second budget in March 1980,
the social security budget looked even more vulnerable. The
Chancellor of the Exchequer told the House that "Social security
cannot be regarded as exempt from re-examination and entitled always
to take absolute priority over spending on defence, the police,
hospitals or schools - or over the need for proper control of public
spending as a whole". (Hansard, vol. 981, col. 1463, 26 March 1980)
It was now "inescapable that this programme must bear some share of the
necessary economies". (Hansard, vol. 981, col. 1660, 27 March 1980)
The budget was followed by a second Social Security Bill, which became
the Social Security (No. 2) Act 1980, which included three measures
to cut back the social security programme and curtail the growth of
expenditure on certain benefits.

The first of these measures reduced the real value of earnings-
related supplement from January 1981. In January 1982 all such
payments were abolished. The Chancellor justified the abolition on
the grounds that earnings-related supplement was diminishing in worth
and effectiveness "with the payment of more generous redundancy payments
and occupational sickness schemes". (Hansard, vol. 981, col. 1461,
26 March 1980) Confirming the announcement, Patrick Jenkin justified
the move because "earnings-related supplement does add to income out
of work and therefore at the margin does not encourage the return to
work". (Hansard, vol. 981, col. 1660, 27 March 1980)

The second major change introduced by the Social Security (No. 2)
Act broke the link between the uprating of all short-term national
insurance benefits and invalidity benefit, and increases in the retail
price index. This measure reflected a concern, which the Chancellor

of the Exchequer said was shared by "The Government and the vast
majority of the British people (who) want hard work and initiative
to be properly rewarded and are vexed by disincentives to work. One
of the biggest problems is the lack of balance between social security
benefits and income in work". (Hansard, vol. 981, col. 1459, 26 March
1980)   As a result of this step, short-term national insurance benefits
and invalidity benefit were uprated by 5 per cent less than the rate
of inflation. [1]   It was estimated that these two measures, the lower
uprating and the abolition of earnings-related supplement would save
£270 million in 1981-82 and £480 million in 1982-83. They would put
an additional 110,000 people on to supplementary benefit by 1982-83,
the first full year of their implementation. (Hansard, vol. 982, col.
536, 14 April 1980)

A third change embodied in the Social Security (No. 2) Act was to
deduct £12 (to be increased automatically in line with inflation) from
the benefit paid to families of strikers. Strikers themselves had
only been eligible for benefit in cases of severe hardship. In
addition, strikers' families ceased to be able to claim urgent needs
payments, except in the most extreme emergency, or single payments.
The Chancellor explained the reasoning behind this change in his
Budget speech: "(social security payments) can be one of several
factors that sometimes tilt the balance of industrial power against
employers and responsible trade union leadership alike. These
payments have helped to sustain some very damaging strikes".
(Hansard, vol. 981, col. 1462, 26 March 1980) He went on to give the
example of the national steel strike which was nearing its end after
a prolonged dispute. In fact, the Supplementary Benefits Commission
later released figures to show that only 30 per cent of steelworkers
had claimed benefits for their families at the height of the dispute.

The reforms of the supplementary benefits scheme made by the
Conservative Government must be seen in the context of the Government's
attitude to social security as a whole. First, its concern with the
"why work" syndrome and a preoccupation with the question of fraud
and abuse. At a time when efforts were being made to reduce the number
of civil servants, the Government announced that an extra 1050 staff
were being added to the DHSS complement "to boost prevention and
detection efforts". (Reg Prentice, Minister of Social Security,
Hansard, vol. 978, col. 710, 13 February 1980) Following a
recommendation resulting from the 'Rayner Scrutiny' into payment of
benefits to the unemployed, the Government announced in March 1981
that further staff would be deployed in this area, mainly to act as
unemployment review officers. (DE/DHSS, 1981)

Secondly, the changes to the supplementary benefits scheme must be
seen in the context of the Government's concern with the complexity
and cost of the whole social security system. Though the reforms
preceded the Government's later more severe cuts in the real value
of some benefits and the range of benefits available, their
introduction cannot be seen in isolation from what was to follow.
Many of the changes included in the Social Security (No. 2) Bill,
which was introduced to Parliament before the first Bill had received
the Royal Assent, undermined or even nullified some of the changes
made in the supplementary benefits scheme by the first Act. Other
changes in the second Act, and in later measures led to increased
dependency on means-tested assistance.

The reform of the supplementary benefits scheme

The fact that the Conservative Government was able to introduce
legislation to reform the supplementary benefits scheme within six
months of coming to office was as much a result of the way in which
the review had been structured and carried out as the result of any
political commitment held by the new Administration. The fact that
the protagonists for a review had been successful in depoliticising
the enquiry and its findings was confirmed when it became clear that
the new Government's reforms derived directly from Social Assistance.
This was confirmed by Patrick Jenkin in the Second Reading Debate,
(Hansard, vol. 976, col. 897, 20 December 1979) and by Reg Prentice,
Minister of Social Security, who said during the Committee Stage, that
the proposed reorganisation of the scheme "follows logically a
sequence of events initiated by the previous Government when they
produced their consultative document". (Hansard, Standing Committee
E, col. 21, 22 January 1980) The new legislation, in fact, included
only two measures not discussed in Social Assistance.

   Analysis of the significance of the open government strategy, in
particular the public debate, to the reforms which were introduced,
must obviously take account of the fact that a general election and
a change of Government intervened between the publication of Social
Assistance and the public consultation which followed, and the
introduction of legislation. Unlike their Labour predecessors, the
incoming Conservative Ministers were not committed to the open
government strategy, a fact best illustrated by the only reluctant
agreement given to the publication of the Analysis of Views and Comments
on the review and the demise of the issues in Social Assistance
deferred for consideration in the second stage of the review.
Consultative papers were produced on only two of the seventeen second
stage subjects. (DHSS, 1979b; DHSS 1979c) Legislative changes were
introduced, however, on a number of issues which had been deferred but
without publication of a discussion document. The first Act included
changes with relation to provision for non-dependants in households
and the recovery of overpayments; the second Act changed the rules
relating to trades disputes. The Government claimed, however, that
in drawing up the proposed changes, it had taken "into account the
very many comments on the report which (had) been sent in by bodies
and interests all over the country". (Hansard, vol. 976, col. 904,
20 December 1979) The second stage of public debate which followed
publication of the review team's findings was used by the Conservative
Government as a justification for omitting the consultation which normally
takes place after a White Paper is introduced and before the proposed
legislation goes before Parliament. The White Paper on the Reform
of the Supplementary Benefits Scheme and the Social Security Bill were
published on the same day. The loss of this period of discussion was
more acute given the tactics adopted by the Opposition during the
Committee Stage of the Social Security Bill. Most of the Committee's
time was taken up with prolonged argument on clause 1, which changed
the uprating rules for long-term benefits. The discussion which did
take place did so without the benefit of knowledge of the regulations
on which the new scheme was to be based. A draft was available but
the final, and revised, regulations were not laid before Parliament
until the summer of 1980, long after the Social Security Bill had
become law.

The incoming Conservative Government was able to use <u>Social Assistance</u> as a basis for its reforms of the supplementary benefits scheme because the proposals in that document had been drawn up within a framework which was consistent with its own priorities of cutting public expenditure, including social security expenditure and the size of the civil service, and rationalising the social security system. It should be unsurprising then that the main opposition to the review team's proposals was largely ignored by the Government. (Walker, 1982) Thus, despite the explicit opposition of one-quarter of all those who wrote into the review team to the no-cost constraint and further opposition to the application of 'rough justice' to the poor, the Government was unmoved. The package of reforms introduced in the Social Security Act 1980 remained "a carefully balanced package; a small number will lose and others will gain by varying amounts". (HMSO, 1979) [3]

The Government later announced that, in fact, 1.75 million claimants would lose from the proposals, more than twice the 0.75 million who would be better off. The remaining half a million claimants would find their net benefit unchanged, though some would both gain and lose from individual changes within the package (see Appendix 4). The number of claimants who actually made a net gain when the reforms were introduced in December 1980 was only one-third of that predicted because most of the gains were nullified by the abatement of short-term national insurance benefits made in the Social Security (No. 2) Act. The 'rough justice' which the reforms meted out worked to the detriment mainly of long-term claimants, especially pensioners. The £60 million which it was estimated would be saved within the package was redistributed towards "claimants with children who are experiencing the most difficulty in managing at supplementary benefit levels". (HMSO, 1979)   (see Table 1)

Numerically, the main losses, of up to 35p per week, were suffered by pensioners and other long-term claimants as a result of the alignment of the long-term supplementary benefits rates with the national insurance rates. Many pensioners figured also amongst the claimants who would no longer be eligible for benefit following the introduction of a £2,000 fixed cut-off for savings. The losses for some pensioners were offset by the introduction of an automatic payment, from November 1979, of the lower rate of heating addition to all households containing a pensioner aged 75 or over. This age limit was reduced to 70 in November 1980. Families with children gained mainly from an increase in some of the children's rates which accompanied the reduction in the number of age bands from five to three, from more generous earnings disregards, especially for lone parents, and from the automatic payment of the lower rate of heating addition to families with a child under five. Few claimants suffered an actual drop in the amount of benefit received as the reforms were introduced at the same time as the November 1980 uprating. Transitional regulations were introduced which allowed a claimant's benefit to be maintained at the current level if implementation of the new regulations would lead to a fall in the cash paid. (SB [Transitional] Regs. 1980, no. 984) Two groups were excluded from the transitional provisions: claimants involved in a trades dispute and those with savings over £2,000 who were disqualified from benefit.

TABLE 6: OVERALL PACKAGE IN THE SOCIAL SECURITY ACT 1980 [1]

000's

Category	LOSERS					No Change	GAINERS				Total number cases
	£3.00 and over	£1.01 - £3.00	0.41p - £1.00	0.01p - 0.40p	Total number losers		0.01 - 0.50p	0.51 - £3.10	Over £3.10	Total number gainers	
Cases without children:											
All supplementary pensioners	8	246	158	1,176	1,587	81	19	43	3	63	1,731
Sick and disabled	1	8	8	47	64	97	19	6	18	43	204
Unemployed	5	8	9	7	29	227	149	10	6	165	421
Other supplementary allowance	1	2	2	11	17	7	5	1	10	16	41
TOTAL without children	15	264	177	1,242	1,697	412	191	60	36	288	2,397
Cases with children:											
All supplementary pensioners	-	2	1	3	5	*	*	1	*	1	6
Sick and disabled	1	2	1	2	4	*	3	8	5	15	20
Unemployed	2	11	5	4	21	*	39	111	5	155	176
Lone parent families	2	13	9	48	72	12	48	120	70	238	322
Other	*	2	1	3	5	*	1	4	2	7	11
TOTAL with children	4	27	16	60	107	13	90	243	82	416	536
GRAND TOTAL	19	291	193	1,302	1,805	424	282	303	118	703	2,932

1 Assumes rent share £3.80:   long-term offsett dropped

* less than 500

Totals may vary because of rounding

Source: Hansard, cols. 483-4   10.12.79

The difference between the nil-cost packages compiled by the
Government and the review team occurred, mainly, because the
legislation did not include the two main expenditure proposals in
Social Assistance. The Government did not extend payment of the
long-term rate of benefit to the unemployed, which was recommended
by the review team and supported by the Commission and all
respondents except staff (13% in favour, 4% against), because, as Reg
Prentice told the House of Commons, it was "not compatible with the
nil-cost package that is the basis of the scheme". It is clear, however,
that the Government's failure to end this long-standing inequity was
due to its over-riding concern with the 'why-work syndrome'. In the
discussions on the Social Security Bill in the Standing Committee of
the House of Commons, Reg Prentice linked the two issues:

> "Of course the majority of people who
> are unemployed ... genuinely want to
> work. In no sense is our decision that
> they cannot go on the long-term rate of
> benefit due to any desire to punish the
> workshy ... It is simply a question of
> costs and priorities. There is no other
> motive behind what we are saying".
> (Standing Committee E, cols. 121-8
> 26 February 1980)

The Government also declined to adopt the review team's recommendation
which was pressed by the SBC, to compensate for the reduced flexibility
in the scheme with automatic lump-sum payments to all claimants. (9%
for, 15% against) This option was opposed by Mr Prentice because "this
is the wrong way to tackle the problem of clothing needs". (Hansard,
vol. 981, col. 519, 15 March 1980) But, as will be seen, the
Government provided no other help with this essential and unavoidable
need, which, as experience had shown, many claimants had great
difficulty in meeting.

Because these two expenditure measures were not implemented, the
Government was able to be more generous in other areas. The number
of children's rates were reduced from five to three by raising the
0-5 and the 11-12 bands up to the level of the band above: an option
rejected by the review team because it was too expensive. Also the
Government did not need to make some of the cuts in ECAs put forward
by the review team. The proposal to abolish dietary additions, opposed
by 14% of respondents, was not implemented. Although the value of
laundry additions was decreased, the criteria governing their payment
were made less severe than those proposed by the review team. The
legislation did not restrict the payment of central heating additions
and, in fact, made more generous provision for heating additions than
had been recommended. This improvement in the level of support given
for heating costs was made politically desirable because of two policy
changes outside the supplementary benefits scheme. First, the decision
made in 1979 to deliberately increase the price of gas above the level
of inflation, and increases in the cost of both electricity and coal.
Secondly, in October 1979, the electricity discount scheme was
terminated at a saving of £45 million. Thus, the Government
compensated supplementary benefits claimants, but not other poor
families, for savings made outside the scheme and therefore outside

the package of reforms, with savings made within the package.

The prediction made by the review team that future Governments would be unlikely to provide the necessary resources to lift substantial numbers of claimants off supplementary benefit was amply fulfilled by the Conservative Administration. Unlike previous Conservative and Labour Governments, there was no mention of a long-term aim to lift people off means-tested supplementary benefit and, as discussed earlier, measures subsequently introduced have increased dependence. The aim of the reforms was "to adapt the structure of the scheme to meet its present (mass) role, as "Social Assistance" suggested". (HMSO, 1979) The tools chosen by the Government were those used by the review team: simplification, the need for which Patrick Jenkin said was the "overwhelming message" in the response to the review; and away from the emphasis on discretion which in the words of the White Paper "(was) unsuited to the scale on which the scheme is now operating"(HMSO, 1979) to a system based on legal entitlement and published rules. Whilst respondents had been in favour of both these aims, they were not acceptable in the context of a nil-cost package. The Government contested that, despite the financial losses suffered by some groups, all claimants would benefit from this change of emphasis and simplification.

Although all but two of the changes included in the Social Security Act were discussed in Social Assistance, and the Government accepted the framework of that document, it did not take on board all the proposals recommended by the review team. However, the views expressed during the period of public debate, or indeed the 200 amendments put down whilst the Social Security Bill was debated in Parliament, were seldom influential factors on whether proposals were included or omitted from the legislation. Some proposals were implemented despite opposition, some proposals opposed by respondents were omitted but for other reasons. In one case, the alignment of the national insurance and supplementary benefits scale rates, the lack of a concerted opposition to this specific proposal, as opposed to implicit criticism in their opposition to nil-cost reform and rough justice, encouraged the Government to include a proposal, which officials had thought would be totally unacceptable to the public.

The Social Security Act 1980: a simpler scheme?

Simplification was the keynote theme underlying the reforms of the supplementary benefits scheme implemented in the Social Security Act 1980. The intention of the legislation was to simplify both the structure and administration by reducing the role of discretion. The attempt to simplify the structure was limited, as Social Assistance had been, by the financial constraint and the reforms were restricted to marginal shifts of existing resources between claimants.

Despite the emphasis on simplification, the Government did not introduce a short-term scheme which the review team had concluded was "one of the most important possibilities for consideration". (DHSS, 1978, p. 104) The omission of this proposal, which was the single issue rejected by all groups of respondents, was not a reflection of the Government bowing to public pressure. Indeed, a recommendation by the Rayner Scrutiny Team to introduce a new procedure for assessing initial claims for the unemployed has been accepted in principle.(DE/DHSS, 1981)   This proposal was not included in the Social Security Act 1980 because, as members of the review team themselves acknowledged during the public debate, its implementation was not feasible until the responsibility for meeting housing costs had been removed from the supplementary benefits scheme. In April 1983, this happened when, with the introduction of the new housing benefit scheme, the local authorities took over this function from the DHSS.

The review team's proposal to align the national insurance and supplementary benefits scale rates was adopted. This measure was described by Patrick Jenkin as the "most important single change" (Hansard, vol. 976, col. 908, 20 December 1979) and by Reg Prentice as "the cornerstone of the simplifications" (Hansard, Standing Committee E, col. 594, 13 February 1980). Any contribution which this step might have made to simplifying the structure of the scheme is debatable (see p 88). However, other policy changes made within the first Act, then in the second Social Security Act and subsequent legislation revealed that, despite Government rhetoric, [4] it was important only because it generated savings of £30 million which could be used for simplifying other aspects of the scheme. It was not a major simplification in itself.

First, any simplification in the structure of the long-term scale rates, which resulted from the alignment, was "seriously undermined" (SBC, 1980, p. 73) by the automatic payment of the lower rate of heating addition to all supplementary pensioners over 70 which effectively created two age-related rates for supplementary pensioners, one for the under 70s and one for those over 70. Changes introduced in the Social Security (No. 2) Act, which came in to effect on the same day as the supplementary benefit changes (24 November 1980) meant that even the limited degree of alignment envisaged by the review team was not achieved. Under the second Act short-term national insurance benefits and invalidity benefit (a long-term benefit) were uprated by five per cent less than other benefits. At that stage, therefore, there continued to be four rates of benefit, though arranged differently: short-term national insurance, short-term supplementary benefit, long-term supplementary benefit and national insurance, and invalidity benefit. The disparity between the short-term national insurance and supplementary benefit rates (£1:25 for a married couple and 70p for a single person at November 1982 rates) is now considerably greater than the nominal sums which applied before November 1980. In November [5] 1982, a difference re-emerged between the long-term rates of benefit, and there are now 5 main rates compared to the 4 which the review team tried to reduce.

Unlike the scale rate alignment, and perhaps the replacement of the special rates for blind people by a weekly addition, other simplific- ations were more than cosmetic. Some, such as the reduction in the [6] number of children's rates and levels of heating additions, brought genuine improvements for claimants. Others had significant administrative advantages but led to cuts in the level of provision. Two measures in particular fell into this category. First, payment of benefit to school-leavers was deferred until the end of the holiday following the term the child had left school. Of the people who responded to the review team, three times as many were against this

proposal as were in favour (27.9% to 7.9%). Careers officers, whose
views had been specifically canvassed, were evenly divided on this.
Those against, who were based mainly in regions of high unemployment,
feared it would encourage school-children to leave before sitting
their examinations. Those who supported the proposal did so on the
grounds that it was undesirable for young people to move direct from
school to benefit. Introduction of this measure, which was supported
by the SBC, was crucial because it released 400 posts, which allowed
the creation of the special case officer posts discussed below. The
second measure implemented to ease administration despite the hardship
caused to the claimants affected was the replacement of the sliding
scale that had been applied to savings by a fixed capital cut-off.
This was set at £2,000, the level chosen by the review team. No
account was taken of the high levels of inflation which had occurred
between 1978 and the date of implementation. (See p. 140)

Both these measures have attracted widespread criticism, in the
media, from Members of Parliament and welfare rights organisations.
The Association of Secondary Heads, which represents three-fifths of
all heads of secondary schools, announced, on the basis of a survey
of its members, that children were leaving school at Easter before
sitting their CSE or GCE examinations in order to claim benefit,
though the Government has since disputed that this is in fact
happening. Criticism of the £2,000 cut-off was so great that the
Supplementary Benefit Policy Inspectorate were asked to conduct a
special study of the way it was working and its impact on those
affected. (DHSS, 1982) The Policy Inspectorate estimated that the
number of claimants who ceased to be eligible for benefit was no more
than 9,000 and probably nearer 5-7,000, considerably fewer than the
original estimate of 13,000. However, the losses for those affected
were large. Over a fifth of pensioners, and over a quarter of those
under pension age, lost £20 per week or more.

Despite the emphasis on simplification four measures were introduced
which complicated administration. The first measure to make extra
demands on the administration arose from provision in the Act, as urged
by the review team, the SBC and commentators, and as required by an
EEC Directive, to take steps towards 'the progressive implementation
of the principle of equal treatment in matters of social security'.
(Council Directive, 76/207 EEC, 9 February 1976) From November 1983,
either partner will be able to claim supplementary benefit if certain
criteria are met. What those criteria will be is still (in March 1983)
unknown but the SBC predicted in 1979 that the new regulation on this
would be 'as unrestrictive as possible, and beyond the "nominated
breadwinner" proposal made in Social Assistance'. (SBC, 1980, p. 15)
We must await further clarification but the continued stress on nil-
cost reform revealed most recently in the new housing benefit scheme
makes the allocation of extra resources unlikely. The issue of written
notices of assessment to all claimants was another change highly
desirable for the claimant but adding to the workload. Thirdly, the
various levels of disregards allowed on benefits and earnings under
the old scheme were standardised - to nothing or £4, with the
exception of tapered earnings disregard for lone parents: an option
dismissed by the review team as being too complicated to administer.
Lone parents are now allowed to keep the first £4 of their earnings
after expenses plus half of anything they earn between £4 and £20.

Fourthly the reduction of the qualifying period for the long-term rate from two years to one, was introduced even though it made demands for extra staff. This measure was the cheaper alternative, however, for the Government's refusal to pay the long-term rate to the unemployed, the change most consistently urged by the critics of the scheme.

From discretion to legal entitlement

The second aim of the 1980 package of reforms was to make the supplementary benefits scheme easier for staff to operate and claimants to understand. The introduction of a more clearly defined legal structure, accompanied by regulations was designed to do this. This was seen by the Government as one of the most significant reforms. This view was shared by the Supplementary Benefits Commission, which, in its last Annual Report, described it as "the single most important reform to emerge from the review". (1980, p. 144) The change in the legal structure favoured by the review team had been an Act supported by a Code of Practice. However, members changed their minds on this issue and it is likely that the more rigid structure implicit in regulations found greater favour with Ministers. This was the option implemented. For the main part, the numerous regulations which have been published (see Appendix 5) merely gave legislative force to policy previously determined and carried out by the SBC. In some important respects, which are discussed below, the regulations were more restrictive. It was as part of this effort to aid clarity and emphasise claimants' rights that the new legislation at last provided for the issue of notices of assessment to all claimants, whenever their entitlement changed. They were not issued, however, after the major 1980 changes.

As predicted by both the Commission and the review team, the shift towards a rule based system removed from the SBC much of its executive and policy-making role. In addition, the new legislation made staff in local offices responsible for their decisions. Local Supplementary Benefits Officers (SBOs) now work under the guidance of a Chief Supplementary Benefits Officer, (CSBO) a civil servant of assistant secretary rank. The first CSBO to be appointed, whose role was vital in interpreting the law and laying down guidance for the discretionary powers which remain in the scheme was Alan Palmer, the leader of the review team.

In Social Assistance, the review team had suggested that:

> "if the scheme's structure is re-cast
> on the lines we favour, we think there
> will still be advantage in having an
> independent body to exercise both a
> policy-making and an advisory function
> in this very sensitive social and
> political area ... The SBC could
> continue to be responsible for
> determining the detailed policies of
> the scheme, by being charged with the
> task of preparing the Code of Practice
> and recommending changes to it".
> (p. 25)

The SBC, in its 1977 Annual Report, also laid emphasis on the importance of the Commission's advisory role and its obligation to:

> "keep under consideration the changing
> number and composition of those in
> poverty, and of the services, specially
> designed for them. No other body has
> so continuing and comprehensive an
> obligation in this field".
> (1978, p. 3)

The Social Security Act 1980 abolished the SBC and the National Insurance Advisory Committee and in their place established a Social Security Advisory Committee (SSAC) to:

> "bring under one umbrella both national
> insurance regulations and supplementary
> benefit regulations so that we may bring
> together our whole system of benefits".
> (Hansard, Standing Committee E, col. 489,
> 12 February 1980)

SSAC has no executive function and its role is wholly advisory. Its precise functions were not spelt out in the regulations. However, besides commenting on draft regulations, it would, said Lynda Chalker, then Under-Secretary of State for Health and Social Security, "be free to initiate ideas and investigations", free to issue reports and give the kind of independent advice proferred by the SBC. (col. 489) SSAC has published one Annual Report (DHSS, 1982a) in which it continued the critical, independent line taken by the SBC under the Donnison Chairmanship. However, the Committee has adopted a much lower profile, rarely does its work come to public attention. It plays a much more reactive role than its predecessor.

The Social Security Act 1980 continued the process of strengthening the legal base of the appeals structure, begun after publication of the Bell Report. (1975) Supplementary benefit appeals tribunals now resemble more closely national insurance tribunals. Appellants may now appeal against a tribunal's findings to the Social Security Commissioner, whose most important decisions form the basis of a body of case caw, which is then binding on staff in local offices and the tribunals.

The absorption of Commission discretion into the new regulations, has left considerably less flexibility in the scheme. The availability of weekly additions to benefit is now prescribed in the regulations, (Supplementary Benefit [Requirements] Regulations 1980, No. 1299, Pt. III) in many cases with the precise amounts payable. Exceptional needs payments have been replaced by 'single payments' which are available only to those in receipt of benefit and those entitled to, but not receiving benefit. (Supplementary Benefit [Single Payments] Regulations 1981 No. 1528) Single payments are not allowed for certain items of expenditure, most contentiously, school clothing. Expenses, not covered by the scale rates, such as maternity and funeral expenses, are set out, together with the level of payment and the circumstances in which the need may be met.

The most serious cutback in single payments, from the point of view of claimants, has been made in relation to items which are supposed to be covered by the scale rates. The circumstances in which clothing grants can be made, for example, are limited to cases where the need has arisen "otherwise than by normal wear and tear". (Sec. 27) As mentioned earlier, the Government rejected the option recommended by the review team and the SBC to compensate for this loss of discretion by introducing regular lump-sum payments. The restriction of discretion without compensation was opposed by nearly one-fifth of the respondents to Social Assistance. Though more were against the lump sum proposal than were in favour, opposition by groups other than staff was on the grounds that the suggested grants were too low or were an unsatisfactory alternative to adequate scale rates. The regulations also restricted the availability of urgent needs payments and those which are now made are more likely to be recoverable. (SB [Urgent Cases] Regulations, 1981, No. 1529)

Although the new supplementary benefit regulations absorbed most 'Commission discretion', the reformed scheme retains several elements of 'officer discretion'. There are still many areas which involve a question of judgement. For example, single payments may be made for items, or in circumstances not specified in the regulations when "in the opinion of the benefit officer, such a payment is the only means by which serious damage or serious risk to the health or safety of any member of the assessment unit may be prevented". (SB [Single Payments] Regs. 1981, sec. 30) In many other instances, it is up to the SBO to assess whether a 'need' exists. The CSBO provides guidance on the use of discretionary powers to local office staff and this is published. There is also an internal S Manual (the successor to the notorious A and AX codes) which translates the law and regulations into a working document for staff. Though it has been announced that this will be made public, two and a half years into the new scheme, its emergence seems no nearer.

In the absence of financial compensation for the cutback in single payments, the 1980 Act brought into being special case officers (SCOs) to tackle the 'minority of cases' which 'present special difficulties'. (SBC, 1980, para 2.14) The DHSS is carrying out its own internal investigation of the way this innovation is working and final judgement must be reserved until these results are made available (that is if they are published) but early indications were that this change had been somewhat less 'revolutionary' than was predicted by the SBC. (para 2.19) The role of the SCO varies between offices but in many offices their workload is very light. In many cases their SCO responsibilities only account for part of their time, the rest being spent on normal duties. In one office visited by the author, twelve months after taking on the post the SCO had had only six or seven cases. It is unlikely that the limited use to which many SCOs have been put reflects the absence of need. It is more likely that other officers are reluctant to pass on cases, either because it reflects failure on their own part or because the SCO has no extra financial resources available, and other SBOs may themselves make arrangements to help with budgeting such as fuel and rent direct payments. Complaints have been made outside the scheme, by social services departments and welfare rights agencies that some particularly difficult cases are not put by SBOs into the 'better trained hands' of the SCO. It has been suggested that others, such as social workers, health visitors

and rights workers more familiar with the difficulties faced by
claimants in managing on supplementary benefit, should be able to
refer cases to the SCO.

The new supplementary benefits scheme: so little reward for so much effort?

At the time of writing the reformed supplementary benefits scheme has
been in operation for two and a half years. Any discussion of its
impact and operation must try to separate out the problem of
implementation of a complex programme of reform from those difficulties
which have arisen from the actual changes. The DHSS has argued that
it would take at least this length of time before such a distinction
could be made. (DHSS, 1982a, para 2.19)

Any assessment of the impact of the 1980 reforms also has to be set
in the context of the enormous increase in the number of claimants
which has occurred since 1979. In the first two years after the
Conservative Government took office the number of people dependent
on supplementary benefit virtually doubled. In November 1982, the
scheme was supporting 7 million people, 1 in 8 of the population.
The main reason for the increase was of course the dramatic rise in
unemployment. In December 1981, the unemployed accounted for over
one-third of the 3.7 million people claiming supplementary benefit;
the number of children being brought up in families dependent on
supplementary benefit had increased by 90 per cent, to 1.7 million
in August 1982. Whilst the rate and size of the increase exceeded
even the most gloomy prognosis made at the time of the review, it was
precisely to cope with the anticipated increase in the number of
unemployed claimants that the reform of the supplementary benefits
scheme had been regarded internally as so urgent. How successfully
has the new scheme been adapted to its 'mass' role? How effective
have the reforms been in making the scheme easier to understand and
easier to operate?

Monitoring the operation of the new scheme was one of the priority
areas selected by SSAC in its first year of office. To that end, the
Committee invited public comment and received submissions from fifty
organisations and nine individuals - a tiny fraction of those who had
commented on Social Assistance. The DHSS has also sponsored
independent research studies on various aspects of the working of the
new scheme and financed CPAG to conduct its own monitoring exercise.
The considerable sums of money put into such monitoring reflects the
importance attached to it by those involved with the review, including
David Donnison, senior DHSS officials, and the review team's research
sub-group. The need for close and continuous assessment of the new
less flexible scheme was made by the SBC in its final Annual Report:

> "if a change (is) proved not to be working
> as intended, or if unexpected side effects
> or implications become evident the rules
> or instructions must be speedily amended.
> The hope is that everything will work smoothly
> from the start. But such a hope must be
> backed by adequate arrangements for quickly

identifying areas in which it is not
being realised, and to take action
where it is needed".
(para 1.21)

The trend towards clearly defined legal entitlement and away from
discretion has made the scheme more open, but not easier for
claimants, staff or even 'experts' to understand. To understand the
new supplementary benefits scheme, it is now necessary to find one's
way around 12 sets of regulations, 22 sets of amended regulations,
Commissioners' decisions, with the help of the memoranda of
guidance from the CSBO. Obtaining such information is well beyond
the resources of any claimant (the original 1980 set of regulations
alone cost £25). Neither is the information easy to understand, as
the latest editions of the Supplementary Benefits Handbook (DHSS, 1982b)
and especially the vastly expanded CPAG, National Welfare Benefits
Handbook, (CPAG, November 1982) can testify.

The problems which have so far emerged from the tighter legal
structure can be attributed to two causes: the first, hopefully only
temporary, the second more intransigent. Many of the initial problems
reported to SSAC arose from the speed with which the supplementary
benefit regulations had been drawn up, and secondly, from the
inadequate training given to staff at the outset. In their evidence,
to SSAC, the CPAG gave the following example:

> "The Department has had two attempts
> at drafting regulations governing lump
> sum payments of maintenance. Amendments
> introduced even before the scheme came
> into operation changed this regulation
> ... The amended regulations have been
> analysed in some depth and found
> unforgiveably wanting. A Commissioner
> 'observed in passing' of the regulation
> that it "would be helpful if ... the
> relevant regulations were amended so
> that what is intended is comprehensible".
> (CPAG, Evidence to SSAC, undated, para 1.3)

Similarly, in its 1981 Annual Report the SSAC found that many of the
problems reported on the urgent needs regulations arose because 'The
regulations are very complicated and we hope that, over time,
simplification will be possible'. (DHSS, 1982a, para 4.30) The
problem of understanding regulations becomes even more acute when they
are amended. (see, for example CPAG 1982a, p. 1)

The difficulty of training large numbers of staff in the intricacies
of numerous sets of regulations, many of which were not even available
until just before the introduction of the new scheme, is obvious. Staff
received only limited training of one or two weeks. The special case
officers received three weeks training. It is not surprising then
that CPAG found that, in the first four weeks "not only (did) the
claimants not know where they stand, but in many cases benefit officers

(did) not know either". (CRO/CPAG, 1981, p. 9)

The initial staff difficulties were compounded by and will
have longer term ramifications because of the Government's desire to
cut civil service manpower. The anticipated 'simplification' provided
a rationalisation for reducing staff. Between April 1981 and April
1982, there was a net staff saving in the DHSS regional and local
offices of nearly 1,900. This reduced figure included the additional
1,050 posts created to tackle fraud and abuse, discussed earlier.
The bulk of the savings came from supplementary benefits, and in
particular from the administration of supplementary benefit to the
unemployed. (see Table 2) These considerable savings took place before

TABLE 2:   ADMINISTRATIVE COSTS AS PERCENTAGE OF EXPENDITURE

	1978/9	1979/80	1980/81	1981/2
NI benefits generally	3.7	3.7	3.9	4.0
SB generally	13.9	15.0	14.3	10.9
UE benefit	10.6	11.4	8.6	8.3
SB to the unemployed	17.8	18.7	15.0	10.9

Source: Social Services Committee, Session 1981/2, Public Expenditure
on the Social Services, vol. II, HMSO, 1982, pp. 204-5

major staff-cutting measures were introduced: postal claims for
the unemployed, housing benefit and the statutory sick pay scheme.

It is not surprising, therefore, that problems in administration figured
prominently in the complaints made to SSAC (DHSS, 1982a; Walker, 1983).
The general impression was that the standard of administration was
at least as bad, if not worse than before November 1980. Staff cuts
in the face of mounting pressure eventually culminated in a national
one day strike in 1983 and several prolonged local disputes in DHSS
offices. A review of local office staffing levels was promised in
order to settle these disputes.

The second set of problems arose not from staffing and training
difficulties, but from an underlying weakness of the reforms: that
of imposing a rigid legal structure on top of inadequate benefits.
There is an essential conflict between trying to contain the availability
of the many additional payments to the minority for whom they are
intended and trying to keep the system simple. This was a problem
foreseen by DHSS lawyers associated with the review, by many critics
but not publicly acknowledged by the team nor heeded by the Government.
Thus, by catering for the many and varied exceptional cases, the

regulations had to be extremely precise and over-definitive and themselves give rise to new anomolies.

The tighter legal framework of the new SB scheme has made it easier for officers to refuse claimants help by putting responsibility for the decision on "the rules" not the individual. Claimants, it seems, readily accept even the boldest of statements justifying refusal of a single payment even that "no grants are made any more". (NWRS, 1981, p. 5) What regulation has not been able to do, especially in the face of work overload in local offices, is to ensure that all claimants know, claim and receive all they are entitled to. The responsibility of the SBO in this respect was discussed in one decision made by the Social Security Commissioner, "it is the duty of the visiting officer to consider whether the claimants have any exceptional needs beyond those mentioned in the claim". (Mesher, 1981) It is already clear that publication of legal rights has not been sufficient to ensure that people actually get those rights. For example, only 1 per cent of claimants received help with their heating bills in the very severe winter of 1981/82 despite legislative provision for this. Nor has it provided any justification for staff cuts. Indeed, it has led SSAC to renew calls for the establishment of advice stations in all social security offices to give general information to callers. (DHSS, 1982a)

Not surprisingly, the restricted availability of lump sum payments, particularly in relation to clothing needs, has led to a substantial drop in the numbers of single payments made. In the first 12 months of the new scheme the proportion of claimants receiving a single payment fell by a quarter despite an increase in claimants of almost a fifth over the same period. The biggest drop was amongst pensioners. The proportion receiving a single payment halved in 1981. Amongst supplementary allowance recipients, the proportion getting such help fell by around 40 per cent. Not surprisingly the main drop was in payments for clothing and shoes. The proportion receiving a grant fell by over two-thirds. The only increase in single payments was amongst those made for furniture. Preliminary figures for 1982 seem to show that the number of single payments is now going up again. This probably reflects a greater understanding, and perhaps exploitation of the new rules,(see Walker 1983) but also the initial over-reaction to the impending cut-backs in single payments prior to their introduction.

In drawing up broad-based rules to replace large areas of discretionary power, the review team noted that it must be done "without leaving the door open to further pressures for complication and extension of the scheme which would quickly get it back to its present unsatisfactory state". (DHSS, 1978, p. 5) The emphasis on law in the new scheme meant that it would be neither quick nor easy to open such doors. However, chinks in the armour have already been made. The contest between the DHSS and pressure groups has centred on the interpretation of the Act's safety clause. In an early decision on this point a Social Security Commissioner concluded that 'shoes that let in water seem to me to present an obvious risk to health'. (CSB, 31/81) In other cases, tribunals have made liberal interpretations of the clause. One ruled that "Children's feet can be permanently damaged by wearing shoes that are too small". (CPAG, 1981, p. 83) More recently, a tribunal ruled that sudden growth spurts common among adolescents fell outside the normal wear and tear provision for clothing, and awarded a payment under section 30. Such decisions stand unless and until challenged by the DHSS to the Social Security Commissioner.

Despite such moves the DHSS feels that it has been successful in operating this regulation according to:

> "its primary purpose of allowing a
> fall-back discretion to be used in
> extreme cases which do not come
> within the scope of the main body
> of the regulations. As was
> intended, it has not provided an
> open door to the kind of wide
> use of discretion that was a
> feature of the old scheme".
> (quoted in DHSS, 1982a para 4.15)

Welfare rights workers have expressed concern both that SBOs have shown reluctance to use this fall-back power and dismay at the CSBOs guidance that 'other means' of obtaining clothing which claimants should be advised to pursue include various forms of credit or borrowing. Claimants are, therefore, being urged to take out expensive forms of credit as a way of coping with the cut in grants. A cut which the SBC and the CSBO, when wearing his hat as leader of the review team, said should only be made if accompanied by automatic lump sum payments to claimants. The DHSS has estimated that only 5,000 to 6,000 such payments were made in 1981, the majority for clothing.

The success of the scheme for claimants and staff will depend on how far future Governments will be prepared to amend the regulations in the light of emerging difficulties and changing needs. If, as seems to be the case, dependence on supplementary benefit is to be allowed to grow and no improvements are made to the real value of benefits, the Government will have to heed any warning signals which emerge. As the SBC pointed out in its final Annual Report

> "unless policy-makers keep closely
> in touch with the way the new scheme
> is working, and respond accordingly,
> the rigidity of the new structure
> will either impose rules which are
> defective and may have harsh effects,
> or lead to the rules being circumvented
> or subtly altered".
> (1980, p. 19)

It is essential that the loss of flexibility to meet individual need is replaced by rules which are fair and open to change.

Thus far, there has been little evidence that the Conservative Government are prepared to make significant changes, particularly if they require extra resources. The Social Security Advisory Committee has already made representations for urgent change of the rule which excludes those not on supplementary benefit from receiving single payments. (DHSS, 1982a, para 4.19) Even though the cost of such a change would be relatively small, and the hardship to the people concerned may be very great, no action has been taken. Furthermore, the Government have allowed the value of the earnings disregards and the level of savings affecting entitlement to single payment to fall since 1979. Only the capital cut-off has been increased (to £2,500 in November 1982 and £3,000 in 1983) as has the automatic deduction to benefit to strikers families (from £12.00 in 1980 to £14.50 in 1982).

Conclusion

The major success of the supplementary benefits review as an exercise in changing policy was that it transcended party politics. It survived a general election and led to reforms of the supplementary benefits scheme despite a change of Government. The fact that the Conservative Government was sympathetic to the assumptions on which Social Assistance had been framed enabled it to introduce reforming legislation within six months of coming to office. The Social Security Act 1980 was said by one member of the review team to have contained '80 per cent of what we wanted'. The other 20 per cent comprised new arrangements for meeting housing costs (since introduced in the 1982 Social Security & Housing Benefit Act) and a short term scheme. Officials have argued that the speed with which the reforms were brought in saved the scheme from the cuts in social security expenditure which were made only 4 months later. It has been asserted more cynically by outsiders that the speed with which the scheme was adapted to its 'mass role' facilitated the cuts and the implications which they had for dependence on supplementary benefit. With hindsight, however, members of the review team and Government advisers regarded the nil-cost basis of the legislative reforms a considerable achievement in the climate of 1979/80.

The open government strategy, and the public discussion in particular, played an important part in influencing the new Government to take swift action. The aim of those who took part in the public debate on Social Assistance, however, was not to ensure changes within the scheme regardless of their quality. Their aim was to influence the content of the reforms and it is in this respect that their involvement was least significant. (Walker, 1982) The deferment of benefit to school-leavers, reductions in discretionary lump sum and urgent needs payments went ahead despite considerable opposition. Other proposals including the abolition of dietary additions and the restriction of central heating additions were dropped but not because of the public response. The Government did not restrict the right of appeal on single payments decisions, as recommended by the review team, but in practice appeals tribunals' powers are far more limited as members are bound by the regulations. Other proposals, such as the payment of the long-term rate of benefit to the unemployed, were not implemented despite considerable public support, the support of the review team and the Supplementary Benefits Commission. The

lack of a wholly negative response to the alignment of the national
insurance and supplementary benefit scale rates, ensured its
introduction despite the doubts of officials about its acceptability when
it was first put forward. The views expressed during the public
discussion had even less influence on the Government's perception of
the role of supplementary benefits. Many of those working close to
the review believe that the overwhelming rejection of the no-cost remit
encouraged the Government not to try to make significant savings in
this area. But the Social Security Act 1980 adapted the scheme to
its mass role - a role rejected by a significant proportion of all
respondents. Changes made in the Social Security (No. 2) Act 1980
increased dependence on supplementary benefit. The new statutory Sick
Pay Scheme, introduced in April 1983 further increased dependency.
The Conservative Government has no long term commitment to lifting
people off means-tested supplementary benefit, rather the opposite.
As Patrick Jenkin declared to the Social Services Select Committee,
the Government's aim was "to make economies in the social security budget
almost entirely in relation to short-term benefits, whilst at the same
time giving high priority to protecting the level of the means-tested
safety net". (Social Services Committee, 1980)

The fact that an impartial official review had succeeded in
producing a set of reforms which made no demands on extra resources,
and that their report had been openly debated, diffused the criticism
of legislation formulated on the same basis. However, at least some
of those involved with the review had hoped that the public debate
would expose the shortcomings of reform on a no-cost basis. It was
a message ignored by the first post-war Government prepared to cut
the social security budget. It was a Government and an attitude which,
some of the protagonists said, could not have been predicted back in
1976.

The final outcome has not been the radical change anticipated when the
review was set up. It is now widely acknowledged that the 1980
legislation has failed to achieve any degree of simplification, -
rather the reverse. This view is widely shared both by outsiders and by
those involved with the operation of the scheme in local offices and
in the policy divisions. The major real simplification to supplementary
benefits has been achieved with the introduction of housing benefit.
Local authorities are now responsible for meeting the housing costs
of the vast majority of claimants living in rented accommodation.
(Owner occupiers still get their mortgage costs met through the
supplementary benefits scheme). The price of internal simplification of
the supplementary benefits scheme has been increased complexity for
the local authorities, and overwhelming confusion for claimants. The
new housing benefit scheme was also introduced on a nil-cost basis
and therefore placed in the same paradox as the reformed supplementary
benefits scheme:

> "to offset or mitigate some of the
> losses, undesirable complexities,
> such as the arrangements for
> topping up payments ... have had
> to be added to the scheme, which
> leave it in many respects even
> more complex than previous
> arrangements. The goal of

> simplification, making the scheme
> easier for claimants to understand
> and for officials to administer has
> sadly not been achieved".
> (McGurk & Raynsford, 1982, p. 5)

Since the introduction of the Social Security Act 1980 claimants'
rights have been laid down in regulations but it does not follow that
they are clear or that claimants are any more aware of those rights
or that they get them. Furthermore, rights are no substitute for cash.
The legislation has accepted that the additional payments made no
longer relate to <u>exceptional</u> needs (viz the change of names from
exceptional circumstances additions and exceptional needs payments
to additional requirements and single payments). However, it does not confront
the main problem faced by claimants, which was acknowledged by the
review team and the SBC and stressed during the public debate, namely
how to manage on inadequate levels of benefit. Under the 1980 Social
Security Act certain categories of need, as well as groups of people,
have been placed beyond the scope of the supplementary benefits scheme.
However, those needs still exist. The danger is that, over time, fewer
demands will be made on the scheme for those expenses which fall outside
its remit and Governments and policy-makers will conclude that such
needs no longer exist. In fact, they will merely have been legislated
out of 'official' existence. And the burden, as ever, will have to
be borne by claimants.

Notes

1. The 'abatement' of benefits was introduced as an interim measure until
   these benefits could be brought into tax. Unemployment benefit has been
   taxed since the summer of 1982, however, it was only after considerable
   pressure from the Tory 'Wets' that the Chancellor promised to make good
   the 5 per cent from November 1983. No action has yet been taken either
   to bring the other benefits concerned into tax, or to make good the
   initial 'abatement'.

2. The first new measure was the abolition of the SBC. The second was the
   introduction of a standard rent addition for non-dependants.

3. Reg Prentice said, in evidence to the Social Services Select Committee,
   that the 1980 reforms would produce a modest saving of £2m. The additional
   savings expected from the anticipated reduction in lump sum payments were
   not included when calculating the overall financial impact of the changes.

4. In the White Paper, it was said that the alignment would "make the
    system easier to understand and make it easier to see how the earnings
    related component of national insurance benefits helps to lift people
    above the supplementary benefit level". (HMSO, 1979, p. 3)

5. Since November 1982, the element for housing costs has been taken out
    of the inflation figure used for the uprating because of the introduction
    of housing benefit. In November 1982, NI benefits were increased by
    11 per cent, and SB by $\frac{1}{2}$ per cent less.

6. The number of children's rates were reduced from five to three. The
    level of benefit of the bands which were abolished were increased to
    the level of the higher age group. A similar procedure was used to reduce
    the number of rates of heating addition from three to two. The
    administrative benefit of the reduction in the number of children's
    rates was undermined by the introduction of an automatic heating
    addition for families with a child under 5, which effectively
    recreated a separate rate for that age group within the 0-10 age
    band.

Chapter 9

Conclusion

The growth of social assistance over the past forty-five years has
been one of the most significant developments in income maintenance
provision in Britain. Yet, whilst its gradual expansion up to 1948
was part of deliberate Government policy to establish a more
acceptable financial safety net for the poor, growth since then has
not been the result of overt social planning. Instead the increasing
dependence has been the negative outcome of successive Governments'
action and inaction in income maintenance and other areas of policy
which had direct or indirect consequences for last resort assistance.
In particular, Governments have failed to provide national insurance
benefits which are adequate in value or duration or to re-examine the
relationship between the two arms of income maintenance provision,
assistance and insurance, in the light of changing social and economic
conditions. Thus, large numbers of the unemployed and lone parents
are dependent on means-tested assistance. Those steps which have
been taken to provide non means-tested support, for example by the
introduction of a non-contributory invalidity pension and an invalid
care allowance, have had little impact on the numbers dependent on
supplementary benefit because they are paid at a lower rate.

The increased burden placed on the scheme by this growing dependency
has been exacerbated by two other factors. First, external economic
and demographic changes have led to a shift in the population of
claimants from the 'deserving' and administratively straightforward
supplementary pensioner to the 'undeserving' and often more complicated
supplementary allowance beneficiary. A second, even more significant
factor, has been the failure of Governments to ensure that the level
of benefit is sufficient to meet basic needs, let alone enable claimants
"to participate in the life of the community". (SBC, 1979, para 1.4)
As a consequence the discretionary powers, which had always been
regarded as an essential element in a last resort assistance scheme,
were used to meet the predictable needs of large groups of
claimants, rather than the truly exceptional needs of the individual.

When the review of the supplementary benefits scheme was announced
in September 1976, it was hoped by outsiders that at last the role
of assistance policy would be re-examined. That the growth of
supplementary benefit from a 'residual' to a 'mass' service and the
inadequacy of the scale rates, the two underlying problems, would be
examined. In reality, the purpose of the review was much more limited.
It was a technical exercise to examine the structure and operation
of the scheme so that the deterioration in the administrative machine
would be stemmed and essential modifications introduced to enable it
to cope with the anticipated further increase of unemployed claimants.

Despite its much more limited goal, the review of the supplementary
benefits scheme was an important development in social policy for two
reasons. First, the review was the first attempt by Government to
take a comprehensive look at the internal working of its assistance
scheme. Previous changes, with the possible, partial exception of
the 1944 simplifications, had not followed such a thorough analysis
of the appropriateness of the machine for the task it was actually

performing. Secondly, the innovative two stage process of the review
introduced a new element to an otherwise fairly routine civil service
enquiry, and opened a hitherto closed area of policy-making to public
scrutiny.

The precise significance of the review in the study of social policy
change can be measured in two ways: first, by an evaluation of the
review as a mechanism for changing policy and secondly, by an
assessment of the impact which this review had on the future development
of the supplementary benefits scheme.

The review as a mechanism for changing policy

Whilst dissatisfaction with the supplementary benefits scheme had been
expressed vehemently, if diversely, by Members of Parliament, pressure
groups, local office staff and the media, it was only when the
Supplementary Benefits Commission and its key officials began to argue
for change, with Ministers and with other departments, that the issue
was taken up effectively by Government. However, the adverse economic
climate and the low esteem in which social security was held by the
general public and the media made 1976 an inauspicious time for
Government to become embroiled in the reform of this politically
sensitive area of policy; or for such an expensive and complex area
of policy to come under scrutiny. As events showed, it marked the
end of an era of expansion in income maintenance policies, and a
trend towards retrenchment and later retreat.

Given the unfavourable economic and social climate, the creation
of the review was a considerable achievement for the main protagonists,
the SBC, especially in the personal form of its Chairman, and its senior
officials. However, in order to obtain the agreement of Ministers
and key Government departments to the establishment of any enquiry,
a number of compromises had to be struck on the nature and scope of
the investigation. A number of new features were built into the review
process to mitigate the limitations which resulted, but the turn of
political events in 1979 meant that they were not effective, at least
in the short term, in broadening the scope of the reforms which were
introduced by the Conservative Government.

The structure of an enquiry and its composition have important
implications for the range of problems which are considered and the
nature of the solutions which are offered. The decision to hold an
internal enquiry has been justified by officials on the grounds that
the review was essentially a technical fact-finding exercise and civil
servants were best qualified to carry it out. However, this is only
one small part of the explanation.

The decision to hold an internal enquiry was also made for political
reasons. It offered Ministers a way of showing concern for the
operation of the supplementary benefits scheme without having to reveal
their own priorities and without making any commitment on future action.
Secondly, it offered the protagonists the best way of taking the review
out of the party political arena. As internal reviews are not directly
associated with party policy, especially when the initiative comes
from within the bureaucracy, their findings could be used by a Government
of either main political party. This depoliticisation was crucial
if the review was to survive regardless of the intervention of a General

Election and not to fall by the wayside like previous attempts at social security reform. Finally, an internal review was acceptable to the Treasury and Civil Service Department, which were extremely reluctant to allow any review of policy, as it was susceptible to the greatest degree of influence and control.

As significant as the composition of an enquiry, are the terms of reference which are set. No clear guidelines were laid down formally for the supplementary benefits review. Instead the general 'comprehensive' remit announced by Ministers was modified in line with 'informal understandings' reached with, most importantly, the Treasury. As a result, the review team was precluded from making recommendations which had policy implications for other departments or which would lead to a net increase in benefit costs or staff resources.

It was decided by the protagonists not to publish the restricted terms of reference, in the hope that, by leaving them vague, the review team would be able to transgress the boundaries more easily and offer a wider range of possible reforms. It was intended at the outset, for example, that the final report would include a list of options, some of which would require extra resources and others of which would make savings. Thus expenditure proposals could be 'slipped past' the Treasury and the no-cost restriction would not be made obvious to outsiders.

Some of the officials interviewed said, with hindsight, that it was a mistake not to publish the terms of reference which made explicit the two restrictions. Lack of clarity on the no-cost remit caused particular problems. On the one hand the decision, contrary to the original intention, to include a package of proposals for change in Social Assistance, meant that the financial constraint became obvious. This package had to be self-balancing in order to get Treasury approval for its publication. On the other hand, because the restrictions placed on the review team were not stated in the report, much of the public discussion centred on why the comprehensive remit had been narrowed and on where responsibility lay, rather than on the quality of the reforms presented. As civil servants, members of the review team were unable to answer these fundamental questions adequately. Their apparent unwillingness to do so provided a poor basis on which to build a constructive dialogue with participants during the second stage.

An internal review, further restricted by limitations imposed by the Treasury and the Civil Service Department, was accepted by the protagonists, including David Donnison who had previously argued for a more comprehensive approach to social policy change, because it was the best and indeed the only kind of enquiry which could be set up at that time. It was also hoped that some of the disadvantages could be ameliorated by the incorporation of some important features and the active role played by the Supplementary Benefits Commission. Throughout the review process, from its creation to the publication of its independent response to Social Assistance, the Commission, and in particular David Donnison strove to keep the debate as wide as possible by exposing issues to public debate. Persistent pressure from David Donnison on the steering group, helped to ensure that a major new proposal like equal treatment of men and women, which did not fit in with the limited aims of the review, was put on the agenda.

In this way, other issues, which strictly fell beyond the scope of
the review, such as the comprehensive reform of fuel or housing
benefits, survived despite the reservations of members
of the steering group.

The decision to conduct the review as an exercise in open government
also lessened the impact of some of the disadvantages of an internal
enquiry. The existence of the review was made public and its findings
were published for public scrutiny. Such openness is not a usual
feature of civil service enquiries. Following the considerable
opposition to the nil-cost, mass role assumptions of Social Assistance
Ministers were left in no doubt of the unpopularity of reform of the
supplementary benefits scheme on these bases. However, the strength
of feeling shown during the public debate did not persuade the
incoming Government to divert extra resources to the scheme, and it
is not at all certain that a Labour Government would have been
significantly more generous. The danger of the acceptance of the
no-cost remit, even as merely the starting point for discussion, was
foreseen by Ruth Lister, Director of the Child Poverty Action Group:

> "There is the danger that Social
> Assistance will provide the politicians
> with an excuse for refusing to divert
> resources to the social security
> scheme, for it creates the comfortable
> illusion that the problems can be
> solved by juggling around the resources
> already devoted to supplementary
> benefit".
> (Lister, 1978)

Whilst the public debate had little effect on the content of the reforms
which were eventually introduced it was a crucial part of the review
process. It provided the impetus for Government. The breadth of the
debate, drawing in pressure groups, staff, and sections of the press,
created an atmosphere in which reform was anticipated. Had the
Government not introduced changes to the supplementary benefits scheme,
it would have been accused of complacency towards the poor and would
have further damaged the morale of the staff. From the Government's
point of view, it was advantageous to introduce such contentious legislation
immediately, and early in its term of office, as all the arguments
had already been made and criticism aired in relation to Social
Assistance. The areas of agreement and disagreement had already been
exposed and certain concessions could be made on some details of the
changes without altering the fundamental nature of the reforms. Thus,
although many pressure groups disliked many aspects of the reforms
included in the Social Security Act 1980, there was no programme of
public meetings called to oppose the legislation, as there had been
to oppose Social Assistance. Indeed the absence of some of the review
team's least popular proposals, in the context of the Government's
unfavourable attitude to social policy in general and social security
in particular, led a representative of one of the major pressure groups
to reflect that 'it could have been worse'.

The depoliticisation of the review and the introduction of the open
government strategy provided the necessary continuity in the policy-

making process. Reforms of the supplementary benefits scheme were introduced despite a change of Government. However, the review process did not survive. Work continued on the issues deferred by the review team only until the summer of 1979 when the officials had to abandon this work to draft the legislation which put the reforms into effect: the Social Security Act 1980.

The change of Government marked, in particular, the end of the open government strategy. Only two further consultative reports were issued, though legislative change was introduced on some of the other issues deferred by the review team. Unlike Social Assistance, the Analysis of Views and Comments was not distributed free and more importantly, this summary of the critical response was given very little publicity. Several months after its publication, only a handful had been distributed. Although the press has campaigned for more open government, in this case they seemed little concerned that, in its supplementary benefits reforms, the Conservative Government was ignoring the views of a wide range of experts which had been expressed in relation to Social Assistance.

The most negative outcome of the open government strategy was that the Conservative Government did not allow time either for discussion of the White Paper on the Reforms of the Supplementary Benefits Scheme or for adequate consideration of the proposed regulations. The White Paper was published on the same day as the Social Security Bill, in which the reforms were included, thus depriving commentators of the usual discussion period. It was argued that debate of these proposals was not necessary because there had been a full discussion on Social Assistance. However, the discussions which had taken place with the review team had been extremely broad and diffuse (see Chapter 7). The lack of clarity on the terms of reference diverted attention away from consideration of specific issues. Also discussion was based on a much wider range of issues than was included in the legislation, and participants could not be expected to comment on all of the hypothetical scenarios.

The haste with which the Government wanted to get the legislation onto the statute book, meant that even in Parliament there was inadequate discussion of the changes. In particular, the detailed regulations which represented a major change of emphasis in social assistance policy were not available in time for consideration at any of the key Parliamentary stages. "Notes" on the Social Security Bill were made available but these provided incomplete information on, for example, the precise availability of exceptional needs payments. (DHSS, 1980)

As a mechanism for changing social policy, the review was far more successful than other enquiries initiated by previous Labour or Conservative Governments. It transcended party politics. Unlike the internal review of benefits for the disabled, on which work was suspended for almost two years after the 1979 election and the demise of the report of the Merrison Commission on the National Health Service, the supplementary benefits review ended with a major reform of the scheme. The reforms which were introduced included most of the options favoured by the review team. However, the changes did not reflect the broader approach favoured by the Commission or the views expressed during the public debate. As a model in open government, the review was successful only in the eyes of the policy-maker, not in the eyes of the participant.

The review and the future of supplementary benefit

The review of the supplementary benefits scheme was a new and, in the context of previous policy changes, bold experiment in a highly sensitive area of social policy. Although the DHSS officials associated with it have indicated considerable support for the review exercise, and especially for its public presentation, it is unlikely that such a staff intensive and time-consuming exercise would be launched in the future. It is unlikely that the Treasury, with the experience of the supplementary benefits review, would agree to a similar enquiry. However, even if the review is remembered by policy-makers and social scientists as a unique and interesting experiment, it will only be significant to those most closely affected by the results of its work, namely staff and claimants, if the supplementary benefits scheme is developed in ways which meet their needs and priorities.

When the Commission and its senior officials were pressing Labour Ministers and the Treasury on the need to set up an enquiry into the state of the supplementary benefits scheme, they accepted a number of crucial compromises on the nature and scope of the review which would be conducted. The much narrowed compromise formula was accepted because it was believed that the scheme was reaching a crisis point and that <u>any</u> enquiry would be acceptable if it prevented the scheme from actually breaking down. It was also hoped that the new features built into this internal review would lessen the impact of the restrictions on the scope of the eventual reform.

When the review was formulated in such a way that it would best promote the successful conclusion of the policy-making process, regardless of a change of Government, none of the protagonists foresaw the election of a Government whose policies on social security would be considerably more reactionary than those of previous administrations. The assumption made at this stage, therefore, was that <u>any change</u> would be for the better. Even when, later, the Commission rejected the nil-cost basis of <u>Social Assistance</u>, it simultaneously urged critics not to reject the review as a basis for reforming the supplementary benefits scheme, but to build on the review team's findings.

> "The needs of poor people are too urgent
> and too obvious to require the lengthy
> deliberations of a Royal Commission ...
> For those who have to live meanwhile on
> means-tested benefits, a fairer and more
> rational system could be devised".
> (DHSS/SBC, 1979, p. 3, p. 14)

There is an obvious danger of depoliticising issues to the extent that they are acceptable to opposing political points of view, to which the reform of SB indeed fell victim. The instigators of this initiative could have no control over the precise content of the policies which were implemented. The Government was even more parsimonious and less sensitive than the review team. The legislation did not incorporate even the limited fine-tuning suggested in <u>Social Assistance</u>. The worst effects of the restricted remit and enquiry structure were not mitigated, as intended by the Commission and officials, by the public discussion. The Government took on board only the first stage of the review - a largely unspectacular internal enquiry. The second stage, the views of outsiders on Social Assistance - including the very critical response of the SBC - were substantially ignored.

The review of the supplementary benefits scheme set up in 1976 remains an important milestone in the development of social assistance policy - regardless of any criticism of its analysis or the adequacy of its proposals. It did lead to the reform of the scheme. It will also undoubtedly be the last examination of supplementary benefits for many years. The SBC, in one of the last public statements before its abolition, welcomed the 1980 reforms, despite their no-cost basis:

> "... the Government have made many
> important and welcome changes, and
> have said that they regard these
> merely as a first stage in a longer
> programme of reform. It is a
> valuable start, but it is no more
> than that. The reforming spirit
> must not be allowed to dissipate,
> and the additional resources for
> further reforms must be found"
> (1980, para 2.3)

However, the first stage of reform got rid of one of the scheme's most influential and persuasive critics: the SBC itself. Although there are obvious advantages to the existence of one committee to oversee all social security benefits, it is impossible for it to devote the same amount of time and detailed attention to supplementary benefit as the Commission had done. It is precisely that kind of constant, in-depth, probing analysis which the current scheme needs, to ensure all aspects of the legislation are working as anticipated.

There now seems no likelihood of the Conservative Government providing the extra resources necessary to pay for real improvements in the scheme. Indeed the first stage provided it with a justification for cutting staff and the rationale for pursuing policies which deliberately increased dependence on supplementary benefits. The Labour Party has said "The new supplementary benefits scheme introduced by the Tories is harsh and unfair. We shall reform it" (Labour Party, 1983, p. 16) But there has been no rejection of the principles on which the reforms were based, which were, of course, accepted by the previous Labour Administration, and certainly no promise of raising the level of benefits. They have promised, however, a 'review' of the national insurance scheme!

Commenting on the Unemployment Assistance Act 1934, B B Gilbert concluded: "The act of 1934 ... had been expected to provide a simpler and less arbitrary apparatus for relieving the poor. Instead it had caused endless complications and hardship. The act had been framed by men who were experts in government rather than experts in human needs. In order to avoid official arbitrariness they had caused personal misery by regulation". (Gilbert, 1970, p. 186) The Social Security Act 1980 also aimed at providing a more rational, rule-based system for assisting the poor. But the review on which it was

based, and the legislation itself tackled only the presenting problems
of the supplementary benefits scheme, the administrative problems,
not the longer term underlying problems of paying inadequate means-
tested benefits to too many people. The reforms made were judged first
by their impact on administration and by their cost implications.
Their impact on the standard of living of claimants ran a poor second.
The 1934 changes had to be amended in the light of a fierce public
outcry. The 1980 changes got a more muted response, largely because
the arguments had been rehearsed before on Social Assistance but also
because little influence could be exerted on a Government with a
formidable parliamentary majority. In addition the effect of this
set of reforms on claimants has been more subtle. Different groups
have been affected differently. Cuts have been hidden in the annual
upratings. The danger is that if the legislation does lead to
"personal misery by regulation", the impact on claimants will remain
hidden in the homes of millions of poor people. Or, that it will be
seen as an 'acceptable' price to pay for more straightforward
administration and rules which are fair in their application but an
inadequate response to the needs of those they affect.

The ability of means-tested assistance to cope on a mass scale is
now being put strenuously to the test. The supplementary benefits
scheme is facing an even greater crisis than that predicted by
Donnison in 1976. If the current strain is proved to be caused by
factors other than the teething problems of new legislation or the
rapid rise in unemployment, which seems likely, the cause will lie
in the supplementary benefit review. The failure of the 1980 reforms
will lie in the compromises which were reached on the structure and
scope of the review. Those same compromises which, in fact, were
essential for its creation and which made the review, as a mechanism
for securing change, such a success.

APPENDIX 1

Background papers relating to the Supplementary Benefits Review

Living standards of supplementary benefit recipients

1. A summary of information from two surveys carried out in 1969 and 1972 by the Department of Health and Social Security.

2. A summary of information about living standards of households receiving supplementary benefit as recorded in the 1975 Family Expenditure Survey.

3. A review of methods of estimating "equivalence scales" used in comparing the living standards of different households.

Contacts with public and other agencies

4. A statistical note on local office contacts with claimants.

5. A note on referrals between local offices and other agencies.

6. A report on public attitudes to supplementary benefit by the Schlackman Research Organisation.

Scope of the scheme

7. A statistical note on types of recipients of supplementary benefit and trends in their numbers.

8. A statistical note on the length and pattern of periods of dependence on supplementary benefit.

Discretion

9. An analysis of discretionary payments in 1975.

10. An account of the development of discretionary powers to increase benefit and make lump-sum payments.

11. A study of decisions on exceptional needs payments in a sample of cases over two years.

12. A study of appeals against decisions relating to exceptional needs payments.

13. A paper on rules and discretion in immigration control and town and country planning (prepared by Professor Jeffrey Jowell and Mr. Rodney Austin. University College, London)

14. A paper on rules and discretion in Local Authority Social Services Departments, with special reference to the Children and Young Persons Act 1963, S.1. (prepared by Mr Michael Freeman, University College, London).

Assessment of benefit

15. An operational research appraisal of the effects of simplified arrangements for dealing with short-term claims.

16. An operational research appraisal of the impact on individual children of changes in the scale rates for children.

17. An operational research appraisal of the impact on families of changes in the scale rates for children, with a mathematical model for estimating family structure.

18. An analysis of the relationship of benefits with incomes in work.

19. A statistical study of the nature and frequency of revisions of supplementary benefit assessments.

Equal treatment for men and women

20. A statistical paper on wives as sole and joint bread-winners.

21. An operational research appraisal of the effect on local office operations of equal treatment measures.

Legislative background to the scheme

22. An account of the historical background to the supplementary benefits legislation.

23. A paper on the legal structure of the supplementary benefits scheme.

Social assistance in other countries

24. A general review of the information immediately available to DHSS at the start of the review.

25. Social assistance in Denmark.

26. Social assistance in the Netherlands.

27. Social assistance in New Zealand.

28. Social assistance in the Federal Republic of Germany.

29. Social assistance in France.

Papers issued for a seminar on the review at the School for
Advanced Urban Studies, Bristol University

30. Scope and purpose of the supplementary benefits scheme.

31. The family.

32. Calculation of requirements and resources.

33. Discretionary payments in the supplementary benefits scheme.

34. The legal structure of the supplementary benefits scheme.

35. Supplementary benefits and the local authorities.

Evidence submitted to the review team

36. Evidence submitted by the Trades Union Congress.

37. Evidence submitted by DHSS Staff Side.

38. Evidence submitted by Child Poverty Action Group (available
     from CPAG, as a pamphlet entitled "Patching Up the Safety Net?").

39. Evidence submitted by the Campaign for Single Homeless People
     (available from CHAR, entitled "Third Class Claimants").

40. Evidence submitted by the team responsible for the Granada
     TV programme "This is your right". A report setting out the
     main topics and problems raised by viewers, plus
     illustrative extracts from viewers' letters.

APPENDIX 2

Issues deferred by the review team for consideration in the second stage

Liaison with other central and local agencies. For example, the relationship with local authorities, including the social services and social work departments on a number of issues, and housing departments about the provision for rent; also, relations with the Manpower Services Commission over the placing and training of the unemployed, and with the Department of Energy and the fuel boards on energy policy. Close co-operation will be necessary over the implementation of changes which emerge as a result of the review.

The existing provisions governing the liability of husbands and wives to maintain each other and of parents to maintain their children; the treatment of maintenance payments made to claimants and their children; and the recovery of benefit paid because of unmet liability. Also, the relationship between the liability to maintain under matrimonial law and under the SB Act.

The implications for the supplementary benefit scale rates for children of developments in child benefit.

The rules on payment of benefit to people involved in trade disputes and their dependants.

The provisions applying to claimants who are voluntarily unemployed, including the reduction of their benefit, the conditions attached to their benefit and the overlap with unemployment benefit law.

The effect of the newly-implemented arrangements governing claims from couples living together as man and wife.

The rules for the assessment of benefit to help with charges levied on boarders and others and with their personal expenses.

The effect of non-dependants on the assessment of benefit; the standard rent addition for non-householders.

People without a settled way of living: whether benefit should be in cash or kind, whether such cases should be dealt with in separate offices, and possible future arrangements for providing the accommodation and other services currently provided by the SBC through reception centres.

The rules governing claims from visitors to the country, and from other people from abroad who are sponsored by relatives resident in this country.

Further consideration of possible alternative ways of dealing with short-term claims.

Further study of the implications for FIS of changes in the supplementary benefits scheme, including in particular the options to secure equal treatment for married women, and of the inter-action between the two schemes.

Subject to the outcome of the current consideration of the possibilities discussed in Chapter 7, examination of methods of simplifying the treatment of rent in the assessment of supplementary benefit; the position of student householders.

The treatment of awards of damages made by the courts in the light of the recent report of the Royal Commission on Civil Liability and Compensation for Personal Injury.

The possibilities of simplifying other means-tests which are at present based on the supplementary benefits scheme, eg for welfare foods and free milk.

Examination of existing penalties and whether they need to be amended to fit in with a revised scheme.

The provisions governing the recovery of overpayments.

A NEW LOOK FOR
SUPPLEMENTARY BENEFIT

report has been published setting out possible changes the scheme.

get a copy:—

—get order form N1 146 here

—write on it your name and address, and the title *SB review report*

HERE IS A CHANCE TO PUT IN YOUR VIEWS.

THE REPORT TELLS YOU WHERE TO SEND THEM.

APPENDIX 4

ESTIMATED EFFECT OF INDIVIDUAL CHANGES IN THE SUPPLEMENTARY BENEFITS SCHEME IN THE SOCIAL SECURITY ACT 1980

Change	Claimant gains	Claimant losses	Effect on staff nos	Benefit cost/saving
Reduction in qualifying period for long-term rate	98,000[1]	-	-	+£2½m-3½m[2]
Reduction in number of children's rates	341,000[1]	-	50[3]	+ up to £32m[2]
Aligning SB/NI rates [4]	553,000[1]	1,889,000[1]	50[3]	- £30m[1]
Deferment of benefit to school leavers	-	400,000[1]	-500[3]	- £4m[2]
£2,000 savings cut-off	36,000[1]	13,000[1]	-	-
Standard contribution for housing costs of non-dependent (£3:80)	106,667[1]	213,334[1]	-150	- £15m[3]
Increased earnings disregard for unemployed	7,000[1]	-	-	+ £¾ m[1]
Tapered disregard for lone parents	21,000[1]	22,000[1]	n/a	+ £½m[4]
Abolition of £1 disregard on occupational pensions	-	202,000[1]	-130[3]	- £10½m[1]
Over 80s addition paid to both partners	7,000	-	-	+£91,000[2]
Special rates for the blind	500[1]	-	-	"small"[1]
No ENPs for non-recipients of SB	-	10,000[1]	-	- £¼m
Restricted laundry additions	-	146,000[1]	-	- £¼m
Notice of assessment	-	-	+100[3]	-
Equal treatment	6,000[3,6]	-	+200[3]	-
Special case officers	-	-	+400[3]	-
No ECAs for home-helps	-	18,000[7]	-	-£140,000[7]
Consolidation of heating additions - under 5s	150,000[8]	-	-	+ £6½m[8]
- over 75s	110,000[8]	-	-	+ £5m[8]

1 Hansard, vol. 975, cols. 371-4, 7.12.79
2 My estimates based on information in the SBC Annual Reports
3 Hansard, vol. 974, col. 66, 3.12.79
4 Figures applicable before the changes in the Social Security (no 2) Act
5 Social Assistance
6 Proposal to pay the long-term rate when either partner reaches 65 only
7 Hansard, vol. 978, col 486, 11.2.80
8 Hansard, vol. 972, col. 35, 22.10.79

APPENDIX 5

Supplementary Benefit Regulations

Regulations

SB (Aggregation) Regulations 1981 No 1524

SB and Family Income Supplement (Appeals) Rules 1980 No 1605

SB (Conditions of Entitlement) Regulations 1981 No 1526

SB (Claims and Payments) Regulations 1981 No 1525

SB (Duplication and Overpayment) Regulations 1980 No 1580

SB (Determination of Questions) Regulations 1980 No 1643

SB (Requirements) Regulations 1980 No 1299

SB (Resources) Regulations 1981 No 1527

SB (Single Payments) Regulations 1981 No 1528

SB (Trades Disputes and Recovery from Earnings) Regulations 1980 No 1641

SB (Urgent Cases) Regulations 1981 No 1529

Social Security (Credits) Regulations 1975 No 556

Amendment Regulations

SB (Aggregation, Requirements and Resources) Amendment Regulations
1980 No 1774

SB (Miscellaneous Amendments) Regulations 1980 No 1649

SB (Miscellaneous Amendment) Regulations 1981 No 815

SB (Requirements and Conditions of Entitlement) Amendment Regulations
1981 No 1197

SB (Requirements and Resources) Amendment Regulations 1981 No 1016

SB and Family Income Supplement (Appeals) Amendment Rules 1982 No 40

SB (Claims and Payments) Amendment Rules 1982 No 522

SB (Housing Benefits) (Miscellaneous Consequential Amendments)
Regulations 1982 No 914

SB (Housing Benefits) (Requirements and Resources) Consequential
Amendments Regulations 1982 No 1126

SB (Miscellaneous Amendments) Regulations 1982 No 907

SB (Requirements and Resources) Amendment Regulations 1982 No 1125

APPENDIX 6

"Package of Proposals" Recommended by the Review Team [1]

Included in the Social Security Act 1980

Changes in the legal structure*

Deferment of benefit to school-leavers until the end of the holiday following the term they left school (2)

Restriction of payment of benefit to sponsored relatives*

to overseas visitors

Entitlement of benefit to continue for some claimants when on holiday abroad*

Definition of full-time work brought into line with Family Income Supplement

Steps to promote greater equality of treatment for married women*

Alignment of the adult national insurance and supplementary benefits scale rates

Simpler rules for the assessment of earnings disregards*

Simpler rules for the assessment of benefits disregards*

Fixed £2,000 disregard on savings

More limited availability of ENPs for items covered by the scale rates

More limited help with special laundry expenses*

Creation of special welfare officers

Changes in heating additions*

Not included in the Social Security Act 1980

Short-term scheme

Automatic six monthly payments

Abolition of ECAs for special diets

Payment of the long-term rate to the unemployed

Abolition of the offset of 50 pence from the long-term scale rates

Central heating additions to be made only for electric central heating

---

1   Social Assistance, DHSS, 1978, ch 13

2   This change was implemented in the Child Benefit (General Amendment) Regulations 1980, No 1045

*   The proposal implemented was at variance with, but similar to, the review team's recommendation

REFERENCES AND SELECTED BIBLIOGRAPHY

a)   Government and official publications

(All publications printed in London, unless otherwise stated)

CPRS (1977), "The Role of the Central Policy Review Staff in
Whitehall", Memorandum submitted by the CPRS to the Expenditure
Committee (General Sub Committee) in the Eleventh Report from
the Expenditure Committee: The Civil Service, 1976-77,
Cmnd 535, HMSO.

Department of Employment/DHSS (1981), Payment of Benefits to the
Unemployed, DHSS.

DHSS (1972), Families receiving supplementary benefit: a study
comparing the circumstances of some fatherless families and
families of the long-term sick and unemployed, HMSO.

DHSS (1976), First Report by the Co-ordinating Committee on Abuse,
Mimeo.

DHSS (1976a), Priorities for Health and Personal Social Services in
England, HMSO.

DHSS (1976b), Sharing Resources for Health in England, Report of the
Resource Allocation Working Party, HMSO.

DHSS (1978), Social Assistance: A Review of the Supplementary Benefits
Scheme in Great Britain, HMSO.

DHSS (1979), Review of the Supplementary Benefits Scheme: Analysis of
Views and Comments, DHSS.

DHSS (1979a), Report of a Survey of Claimants' Attitudes to Central
Issues of the Supplementary Benefits Review, DHSS.

DHSS (1979b), Relations with Social Services, DHSS.

DHSS (1979c), Boarders and People in Residential Accommodation, DHSS.

DHSS (1980), Social Security Bill & Notes on Clauses, DHSS.

DHSS (1982), Report of the Supplementary Benefits Policy Inspectorate on the effects of the New Capital Rule, DHSS.

DHSS (1982a), First Report of the Social Security Advisory Committee, 1981, HMSO.

DHSS (1982b), Supplementary Benefits Handbook, HMSO.

DHSS/SBC (1975), Exceptional Needs Payments, SBA Papers No 4, HMSO.

DHSS/SBC (1976), Living together as Husband and Wife, SBA Papers No 5, HMSO.

DHSS/SBC (1977), Supplementary Benefits Handbook, SBA Papers No 2, HMSO.

DHSS/SBC (1977), Low Incomes: Evidence to the Royal Commission on the Distribution of Income and Wealth, HMSO.

DHSS/SBC (1978), Take-up of Supplementary Benefits, SBA Papers No 7, HMSO.

DHSS/SBC (1979), Response to the Supplementary Benefits Commission to "Social Assistance: A review of the supplementary benefits scheme in Great Britain, SBA Papers No 9, HMSO.

Department of the Environment/Welsh Office (March 1981), Consultative Document, Assistance with Housing Costs.

EEC (1977), The Perception of Poverty in Europe.

Expenditure Committee (General Sub-committee): (July 1977), The Civil Service, Vols I-III, 1976-77, HMSO.

Financial and Other Circumstances of Retirement Pensioners, (1966), HMSO.

Income during Initial Sickness, (1980), Cmnd 7864, HMSO.

Proposals for a Tax Credit System (1972), Cmnd 5116, HMSO.

Report of the National Assistance Board 1948 (1949), Cmnd 7767, HMSO.

Report of the National Assistance Board 1950 (1951), Cmnd 8276, HMSO.

Report of the National Assistance Board 1955 (1956), Cmnd 9781, HMSO.

Report of the National Assistance Board 1965 (1966), Cmnd 8900, HMSO.

People and Planning (The Skeffington Report) (1969), HMSO.

Proposals for a Tax Credit System, (1972), Cmnd 5116, HMSO.

Public Expenditure to 1979-80 (1976), Cmnd 6393, HMSO.

Reform of the Supplementary Benefits Scheme (1979), Cmnd 7773, HMSO.

Social Insurance and Allied Services (The Beveridge Report) (1942),
    Cmnd 6404, HMSO.

Report of the Committee on One Parent Families (Finer Report) (1974),
    Cmnd 5629, HMSO.

Report of the Committee on Abuse of Social Security Benefits (Fisher
    Committee) (1973), Cmnd 5228, HMSO.

The Civil Service (1966-68) (The Fulton Report) (1968a), Cmnd 3638,
    HMSO.

Report of the Royal Commission on the National Health Service (Merrison
Commission) (1979), Cmnd 7615, HMSO.

Royal Commission on Civil Liability and Compensation for Personal
    Injury (The Pearson Commission), (1978), Cmnd 7054, HMSO.

Report of the Committee on Control of Public Expenditure (Plowden
    Report) (1961), Cmnd 1432, HMSO.

Report of the Committee on Local Authority and Allied Social Services
    (Seebohm Report) (1968), Cmnd 3703, HMSO.

Report of the Committee of Enquiry into the Education of Handicapped
    Children and Young People (the Warnock Report) (1978), Cmnd 7212,
    HMSO.

"Supplementary Benefits Commission Annual Report 1967" (1968), in Report of the Ministry of Social Security for the Year 1967, Cmnd 3693, HMSO.

SBC Annual Report 1975 (1976), Cmnd 6615, HMSO.

SBC Annual Report 1976 (1977), Cmnd 6910 HMSO.

SBC Annual Report 1977 (1978), Cmnd 7392 HMSO.

SBC Annual Report 1978 (1979), Cmnd 7725, HMSO.

SBC Annual Report 1979 (1980), Cmnd 8033, HMSO.

Social Services Committee (1980), The Arrangements for Paying Social Security Benefits, Session 1979-80, HMSO.

Social Services Committee (1980a), The Government's White Papers on Public Expenditure: the Social Services, Session 1979-80, HMSO.

Social Services Committee (1982), 1982 White Paper: Public Expenditure on the Social Services, Session 1981-82, HMSO.

Report of the Unemployment Assistance Board 1935 (1936), Cmnd 5177, HMSO.

Report of the Unemployment Assistance Board 1936 (1937), Cmnd 5526, HMSO.

Report of the Unemployment Assistance Board 1937 (1938), Cmnd 5752, HMSO.

Report of the Unemployment Assistance Board 1938 (1939), Cmnd 6021, HMSO.

b)   Books and articles

Abel-Smith B and Townsend P (1965), The Poor and the Poorest,
   Bell.

Adler M and Bradley A (1975), Justice, Discretion and Poverty:
   Supplementary Benefits Appeals Tribunals in Britain, Professional
   Books.

Arnstein S (1969), "A Ladder of Citizen Participation", Journal of
   American Institute of Planners, vol 35, no 4.

Atkinson A (1970), Poverty in Britain and the Reform of Social
   Security, CUP.

Bachrach P and Baratz M (1970), Power and Poverty: Theory and
   Practice, OUP.

Banting K (1979), Poverty, Politics and Policy, MacMillan.

Batley R (1972-3), "An Explanation of Non-participation in Planning",
   Policy and Politics, vol 1, no 2.

Bell K (1975), Research Study on Supplementary Benefits Appeals
   Tribunals: Summary of Main Findings: Conclusions: Recommendations
   HMSO.

Bosanquet N and Townsend P (eds) (1980), Labour and Equality,
   Heinemann.

Briggs E and Deacon A (1973), "The Creation of the Unemployment
   Assistance Board", Policy and Politics, vol 2, no 1.

Briggs E and Rees A (1980) Supplementary Benefits and the Consumer,
   Bedford.

Broad P (1977), Pensioners and their Needs, OPCS.

Bull D (1979), "Open Government and the Review of Supplementary
   Benefits", in Baldwin S and Brown M (eds), The Yearbook of Social
   Policy 1978, Routledge and Kegan Paul.

Bulmer M (ed) (1980), Social Research and Royal Commissions, Allen and
   Unwin.

Burgess P (1978), "Civil Service Shock Troops", Community Care,
15 December.

Burghes L (1980), Living from Hand to Mouth: a study of 65 families
living on SB, FSU/CPAG, Poverty Pamphlet No 50.

Chapman R A (1973), The Role of Commissions in Policy-Making,
Allen and Unwin.

CHAR (1978), Third Class Claimants, duplicated.

Clarke J S (1943), "The Assistance Board", in Robson W (ed), Social
Security, Allen and Unwin.

Clarke Sir R (1978), Public Expenditure, Management and Control
MacMillan.

Cole D with Utting J (1962), The Economic Circumstances of Old
People, Welwyn Codicote.

Coleman R J (1971), SB and the Administrative Review of Administrative
Action, Poverty Pamphlet No 7, CPAG.

Coussins J (ed) (1980), Dear SSAC, CPAG, Poverty Pamphlet No 49, CPAG.

CPAG (undated), The Great Child Benefits Robbery, CPAG.

CPAG (1980), National Welfare Benefits Handbook, CPAG.

CPAG (1982), "Consolidating Regulations", Welfare Rights Bulletin
no 46.

CRO/CPAG (1981), Four weeks past A-day: the new supplementary benefits
scheme in practice, duplicated.

Crossman R (1972), The Politics of Pensions, Liverpool University Press.

Davison R C (1938), British Unemployment Policy: The Modern Phase
since 1930, Longman Green.

Davison R C (1934), "The New Scheme of Unemployment Relief", Political
Quarterly, vol 5.

Deacon A (1976), In Search of the Scrounger, Bell.

Deacon A (1978), "The Scrounging Controversy", Social and Economic Administration, vol 12, no 2.

Deacon A (1981) "The Duration of Unemployment Benefit under the National Insurance Act 1946", in Burghes L and Lister R (eds), Unemployment: Who Pays the Price, Poverty Pamphlet No 53, CPAG.

Deacon A (1982) "An End to the Means-test: Social Security and the Attlee Government", Journal of Social Policy, vol II, pt 3.

Dennis N (1970), People and Planning, Faber and Faber.

Derthick M (1979), Policymaking for Social Security, Washington, Brookings.

DIG (1979), "A Response by the Disablement Income Group to the Review produced by the Department of Health and Social Security", DIG Occasional Paper No 2.

Donnison D (1972), "Ideologies and Policies", Journal of Social Policy, vol 1, pt 2.

Donnison D (1976), "Supplementary Benefit: Dilemmas and Priorities", Journal of Social Policy, vol 5, pt 4.

Donnison D et al (1975), Social Policy and Administration Revisited, Allen and Unwin.

Donnison D (1977), Speech to the Family Welfare Association, mimeo, 24 February.

Donnison D (1982), The Politics of Poverty, Oxford, Martin Robertson.

Elks L (1974), The Wage Stop: Poor by Order, Poverty Pamphlet No 17.

Fabian Society (May 1971), People in Participation and Government, Fabian.

Fagence M (1977), Citizen Participation and Planning, Oxford, Pergamon Press.

Field F (1976), "An Agenda for the Poor", New Society, 23 September.

Field F and Grieve M (1972), Abuse and the Abused, Poverty Pamphlet No 10, CPAG.

Fimister G (1978), Tidying up the Poor, Tyneside CPAG.

Forder A (1974), Concepts in Social Administration, Routledge and Kegan Paul.

Fulbrook J (1975), Justice for the Claimant, Poverty Pamphlet, CPAG.

Fulbrook J (1978), Administrative Justice and the Unemployed, Mansell.

Gilbert B B (1970), British Social Policy 1914-39, Batsford.

Glennerster H (1962), National Assistance: Service or Charity, Fabian Society.

George V (1973), Social Security and Society, Routledge and Kegan Paul.

Golding P and Middleton S (1982), Images of Welfare, Oxford, Martin Robertson.

Golding P and Middleton S (July 1978), Information and the Welfare State, Centre for Mass Communications Research, University of Leicester.

Greenwood W (1933), Love on the Dole, Jonathan Cape.

Hall P (1976), Reforming the Welfare: The Politics of Change in the Personal Social Services, Heinemann.

Hall P, Land H, Parker R and Webb A (1975), Change Choice and Conflict in Social Policy, Heinemann.

Hannington W (1940), Ten Lean Years, Gollancz.

Heclo H (1974), Modern Social Politics in Britain and Sweden, Yale.

Heclo H and Wildavsky A (1974), The Private Government of Public Money, MacMillan.

Heidenheimer A, Heclo H and Adams C T (1976), Comparative Public Policy, MacMillan.

Heidenheimer A, Heclo H and Adams C T (1983), Comparative Public Policy, second edition, MacMillan.

Help the Aged (1978), "Comment on Social Assistance", mimeo.

Herman M (1972), Administrative Justice and Supplementary Benefit, Bell.

Hill M (1969), "The Exercise of Discretion in the National Assistance Board", Public Administration, 47.

Hill M and Laing P (1978), Money Payments, Social Work and Supplementary Benefits, SAUS, Bristol.

Hill M J (1972), The Sociology of Public Administration, Weidenfeld and Nicolson.

Hill M (1976), The State, Administration and the Individual, Fontana.

Houghton D (1967), Paying for the Social Services, Institute for Economic Affairs.

Jones K, Brown M and Bradshaw J (1978), Issues in Social Policy, Routledge and Kegan Paul.

Jordan B (1978), "Personal View: Flexibility – the better part of discretion", Social Work Today, vol 10, no 13, 21 November.

Kerr S (1983), Making Ends Meet: An investigation into the non-claiming of Supplementary Pensions, Bedford Square Press/NCVO.

Kincaid J C (1975), Poverty and Equality in Britain, Harmondsworth, Penguin.

The Labour Party (1983), Labour's Plan: The New Hope for Britain, Labour Party.

Lafitte F (1945), Britain's Way to Social Security, Pilot Press.

Leaper R A B (1979), "Social Assistance: a Watershed?", Social Policy and Administration, vol 13, no 1.

Leman C (1980), The Collapse of Welfare Reforms: Political Institutions, Policy and the Poor in Canada and the United States MIT.

Lister R (1975), Social Security: The Case for Reform, Poverty Pamphlet No 22, CPAG.

Lister R (1977), Patching up the Safety Net? Evidence to the review of the supplementary benefits scheme, Poverty Pamphlet No 31, CPAG.

Lister R (1978), Social Assistance: The Real Challenge, Poverty Pamphlet No 38, CPAG.

Lister R (1979), The No-Cost No-Benefit Review, Poverty Pamphlet No 39, CPAG.

Lister R (1979a) "Social Assistance: A Civil Servant's Review", Journal of Social Welfare Law, vol 1.

Long A R (1975), "Participation and the Community", Progress in Planning, vol 5, no 2.

Lucas J R (1976), Democracy and Participation, Harmondsworth, Penguin.

Lynes T (1967), National Assistance and National Prosperity, Bell.

Lynes T (1977), "Supplementary Benefits: the legislative history", in SBC Annual Report 1976, (1977), Appendix A.

May J and Wildavsky A (eds) (1979), The Policy Cycle, Sage.

Marsh D (1979), Introducing Social Policy, Routledge and Kegan Paul.

McClements L (1978), The Economics of Social Security, Heinemann.

McGurk P and Raynsford N (1982), A Guide to Housing Benefits, Institute of Housing /SHAC.

Mesher J (1981), "Recent Social Security Commissioners' Decisions, Journal of Social Welfare Law.

Millett J (1940), The Unemployment Assistance Board, Allen and Unwin.

National Consumer Council (1976), Means Tested Benefits: Discussion Paper, NCC.

Nelson B J and Lindenfeld T (1979), "Setting the Agenda: the case of child abuse", in May J and Wildavsky A (eds), The Policy Cycle, Sage.

Newcastle Welfare Rights Service (1981), "Fairer and more easily understood - Nine months of the new SB scheme in Newcastle upon Tyne", NWRS.

Parker H (1980), Goodbye Beveridge, Outer Circle Policy Unit.

Partridge M (1979), "The Review of the SB scheme: an exercise in open government" (unpublished).

Partridge M (1979a), "Why Social Workers Should Welcome the SB Review", Community Care, 8 February.

Piachaud D (1979), The Cost of a Child, Poverty Pamphlet No 43, CPAG.

Piachaud D (1981), "Social Security" in Bosanquet N and Townsend P (eds), Labour & Equality, Heinemann.

Pinker R (1971), Social Theory and Social Policy, Heinemann.

Rhodes G (1975), Committees of Enquiry, Allen and Unwin.

Ritchie J and Wilson P (1979), Social Security Claimants, OPCS.

Robson W (ed) (1943), Social Security, Allen and Unwin.

Robson W and Crick B (eds) (1971), The Future of the Social Services, Harmondsworth, Penguin.

Rose H (1976), "The icing on the welfare cake", Year Book of Social Policy 1975, Routledge and Kegan Paul.

Rose R (ed) (1969), Policy-making in Great Britain, MacMillan.

Senior D (1971), "Public involvement in planning", in Robson W and Crick B (eds), The Future of the Social Services, Harmondsworth, Penguin.

Slack K (1969), Social Administration and the Citizen, Michael Joseph.

Smee C and Stern J (1978), The Unemployed in a Period of High Unemployment, Economic Adviser's Office/DHSS.

Self P (1977), Administrative Theories and Politics, Allen and Unwin.

Smith B (1976), Policy Making in British Government, Martin Robertson.

Stein B and Miller S (eds) (1974), Incentives and Planning in Social Policy, Chicago, Aldine.

Stevenson O (1973), Claimant or Client? A Social Worker's View of the SBC, Allen and Unwin.

Stowe K R (1961), "Staff Training in the National Assistance Board: Problems and Policies, Public Administration, Columbia.

Titmuss R (1969), "New Guardians of the Poor", in Jenkin S (ed), Social Security in International Perspective, Columbia.

Titmuss R (1971), "Welfare 'Rights' Law and Discretion", Political Quarterly, vol 42, no 2, April.

Townsend P et al (1970), Social Services for All, Fabian Society.

Townsend P (1981), "Social Planning and the Treasury", in Bosanquet N
and Townsend P (eds), Labour & Equality, Heinemann.

Walley Sir J (1972), Social Security: - Another British Failure,
Charles Knight.

Walker C (1982), "Social Assistance: the reality of open government",
Policy & Politics vol 10, no 1.

Walker C (1983), "The Reform of the Supplementary Benefits Scheme:
for whose benefit" in Jones C and Stevenson J (eds), The Year Book
of Social Policy in Britain 1981-82,Routledge & Kegan Paul.

Willson F (1969), "Policy-Making & the Policy-Makers", in Rose R,
Policy-Making in Britain, MacMillan.